CASSELL

Dictionary of
Word and Phrase Origins

CASSELL

Dictionary of
Word and Phrase Origins

NIGEL REES

CASSELL

This edition first published in the UK 1996 by
Cassell
Wellington House, 125 Strand, London WC2R 0BB

Distributed in the United States by
Sterling Publishing Co. Inc.
387 Park Avenue South, New York, NY 10016, USA

British Library Cataloguing-in-Publication Data
A catalogue record for this book is available from the British Library

ISBN 0-304-34803-1

Typeset in Monophoto Garamond
by Latimer Trend & Company Ltd, Plymouth
Printed and bound in Great Britain by
Biddles Ltd, Guildford and King's Lynn

Contents

Introduction

Why do we say a person is a 'nerd' or a 'wally' or a 'twerp'? Or makes money 'hand over fist'? Or is the 'spitting image' of someone else?

Why is a lavatory also known as a 'loo', a 'john', a 'jakes' or a 'crapper'? Why do we 'take a rain-check'? Why shouldn't you 'teach your grandmother to suck eggs'?

These are the sort of questions that normal dictionaries duck out of by saying 'orig. obsc.' or 'orig. uncert.' or 'orig. unknown'. On the other hand, books which specialize in word and phrase origins often seem to assert that one explanation (and one explanation only) can be provided.

The method of this *Cassell Dictionary of Word and Phrase Origins* is to compare the several explanations that may be on offer and to test them, even if in the end it serves to emphasize that in this field hard and fast conclusions are difficult to come by.

The especial need for this approach derives from the fact that a good deal of amateur etymological folklore has been established. It is now very difficult, for example, to persuade people that the word 'posh' is *not* an acronym derived from the request for cabins 'Port Out, Starboard Home' on ships going to and from India in the days of the British Raj. Or to convince them that the word 'crap' had existed for centuries before Thomas Crapper, the Victorian sanitary engineer, came along.

In addition, a number of quizzes and newspaper strips have arisen recently claiming to explain the origins of well-known words and phrases with difficult and/or colourful roots. Frequently, however, these merely pass on old myths and legends, unsubstantiated by evidence.

This book tries to sift through the lore and disentangle the misconceptions. Sometimes it exposes an impostor; sometimes it throws up its hands and offers no solution of its own because in this area of folklore an origin is never realistically going to be found. In one or two cases I examine words and phrases which seem to have been neglected entirely by the substantial number of reference books I have consulted. In these cases, as in others, I hope that I have not created any new misconceptions.

The choice of words and phrases examined may at times seem eccentric. It ranges from words and phrases that have entered the language within recent years to venerable examples that still present a puzzle. The book is certainly not intended to be comprehensive – how could it be? – and my usual criterion for including a word or phrase is simply whether there is anything interesting or new to say about it.

This dictionary was first published by Blandford Press under the title *Why Do We Say ...?* in 1987. In 1992, it became the *Cassell Dictionary of Word and Phrase Origins*. Now, in 1996, it is time for an expanded edition under the second title.

The process of revision has benefited enormously from the great deal of interest shown by readers all over the world. In particular I would acknowledge the advice and suggestions of: Roy Alexander, Paul Beale, R.K. Dann, Jaap Engelsman, Mark English, Frank Loxley, Ronald Monroe, Michael Grosvenor Myer, the late Vernon Noble, Norman H. Page and John Yates.

HOW TO USE THIS BOOK

Words and phrases are listed in word-by-word order. The first significant word in a phrase usually dictates its place in the alphabetical order.

Cross-references are given in SMALL CAPITALS.

Quotations from the Bible are from the Authorised Version, 1611 (except where stated otherwise).

Quotations from Shakespeare are as in *The Arden Shakespeare* (2nd series).

The reference *OED2* is to *The Oxford English Dictionary* (2nd ed.) 1989, (CD-ROM version), 1992; Partridge/*Catch Phrases* is to Eric Partridge, *A Dictionary of Catch Phrases* (2nd ed., edited by Paul Beale),

1985; Partridge/*Slang* is to Eric Partridge, *A Dictionary of Slang and Unconventional English* (8th ed., edited by Paul Beale), 1984; *DOAS* is to *Dictionary of American Slang* (2nd ed., compiled by Harold Wentworth and Stuart Berg Flexner), 1960; and *Brewer* is to *Brewer's Dictionary of Phrase & Fable* (15th edition, revised by Adrian Room, 1995).

Citations are printed as they appeared in the original publication named.

Dating is given according to the first recorded appearance of words and phrases. They may, however, have been in existence long before.

A

a/an. Why do people say or write 'an hotel' when it is perfectly all right to say simply 'a hotel'? Presumably, because they think there is some rule of grammar which says they should. But there is not. As *Fowler's Modern English Usage* (2nd edition, 1965) explains: '*An* was formerly usual before an unaccented syllable beginning with h (*an historian, an habitual offender* . . .) But now that the h in such words is pronounced the distinction has become anomalous and will no doubt disappear in time. Meantime speakers who like to say *an* should not try to have it both ways by aspirating the h.'

> He was sojourning at an hotel in Bond Street.
> Anthony Trollope, *The Belton Estate* (1865)

> Guest. A temporary inmate of an hotel, inn, or boarding house.
> *Oxford English Dictionary* (2nd ed., 1989)

à go-go. *See* WHISKY À GOGO.

abominable snowman. Phrase used to describe anyone or anything indescribable and unpleasant. Originally, an unidentified creature of the Himalayas, which derives its name from the Tibetan *meetoh kangmi* [abominable snowmen] or *yeti*. It is said to raid mountain villages and to be tall, powerful and bearlike, with a near-human face. The name became known to European mountaineers attempting to climb Mount Everest in the 1920s and was popularized by climbing expeditions in the 1950s. In 1960 Sir Edmund Hillary found footprints which seemed to be those of an animal such as a bear. The mystery surrounding this creature gave rise to the detective novel *The Case of the Abominable Snowman* (1941) by Nicholas Blake. There was also a separate film on the subject, *The Abominable Snowman* (UK, 1957).

In 1953, David Eccles, Minister of Works responsible for the Coronation decorations in London, became known as 'the Abominable *Showman*'. General de Gaulle, having obstructed British entry

1

to the European Common Market in the 1960s by saying '*Non!*', was dubbed 'the Abominable *No-man*'.

absit omen!   *See under* GESUNDHEIT!

— abuse.   This phrase-making suffix is used when describing (1) misuse of any substance, and (2) maltreatment of another person. Hence such phrases as: 'alcohol abuse', 'child abuse', 'drug abuse', 'heroin abuse', 'ritual abuse', 'satanic abuse', 'solvent abuse', 'substance abuse'. The format has been used in the first sense since the 1960s and in the second since the 1970s, but both constructions were especially prevalent in the 1980s. When applied to drugs and other 'substances', it seems an inappropriate construction, as though any blame for misuse could be placed on the substance itself rather than the user. It also rather begs the question of whether drugs and alcohol can ever be used 'properly'. In the US, the phrase 'substance abuser' has now largely replaced 'drug addict' and 'drunk'.

according to Hoyle.   Meaning 'exactly; correctly; according to the recognized rules; according to the highest authority'. The phrase comes from the name of the one-time standard authority on the game of whist (and other card games). Edmond Hoyle was the author of *A Short Treatise on the Game of Whist* (1742).

> If everything goes according to Hoyle, I'll go into semi-retirement there.
> *Melody Maker* (21 August 1971)

ace in the hole.   A hidden advantage or secret source of power. An American phrase used as the title of a Cole Porter song in the show *Let's Face It* (1941), and of a Billy Wilder film (US, 1951), it came originally from the game of stud poker. A 'hole' card is one that is not revealed until the betting has taken place. If it is an ace, so much the better.

DOAS dates the use of the expression, in a poker context, to the 1920s, *OED2* to 1915. In British English the nearest equivalent would be to talk of having an 'ace up one's sleeve'.

> In the long haul ... AM's ace in the hole may be the $213 million net operating loss carryforward it still has left from its 1981–2 losses.
> *New York Times* (6 May 1984)

act. *See* CAUGHT IN THE ...

aerobics. The name of a physical fitness programme created by Dr Kenneth Cooper, a former USAF flight surgeon, who coined the phrase for a book called *Aerobics* (1968). The adjective 'aerobic' means living on free oxygen and comes from the Greek words for 'air' and 'life'.

> The ... stuffy gym reverberated with the insistent drum notes as thirty pairs of track shoes beat out the rhythm of the aerobics routine.
> Pat Booth, *Palm Beach* (1986)

age of kings. Name given to the period of history between the assassination of Henry IV of France in 1610 to the eve of the American War of Independence. This was the period of absolute monarchy, characterized by a series of powerful monarchs.

The term was borrowed for an outstanding BBC TV drama series *An Age of Kings* (1960) in which Shakespeare's English history plays were performed in sequence from *Richard II* to *Richard III*.

ageism/agism. Discrimination and prejudice against people on the grounds of their age, directed especially at the middle-aged and the elderly, but also (theoretically) at the young. Most commonly, ageism is the oppression of the young and of the old by the age group in the middle. The term was coined in 1969 by Dr Robert Butler, a specialist in geriatric medicine, of Washington DC:

> [Dr Butler said] 'We shall soon have to consider a form of bigotry we now tend to overlook: age discrimination or age-ism, prejudice by one age group toward other age groups.'
> *Washington Post* (7 March 1969)

> Agism is bad for men but worse for women. An older woman – unless she has made the top – is invisible. No longer desirable, she is expected to be even more deferential and servile.
> *Guardian* (13 May 1986)

agitprop. The use of literature, art and music for (usually) Communist propaganda purposes. A term of Russian origin, from *agitatsiya propaganda* [agitation propaganda]. It was coined by Georgy Plekhanov and later adopted by Lenin in *What Is To Be Done* (1902). The original use was simply concerned with political training and agitprop was the organ of indoctrination of the Central Committee. The secondary meaning became popular in the West during the 1960s, when really for the first time such means as pop music were indeed used to promote social and political ideas.

> The whole tone [of the play] is ten times heavier and cornier than any of the agitprop from the old Unity Theatre.
> *Spectator* (6 November 1959)

> All that is missing in the film is some touches of imagination and human detailing that transcend agitprop. Life, even for highly-motivated gays and blacks, does not consist wholly of zigzagging polemically from one socio-cultural Aunt Sally to the next.
> *Independent* (23 August 1991)

ahoy! *See under* HELLO.

aisle. *See* GO UP THE . . .

Alfa-Romeo. The Italian sports car line gets its name from the initials '*A*nonima *L*ombarda *F*abbrica *A*utomobili' ('Lombardy Automobile Works Company') coupled with the name of N. Romeo, the firm's manager from 1914.

Alice-blue gown. Celebrated in song, the colour of this garment, a light greenish blue, takes its name from a particular Alice – the daughter of President Theodore Roosevelt. The song 'Alice-blue Gown' was written for her by Joseph McCarthy and Harry Tierney in 1900, when she was sixteen, though apparently not published until 1919. In the late 1930s, there was another (British) song, called 'The Girl in the Alice-blue Gown'.

all in a lifetime. An expression implying that the speaker is resigned to whatever has happened: 'Ah well, it's all in a lifetime,' he or she might say. The *OED2*'s earliest citation is from 1849. Walter Allen entitled a novel *All In a Lifetime* (1959).

all in the family. *All In the Family* was the title of the American TV version (from 1971) of the BBC's sitcom *Till Death Us Do Part*. The respective main characters were Archie Bunker and Alf Garnett, racists and bigots both. But what of the American title? It is not a phrase particularly well known elsewhere.

The implication would seem to be '. . . so there's no need to be over-punctilious, stand on ceremony, or fuss too much about obligations' (often with an ironical tinge). Compare 'we are all friends here!'

There is not a trace of the phrase in the *OED2*. However, there is an 1874 citation 'all *outside* the family, tribe or nation were usually held as enemies' which may hint at the possible existence of an opposite construction.

The phrase does occur in Chapter 21, 'Going Aboard', of Herman Melville's *Moby Dick* (1851) – emphasizing a likely American origin. Elijah is trying to warn Ishmael and Queequeg against the *Pequod* and its captain: '"Morning to ye! morning to ye!" he rejoined, again moving off. "Oh! I was going to warn ye against – but never mind, never mind – it's all one, all in the family too; – sharp frost this morning, ain't it? Good bye to ye. Shan't see ye again very soon, I guess; unless it's before the Grand Jury."'

all my eye and Betty Martin. Meaning 'nonsense'. *OED2* finds a letter written in 1781 by one S. Crispe stating: 'Physic, to old, crazy Frames like ours, is all my eye and Betty Martin – (a sea phrase that Admiral Jemm frequently makes use of)'. The shorter expressions 'all my eye' or 'my eye' predate this. As to how it originated, Edwin Radford, *To Coin a Phrase* (edited and revised by Alan Smith, 1974) repeats the suggestion that it was a British sailor's garbled version of words heard in an Italian church: '*O, mihi, beate Martine*' [Oh, grant me, blessed St Martin], but this sounds too ingenious. Probably there *was* a Betty Martin of renown in the eighteenth century (Partridge/*Catch Phrases* finds mention of an actress with the name whose favourite expression is supposed to have been 'My eye!') and her name was co-opted for popular use.

all of a tiswas. Meaning 'confused, in a state'. Known by 1960, this might be from an elaboration of 'tizz' or 'tizzy' and there may be a hint of 'dizziness' trying to get in somewhere. But no one really knows. The acronym of 'Today Is Saturday, Wear A Smile' seems not to have anything to do with the meaning of the word and to have been imposed later. The acronym-slogan was the apparent reason for the title *Tiswas* being given to a children's ITV show of the 1970s, famous for its bucket-of-water-throwing and general air of mayhem. Broadcast on Saturday mornings, its atmosphere was certainly noisy and confused.

all over bar the shouting.   Almost completely over, finished or decided, except for the talking and argument which will not alter the outcome. Said of a contest or event. Of sporting origin, with the shouting referred to being cheering or, say, the appeal against the referee's decision in boxing. Known since 1842 (in the form '. . . *but* the shouting').

> But if the Rhodesia affair is all over bar the shouting, can the same be said about South Africa?
> *Western Morning News* (25 September 1976)

> Fewer than half of the trusts had made 3 per cent offers and only half of those were without strings. 'He seems to be giving the impression the pay round is all over bar the shouting. He couldn't be more wrong,' she said.
> *The Times* (15 May 1995)

all sorts.   All kinds of people, as in the proverb (known in this form by 1844, but the idea since the seventeenth century), 'It takes all sorts to make a world', usually said in bafflement at some aspect of human behaviour. Also used to hint darkly at things the speaker does not choose to be precise about: 'Oh, that couple – they get up to all sorts, they do.' Probably from Northern English use and popularized on a national scale when Liquorice All Sorts (i.e. in many different shapes and colours) became the brand name of a type of sweet or candy.

alternative.   As a prefix, this word became popular from the 1960s onwards, hence 'alternative comedy, lifestyles, medicine, society, theatre' etc. The basic notion is that the subject differs from the established norm (because that is regarded as dull, conventional and unsatisfactory in some way).

ambition.   *See* POVERTY OF . . .

(and remember) you heard/read it here first!   Promotional tag uttered by radio presenters or written by newspaper columnists when imparting a tasty piece of advance news or gossip. American origin. Noted 1995, but of long standing.

> Other possibilities [as Chairman of the BBC] are Sir Christopher Bland, who is said to have walked away with a handy £12m when LWT lost out to Granada last year . . . All of which, apparently, rules out David

Owen, who also fancies the job. Watch out, Duke is about. You read it here first.
Independent (11 August 1995)

and so it goes. An expression of mild irritation or amused philosophicality at being presented with yet another example of the way things are in the world. A catchphrase in Kurt Vonnegut's novel *Slaughterhouse-Five* (1969). *So It Goes* was the title of a British TV pop show devoted mainly to punk in the late 1970s.

> And so it goes: hassle, hassle, hassle, one horrible death after another, and yet the put-upon lad's soul is a butterfly that transmutes (on the spiritual sphere, you understand) into an Airfix Spitfire. By MTV standards, Hirst could be the next Francis Ford Coppola.
> *Observer* (25 February 1996)

> Sausages are brilliant all-rounders, everyone knows that. Fried up for breakfast, sandwiched between two slices of bread at lunch, grilled with mustard and mash for supper, cold on sticks at children's parties, hot on sticks with a spicy dip at grown-up dos, and so it goes.
> *Sunday Times* (25 February 1996)

angel. An investor or backer of theatrical productions, in the US, originally – a fairly obvious extension of 'guardian angel'. Perhaps the most far-fetched version of the phrase's origin is that one Luis de Santangel was the man who put up the money for Christopher Columbus's voyage to America. The use of the word 'angel' in this sort of context seems not to date from much before the 1920s, however.

answer the call of nature, to. A euphemism for urinating or defecating. Known since 1761 (Laurence Sterne, *Tristram Shandy*).

> The calls of nature are permitted and Clerical Staff may use the garden below the second gate.
> *Tailor & Cutter* (1852)

> Call of nature 'sent Maxwell overboard'...'He would frequently get up in the middle of the night and found it more convenient, as a lot of men do on a boat, to relieve themselves over the side as it was moving.'
> Headline and text, *Independent* (21 October 1995)

The **call of the great outdoors** may also be used in the same way. Originally the phrase 'great outdoors' was used simply to describe 'great open space' (by 1932).

antimacassar. A name given to coverings thrown over the backs of chairs and sofas from Victorian times onwards to protect them from hair-oil stains. Known by 1852. The impressive-sounding name reflects that 'Macassar' was the proprietary name of a hair oil and so the coverings acted 'anti' [against] it. They really do exist, which is more than can be said for the legendary coverings said to have been put over too-shocking piano legs in Victorian times.

anyone we know? Originally, a straightforward request for information when told, say, that someone you know is getting married and you want to know to whom. Then an increasingly joky catchphrase. 'She's going to have a baby' – 'Who's the father – anyone we know?' The joke use certainly existed in the 1930s. In the film *The Gay Divorcee* (US, 1934), Ginger Rogers states: 'A man tore my dress off.' A woman friend asks: 'Anyone we know?'

> The moment from which many of us date the genre was when the curtain rose on a production by Harry Kupfer in the late 1970s – I think of a work by Richard Strauss – to reveal a set dominated by a huge phallus, occasioning, from one male in the stalls to his gentleman friend, the loud whisper: 'Anyone we know, duckie?'
> *The Times* (17 May 1986)

a-OK. Another way of saying 'OK' or 'All systems working'. From NASA engineers in the early days of the US space programme 'who used to say it during radio transmission tests because the sharper sound of A cut through the static better than O' (according to Tom Wolfe, *The Right Stuff*, 1979). Now largely redundant, it seems never to have been used by astronauts themselves. President Reagan, emerging from a day of medical tests at a naval hospital in June 1986, pronounced himself 'A-OK'. Another derivation is a melding of 'A1' and 'OK'.

appeasement. A name given to the policy of conciliation and concession towards Nazi Germany, around 1938. The word had been used in this context since the end of the First World War. On 14 February 1920, Winston Churchill was saying in a speech: 'I am, and have always been since the firing stopped on November 11, 1918, for a policy of peace, real peace and appeasement.' The word may have become fixed following a letter to *The Times* (4 May 1934) from the 11th Marquess of Lothian: 'The only lasting solution is that Europe should gradually find its way to an internal equilibrium and a limitation of armaments by political appeasement.'

apple of one's eye. What one cherishes most. The pupil of the eye has long been known as the 'apple' because of its supposed round, solid shape. To be deprived of the apple is to be blinded and lose something extremely valuable. The Bible has: 'He kept him as the apple of his eye' (Deuteronomy 32:10).

apple pie. *See* IN . . . ORDER.

apply Morton's fork, to. A kind of test where there is no choice, dating from England in the fifteenth century. John Morton (*c*.1420–1500) was Archbishop of Canterbury and a minister to Henry VII. As a way of raising forced loans he would apply his 'fork' – the argument that if people were obviously rich, then they could afford to pay. And, if people looked poor, then they were obviously holding something back and so could also afford to pay. An early form of Catch-22. Known by 1889.

arbitrageur. A person who engages in arbitrage – the buying and selling of stocks and bills of exchange to take advantage of price variations in different markets. One of the more extraordinary words to be noticed in the English language during the 1980s. In fact, it has been known since at least the 1870s, sometimes being anglicized as 'arbitrager'.

argy-bargy. Nagging argument, a continuing aggravated exchange of insults and abuse. Rather a good word. Originally a Scottish dialect expression (recorded in 1887) which derives from 'argle-bargle', a version of 'argue' perhaps combined with 'haggle'.

as bald as a badger/bandicoot/coot. Phrases used to mean 'completely bald'. 'Bald as a coot' has been known since 1430. The aquatic coot, known as the Bald Coot, has the appearance of being bald. The Australian marsupial, the bandicoot, is not bald but presumably is evoked purely for the alliteration and because the basic coot expression is being alluded to. As for badger, the full expression is 'bald as a badger's bum'. There was once a belief that bristles for shaving brushes were plucked from this area. Christy Brown, *Down All the Days* (1970) has, rather, 'bald as a baby's bum'.

as happy (or **jolly**) **as a sandboy.** Extremely happy. Presumably these expressions refer to the boy who used to hawk sand from door to door but why he was especially remarkable for his happiness is hard to say. The *OED2* finds a quotation from Pierce Egan (1821): 'As happy as a sandboy who had unexpectedly met with good luck in disposing of his hampers full of the above household commodity.' Dickens in *The Old Curiosity Shop* (1840–1) has 'The Jolly Sandboys' as the name of a pub, with a sign, 'representing three Sandboys increasing their jollity with as many jugs of ale and bags of gold'. Angus Easson in his Penguin edition, notes: 'Sand was sold for scouring, as a floor cover to absorb liquids, and for bird cages. Sandboys were proverbially happy people, as indeed they might be in 1840 when they could buy a load of about $2\frac{1}{2}$ tons for 3s. 6d. ($17\frac{1}{2}$p), and take £6 or £7 in a morning … During the century, sawdust tended to replace sand for floors … and, by 1851, those in the trade were much less happy.'

as happy as Larry. Meaning 'extremely happy'. Usually considered an Australian expression and supposedly referring to the boxer Larry Foley (1847–1917). The first *OED2* citation (indeed Australian) is from 1905. Another suggestion is that the phrase derives from the Australian 'larrikin', meaning 'lout, hoodlum, mischievous young person'.

as like/different as chalk and/from cheese. Very different indeed (despite the superficial similarity that they both look whiteish). Known since 1393. Sometimes to be found in the phrase 'not to know chalk from cheese' – unable to tell the difference.

Aston Martin. Fast, smart sports cars have been made with this name by the Aston Martin Lagonda company since 1921. According to Adrian Room, *Dictionary of Trade Name Origins* (1982), the company was founded by Lionel *Martin* who used to race cars near *Aston* Clinton in Buckinghamshire.

at one fell swoop. At one time, in a single movement. 'Fell' here means 'fierce' and originally had a 'deadly' connotation. Indeed, the image in the full phrase is of a hawk swooping on its prey. Apparently, a Shakespearean coinage. In *Macbeth*, IV.iii.219 (1606), when Macduff is told that his wife and children have all been slaughtered, he exclaims:

O Hell-kite! – All?
What, all my pretty chickens, and their dam,
At one fell swoop?'

at the eleventh hour. Meaning 'at the last moment', this phrase's origin lies in the parable of the labourers, of whom the last 'were hired at the eleventh hour' (Matthew 20:9). It was used with a different resonance at the end of the First World War. The Armistice was signed at 5 a.m. on 11 November 1918 and came into force at 11 a.m. – 'at the eleventh hour of the eleventh day of the eleventh month'.

Autocue. Originally, the proprietary name for a prompting device used in television production. By use of angled glass, it enables the performer to read a script which is unrolled as required, whilst he or she looks straight into the camera and does not betray that any such device is being used. Originally the script was on paper; more recently on a computer screen. A British proprietary name, known by 1958. The name has often been used interchangeably with the generic term 'teleprompter' (originally an American proprietary name, known by 1951).

AWOL. *A*bsent *W*ith*O*ut *L*eave – unwarranted absence from the military for a short period, but not desertion. This expression dates from the American Civil War when offenders had to wear a placard with these initials printed on it. During the First World War, the initials were still being pronounced individually; not until just before the Second World War was it pronounced as the acronym 'Awol'. It does not mean 'absent without *official* leave'.

axe to grind. *See* HAVE AN ...

B

baby boomer. A person born just after the Second World War during the 'baby boom'. This US term was hardly known in Britain until a 'Baby Boomer' edition of the Trivial Pursuit board game arrived in 1986. It was intended to appeal to those who had reached maturity during the 1960s. For a while, British journalists took to using the phrase 'baby boom' and even 'baby boomers' in preference to the **bulge** or **post-war bulge** which had been used hitherto (a much better way, surely, to describe a pregnancy-related phenomenon). In fact, both 'baby boom' and 'bulge' had been used to describe the rise in births after the *First* World War and, specifically, the effect this had when those children became of school age. The Japanese also have a phrase for the phenomenon: *dankai no sedai* [the cluster generation].

Baby Ruth. The name of the popular US candy bar does *not* derive from the name of George Herman Ruth (1895–1948), the US professional baseball player known as 'Babe Ruth'. One story has it, however, that the manufacturers had wanted to call the bar a 'Babe Ruth'. They offered him $20,000 but he held out for $50,000. So they settled instead for an approximation and did not have to pay a nickel.

The bar is also said to have taken its name from President Grover Cleveland's daughter, Ruth, who was born in the White House. However, that event took place in 1891 and the bar did not make its first appearance until the 1920s.

More probably, it was thus dubbed by Mrs George Williamson, whose husband was president of the Williamson Candy Company which originally made the bar. She named it after a granddaughter. Babe Ruth himself had to be content with giving his name to a home run in baseball.

back to square one. Meaning 'back to the beginning', this phrase is sometimes said to have gained currency from the 1930s onwards through its use by British radio football commentators. *Radio Times* used to print a map of the football field divided into numbered squares, to which commentators would refer thus: 'Cresswell's going to make it – FIVE. There it goes, slap into the middle of the goal – SEVEN. Cann's header there – EIGHT. The ball comes out to Britton. Britton manoeuvres. The centre goes right in – BACK TO EIGHT. Comes on to Marshall – SIX' (an extract from the BBC commentary on the 1933 Cup Final between Everton and Manchester City). The idea had largely been abandoned by 1940.

Against this proposition is the fact that square 'one' was nowhere near the beginning. The game began at the centre spot, which was at the meeting point of squares three, four, five and six.

Indeed, Partridge/*Catch Phrases* prefers an earlier origin in the children's game of hopscotch or in the board game Snakes and Ladders. If a player was unlucky and his or her counter landed on the snake's head in Square 97 or thereabouts, it had to make the long journey 'back to square one'.

backroom boys. A nickname given to scientists and boffins – and specifically to those relied on to produce inventions and new gadgets for weaponry and navigation in the Second World War. Compare *The Small Back Room*, the title of the novel (1943) by Nigel Balchin.

The phrase was originated, in this sense, by Lord Beaverbrook as Minister of Aircraft Production when he paid tribute to his research department in a broadcast on 19 March 1941: 'Let me say that the credit belongs to the boys in the backrooms [*sic*]. It isn't the man who sits in the limelight who should have the praise. It is not the men who sit in prominent places. It is the men in the backrooms.' In the US, the phrase 'backroom boys' can be traced at least to the 1870s, but Beaverbrook can be credited with the modern application to scientific and technical boffins. His inspiration quite obviously was his favourite film, *Destry Rides Again*, (1939), in which Marlene Dietrich jumps on the bar of the Last Chance saloon and sings the Frank Loesser song 'See What the Boys in the Back Room Will Have'.

bacon. *See* BRING HOME THE ...

bad hair day. A day on which you feel depressed, possibly because – as it used to be put – you 'can't do a thing' with your hair. American origin, early 1990s.

'Having a bad hair day', in the fast-changing slang favoured by Californian teenagers, is how you feel when you don't want to leave the house: out of sorts, ugly and a bit depressed ... having a bad hair day is meant to be a metaphor for a bad mood.
Daily Telegraph (19 December 1992)

The Chanel public relations director is having what Manhattanites describe as a bad hair day. But, somewhat perversely, she is quite enjoying herself.
The Times (13 January 1993)

[Hillary Clinton] stopped saying 'two-fer-one' and 'vote for him, you get me' – but still, one bad hair day was following the next. Soon she started making jokes about it with her campaign staff. 'How 'bout it?' she'd say. 'Another bad hair day?'
Guardian (19 January 1993)

bad name. *See* GIVE A DOG A ...

badger. *See* AS BALD AS A ...

bag. *See* LET THE CAT OUT OF THE ...

baker's dozen. In use by the sixteenth century, this phrase to denote the number thirteen may date from the medieval baker's habit of giving away an extra loaf with every twelve to avoid being fined for providing underweight produce. The surplus was known as 'inbread' and the thirteenth loaf, the 'vantage loaf'. A **devil's dozen** is also thirteen – the number of witches who would gather when summoned by the devil.

bald. *See* AS ... AS A BADGER ...

baldheaded. *See* GO AT SOMETHING ...

Baldock. The Hertfordshire town takes its name from the city of Baghdad which became the capital of Iraq. The Knights Templar who once held the local manor named it in honour of the Levantine city which was known as Baldac in Old French.

ball rolling. *See* KEEP THE . . .

balloon's gone up. Current by 1924 and meaning 'the action or excitement has commenced', particularly in military activities, this expression derives from the barrage balloons introduced during the First World War to protect targets from air raids. The fact that these balloons – or observation balloons – had 'gone up' would signal that some form of action was imminent. C.H. Rolph in *London Particulars* (1980) suggests that the phrase was in use earlier, by 1903–4.

> Oh, and of course the moment when the boss walks in and says 'OK, Carruthers, the balloon's gone up, this is the big one and you're the chap to handle it' – which, naturally, happens all the time.
> *Scotsman* (30 August 1994)

bang to rights. As in 'You've got me bang to rights!' said by a criminal to an arresting policeman, this is an alternative to 'It's a fair cop!' [You are quite right to have caught me, constable!]. There is also an element of 'You've caught me red-handed, in an indefensible position'. Partridge/*Slang* dates this from the 1930s, but *OED2* finds a US example in 1904. Possibly derived from nineteenth-century usage – from the idea of being 'bang-on right' – in absolute certainty. Compare the somewhat rare Americanism 'bang' for a criminal charge or arrest, as in 'it's a bum bang', perhaps having some connection with the banging of a cell door.

banger. (1) A decrepit old car – presumably from its tendency to backfire (so known, usually, as 'old banger' by 1962). (2) A sausage (so known by 1919), presumably from the popping noises made during cooking.

banjaxed, to be. An Irishism meaning 'banged about; smashed' and introduced into popular British speech by the broadcaster Terry Wogan in the early 1970s. Possibly from Dublin slang of the 1920s. When he wrote a book called *Banjaxed* (1979), Wogan supplied this definition of the verb: 'To hornswoggle, corpse, knacker, rasher, caramelize, malfooster, malavogue, powfagg, keelhaul, macerate, decimate, pulverize, make rawmeish of. Hence *banjaxed*, reduced to the condition of a pig's breakfast, and *banjaxing*, tearing a plaster from a hairy leg.'

bar the shouting.   *See* ALL OVER . . .

Barbarella.   Name of a sexy, blonde astronaut who made her debut as the heroine of a comic strip in the French *V* magazine in 1962, and who was celebrated in the French/Italian film *Barbarella* (1967) with Jane Fonda in the title role. Like the British 'Jane' during the Second World War, she was always falling out of her clothes.

barbarians (are) at the gate(s).   Meaning 'the end of civilization is at hand'. Hyperbole. In 1990 *Barbarians at the Gate* was used as the title of a book by Bryan Burrough (subtitled 'The Fall of RJR Nabisco') about goings-on in Wall Street – suggesting that unregulated, or at least ungentlemanly, behaviour had broken out.
    Appropriately enough, the phrase is used literally in Edward Gibbon's *Decline and Fall of the Roman Empire*, I.303 (1776–88): 'Such was the public consternation when the barbarians were hourly expected at the gates of Rome.'

bargepole.   *See* TOUCH SOMEONE/THING WITH A . . .

bark up the wrong tree, to.   This phrase meaning 'to follow a false scent' is of US origin (by 1832) and *appears* to come from racoon hunting. As this is done at night (racoons being nocturnal animals) and as, if chased, racoons run up trees, it would be quite possible for a dog to bark mistakenly under the wrong tree.

> Perhaps at this point a dutiful biographer, loyal to his calling, should seek to refute such charges. Actually, I am inclined to accept some of them, and simply say that the critics are barking up the wrong tree.
> *Times Higher Education Supplement* (7 July 1995)

barmy.   *See* GINGER, YOU'RE . . .

barnstorm, to.   (1) (Of actors) to perform unsubtly. (2) (Of US politicians) to give speeches drumming up votes in rural areas.
    The word originated in the US in the early nineteenth century when actors did indeed go bustling around the countryside performing in barns and similar informal venues. Their style was akin to that found in melodrama.
    It was possibly more the makeshift, improvised nature of the touring which led to the word being used (from the 1890s) in

connection with politicians who stomped about seeking votes. In time, 'barnstorming' was largely superseded by 'whistle-stop touring'.

bat out of hell.   *See* LIKE A . . .

bats in the belfry.   *See* HAVE . . .

battle royal.   *See* WAGE A . . .

BCE.   An abbreviation to be used in dating instead of B.C. (Before Christ). The initials stand for 'Before the Common Era' – a rather vague coinage which has, however, appealed principally to Jewish people because the unacceptable Christian element has been removed.

> A glance at the Babylonian captivity (587–536 BCE.).
> K. Magnus, *About the Jews* (1881)

Hence, also **CE**, the abbreviation for 'Common Era' – originally and still an almost exclusively Jewish usage designed to remove the Christian element from dating, as in AD meaning '*Anno Domini*' [in the year of Our Lord]. However, it has sometimes been taken to mean 'Christian Era', which surely defeats the object of the exercise.

> *Outlines of Jewish History from BCE 586 to CE 1885*
> Title of book by K. Magnus (1886)

beans.   *See* SPILL THE . . .

Beatle.   *See* FIFTH . . .

Beaujolais nouveau.   Selling Beaujolais wine during the first year of a vintage became a marketing ploy in Britain during the early 1970s. For a number of years, a race was held to see who could bring the new stock most quickly from France to Britain. The slogan was '*Le Beaujolais Nouveau est arrivé! . . .*'

b/Beaver.   (1) The cry identifying a man with a beard appears to have been common among children in the 1910s and 20s, though now redundant. In 1922, *Punch* had several jokes and cartoons on this theme and noted (19 July) in a caption: 'To Oxford is attributed the credit of inventing the game of "Beaver" in which you score points for spotting bearded men.'

But why *beaver*? Stuart Berg Flexner in *I Hear America Talking* (1976) notes the use of the animal's name to describe a high, sheared-fur hat in the US. The beaver's thick dark-brown fur, he says, also refers 'to a well-haired pudendum or a picture showing it, which in pornography is called a "beaver shot".' Beaver for beard may derive rather from the Middle Ages when the 'beaver' was the part of a soldier's helmet which lay around the chin as a face-guard (the 'vizor' was the bit brought down from the forehead). In Shakespeare's *Hamlet*, I.ii.228 (1600), the Prince asks: 'Then saw you not his face?' (that of his father's ghost). Horatio replies: 'O yes, my lord, he wore his beaver up.'

(2) Nickname of William Maxwell Aitken, 1st Baron Beaverbrook (1879–1964), newspaper magnate and politician in Britain. He took his title from the town in New Brunswick, Canada, where he had a home. Called 'Max' by his friends, he was known to his staff as 'the Beaver', a name explained by Tom Driberg (his first 'William Hickey' columnist on the *Daily Express*) as conveying a 'zoological symbol of tireless industry'.

because the scenery is better.   An argument in promoting the superior imagination-stirring qualities of radio as a creative medium. It may have originated in a letter to *Radio Times* in the 1920s, quoting a child who had said rather, 'The pictures are better' when comparing the radio version of a story with that seen on the stage. Known by the early 1960s, certainly, but somewhat overworked and inevitable now.

> Do you ever listen [to the radio]? I do. I like it best. As a child I know says: 'I see it much better on radio than on TV.'
> Joyce Grenfell (letter of 22 September 1962, included in *An Invisible Friendship*, 1981)

> 'I like the wireless better than the theatre,' one London child wrote in a now legendary letter, 'because the scenery is better.'
> Derek Parker, *Radio: The Great Years* (1977)

bed.   *See under* IN APPLE-PIE ORDER; GET OUT OF THE WRONG SIDE OF THE . . .

bee's knees, to be the.   To be the very best around; absolutely TOP HOLE. There has always been a fascination with bees' knees. In the eighteenth century there was the expression, 'as big as a bee's knee' and, in the nineteenth, 'as weak as a bee's knee'. But the bee whose knees became celebrated in US slang by 1923 was probably only there because of the rhyme. At about the same time, we find the **kipper's knickers**, the **cat's whiskers** (perhaps because of the importance of these in tuning wireless crystal sets in the 1920s), the **cat's pyjamas** (still new enough to be daring), 'the cat's miaow/eyebrows/ankles/tonsils/adenoids/galoshes/cufflinks/roller skates'. Not to mention 'the snake's hips', 'the clam's garter', 'the eel's ankle', 'the elephant's instep', 'the tiger's spots', 'the flea's eyebrows', 'the canary's tusks', 'the leopard's stripes', 'the sardine's whiskers', 'the pig's wings' – 'and just about any combination of animal, fish, or fowl with a part of the body or clothing that was inappropriate for it' (Stuart Berg Flexner, *I Hear America Talking*, 1976).

beeline. *See* MAKE A . . .

beggar this for a game of soldiers! Expression signifying that one is giving up some activity through exhaustion or disillusionment. 'Beggar' is, of course, a soft form of 'bugger', but quite what is meant by a 'game of soldiers' is not totally clear. Perhaps the speaker considers the activity being abandoned as pointless as a game of toy soldiers or as futile as the 'army game' (life as a professional soldier). **Sod this for a game of soldiers** is a fraction more alliterative. There is also **f*** this** (or **that**) for a game of soldiers. Perhaps none of these date from before the Second World War.

> I met him in the pub one summer. I'd just been stood up by a man I was having a relationship with. Blow that for a game of soldiers, I thought, when suddenly Jim appeared from one corner of the pub and offered me a drink.
> *Independent on Sunday* (13 February 1994)

bells on. *See* WITH KNOBS ON.

belt and braces. The name applied to a system with its own back-up, suggesting that if one part falls down, the other will stay up; a double check. An engineer's expression, used for example by a BBC man to describe the two microphones placed side by side when broadcasting the sovereign's Christmas message. In the days when this was broadcast live, it ensured transmission. Possibly known by the 1930s. Belt and Braces was also the name of a British theatre group of the 1970s.

An Australian engineer commented (1993) that some of his colleagues would talk of 'belt, braces and bowyangs, too' – bowyangs being ties round a worker's trousers to keep out cold and mud.

> Antibiotics . . . tend to neutralise the contraceptive pill. Mumbled warnings about the need for 'belt and braces' if hubby gets a bit amorous are useless.
> *Guardian* (29 March 1994)

Benedict. *See* EGGS . . .

Bennett. *See* OMELETTE ARNOLD . . .; GORDON . . .

berk. The American *Morris Dictionary of Word and Phrase Origins* (1977) cites entertainer Dudley Moore as saying of his colleague Peter Cook (in a magazine interview): 'It is hard to distinguish sometimes whether Peter is being playful or merely a berk.' Morris then goes on, coyly, to say '*berk* is British slang – originally a bit of Cockney rhyming slang – meaning "fool"' – and leaves it at that. In fact, 'berk' *is* rhyming slang but short for 'Berkeley/Berkshire Hunt' ('c***'). Spelling the word 'birk' or 'burk(e)' helps obscure the origin. Theoretically, if it comes from this source, the word should be pronounced 'bark'. The use probably does not date from before 1900.

Bermuda Triangle. An area of sea between Bermuda and Florida where a number of ships and aircraft inexplicably disappeared. So described by the early 1960s and celebrated in a best-selling book *The Bermuda Triangle* (1974) by Charles Berlitz. Then, allusively, the name given to any thing or place into which people or things simply vanish.

berserk. Frenziedly mad, as in 'he went berserk'. The word derives from the Berserkers, legendary Norse warriors who fought frenziedly in battle. The name may have to do with their clothing, 'bear-sark' = 'bear-coat'.

better days. *See* HAVE SEEN . . .

Betty Martin. *See* ALL MY EYE AND . . .

between a rock and a hard place. In a position impossible to get out of, literally or metaphorically. Popular in the 1970s and almost certainly of North American origin. An early appearance occurs in John Buchan, *The Courts of the Morning* (1929) but the phrase was being discussed in *Dialect Notes*, No. 5 (1921) where it was defined as 'to be bankrupt … Common in Arizona in recent panics; sporadic in California'.

> The phrase 'between a rock and a hard place' is, to my knowledge, a ruralism. I first heard it in Arizona about 1940 and had the impression it had been used long before that. Country sayings almost invariably have a much higher poetic component than their big-city equivalents.
> Letter, *Time* Magazine (2 April 1984)

between/betwixt the devil and the deep (blue) sea. Meaning 'having two courses of action open, both of them dangerous' (as with the classical Scylla and Charybdis), the phrase should not be taken too literally. The 'devil' here may refer to the seam of the wooden ship's hull or to a plank fastened to the side of a ship as a support for guns. Either of these was difficult of access, a perilous place to be, but better than in the deep blue sea. An earlier form was 'between the devil and the Dead Sea' (known by 1894). Nowadays, when expressing an impossible position, it has largely been replaced by BETWEEN A ROCK AND A HARD PLACE.

beware Greeks bearing gifts. A warning against trickery, this is an allusion to the most famous Greek gift of all – the large wooden horse which was built as an offering to the gods before the Greeks were about to return home after besieging Troy unsuccessfully for ten years. When it was taken within the city walls of Troy, men leapt out from it, opened the gates and helped destroy the city. Virgil in the *Aeneid* (II.49) has Laocoön warn the Trojans not to admit the horse, saying *timeo Danaos et dona ferentes* [I still fear the Greeks, even when they offer gifts].

beyond the pale. Meaning, 'outside the bounds of acceptable behaviour'. The Pale was the area of English settlement around Dublin in Ireland, dating from the fourteenth century, in which English law had to be obeyed. There have also been areas known as pales in Scotland, around Calais, and in Russia. The derivation is from Latin *palus*, meaning 'a stake'. Anyone who lived beyond this fence was thought to be beyond the bounds of civilization. The allusive use does not appear earlier than the mid-nineteenth century.

Big Bang. On 27 October 1986, the London Stock Exchange deregulated the British securities market in a sweeping move to which the light-hearted appellation 'Big Bang' was applied by those hoping for a 'boom' and fearing a 'bust' (which duly followed a year later). The system of fixed commissions on stock trading was eliminated in favour of negotiated rates. At the same time, the practice of separating brokers (who take orders and execute trades on behalf of investors) from jobbers (who buy and sell stock on their own account in order to make a market in that stock) was abolished. The previous March, banks and brokerages, domestic and foreign, were allowed to become members of the exchange in a move dubbed 'Little Bang'. The so-called 'Big Bang' theory of the beginning of the universe had been discussed during 1950 by Fred Hoyle in his book *The Nature of the Universe* and the phrase obviously predated the specific application to deregulation in the City.

big conk, big cock! Phrase expressing the age-old superstition that there is a correlation between the size of a man's nose and his penis. Erasmus (1466–1536), of all people, is supposed to have included the aphorism (in Latin) in one of his works. The obverse is contained in the superstition, 'small feet, small cock!'

big girl's blouse. Phrase used about a man who is not as manly as he might be. *Street Talk, the Language of* Coronation Street (1986) states, rather, that it 'describes an adult male who has a low pain threshold, a "sissy". When trying to remove a splinter someone might say: "Hold still you big girl's blouse. It won't hurt."' The phrase has also been associated with the British comedienne Hylda Baker (1908–86), especially in the TV series *Nearest and Dearest* which, if the case, would take back its use to the early 1970s, at least. Either way, it looks as though it is of Northern English origin.

> The house is utterly still (except where Balthazar is trying to screw the spout of his frankincense pot into Melchior's ear, to even things up for being called a big girl's blouse on the way in from the dressing room).
> *Guardian* (20 December 1986)

> His acid-tongued father [Prince Philip] might be reinforced in his view of him as a big girl's blouse, but Prince Charles is actually a big boy now. His children, locked away in the posh equivalent of care, are not.
> *Herald* (Glasgow) (20 October 1994)

bigwig. An important person, a magnate. From the large and imposing wigs worn by the aristocracy in Britain and France during the seventeenth and eighteenth centuries. Word known by the 1780s.

bikini. Bikini was originally the name of an atoll in the Pacific Marshall Islands. In July 1946 it was chosen as the site for US atomic bomb tests and the following summer, in France, the word 'bikini' was taken to apply to the skimpy two-piece women's bathing costume which had become all the rage. An unlikely pairing, but it is a word with an interesting sound and, just possibly, Louis Réard, the French motor engineer who designed the garment, was not too worried when what *he* called *le minimum* was replaced by a name which expressed the explosive effect of the new fashion. *Le Monde Illustré* (August 1947) wrote of, '*Ce mot cinglant comme l'explosion même*' [This word having the force of the explosion].

According to the *Guardian* (20 December 1988), Mrs Annie Castel, who took over the Réard company, thought that M. Réard in rechristening the garment had been thinking of the minute size of Bikini atoll rather than its explosive connotations.

Bill. *See* OLD ...

bill stickers will be prosecuted. The traditional British warning to anyone about to paste a poster on a wall. When could the words have been chosen? The term 'bill-sticker' was known by 1774, but the earliest evidence found of the warning is in a *Punch* cartoon in the edition of 26 April 1939. The graffitoed response, 'Bill Stickers is innocent', was current by the 1970s.

billion/trillion. Britons and Americans use these words differently. So:

    1 billion (US) = a thousand millions
    1 billion (UK) = a million millions
    1 trillion (US) = a million millions
    1 trillion (UK) = a billion millions.

In other words, the British amounts are *bigger* in each case, though the US values are beginning to predominate.

bimbo. In 1987–8, there was an explosion in the use of this word in the British press to describe a type of empty-headed but sexually attractive young woman. In fact, coinciding as it did with another explosion in the use of the verb BONK, the world seemed suddenly full of allusions to 'bonking bimbos'.

In Italian *bimbo* (like *bambino*) is the word for a baby or infant. From this, probably, we get the US slang use of the word for a foolish man ('poor bimbo') or whores ('blonde bimbos'). *OED2* finds both these senses current around 1920. There was also a song in 1954 by Rodney Morris which went: 'Bimbo, Bimbo, does your Mummy knowio/You're going down the road to see a little girlio'.

The resurgence in the use of the term occurred in 1987 when US girls Donna Rice and Jessica Hahn, who had had much-publicized flings with a presidential candidate and TV evangelist respectively, both felt it necessary to declare that they were not 'bimbos in bathing-suits'. By this time, the roots of the word, whatever they might be, had long been obscured. Simon Carr in the *Independent* (23 July 1988) mused that the word was right because it had a 'certain pneumatic promise . . . a pleasant combination of bulge and bubble-headedness'.

Bingo! A generalized exclamation on achieving anything, similar to 'Eureka!' In 1919, at a carnival near Jacksonville, Florida, Edwin Lowe saw people playing what they called 'bean-o' – putting beans on a numbered card. This game of chance was already established elsewhere under the names 'Keno', 'Loo', and 'Housey-Housey'. Lowe developed the idea and launched a craze which netted him a fortune. One of his friends stuttered, 'B . . . b . . . bingo!' on winning, and that is how the game is said to have got its name. The word had already been applied to brandy in the seventeenth century, but – as a result of this development from 'bean-o' – it turned not only into an exclamation on winning Lowe's game but also into a generalized cry.

bird. *See* GET THE . . .

Birds Eye. It may come as a surprise to consumers of the frozen foods sold under this brand name that the allusion is to one Clarence Birdseye (1886–1956). An American, he thought up the freezing process while fur-trapping in Labrador. In 1923, he launched Birdseye

Seafoods Inc. in New York. Eventually the company was absorbed by General Foods Corporation. The two-word form of the name may be appropriate as family tradition holds that it was given to an English ancestor, a royal page at court, who once shot a hawk through the eye.

bistro.   A small restaurant or bar. Another Russian word that has entered the English language (sometimes *bistrot*). It reaches us via French, but the Russian word says it all: 'quick'. However, some question this derivation. In English use by 1922.

bite the dust.   *See under* KICK THE BUCKET.

bitter end.   Meaning 'the last extremity; the absolute limit', and a common phrase by the mid-nineteenth century. Bitterness doesn't really enter into it: the nautical 'bitt' is a bollard on the deck of a ship, on to which cables and ropes are wound. The end of the cable that is wrapped round or otherwise secured to the bollard is the 'bitter end'. On the other hand, ends have – for possibly longer – been described as bitter in other senses. Proverbs 5:4 has: 'But her end is bitter as wormwood, sharp as a two-edged sword'.

> There's something quite refreshing about admitting you're bored with a performance instead of staying to the bitter end, worrying about how much you've paid for the ticket.
> *Independent on Sunday* (25 February 1996)

black box.   After a plane crash there is usually a scramble to retrieve the aircraft's 'black box' – or, more properly, its 'flight data recorder'. This contains detailed recordings of the aircraft's performance prior to the crash and can be of value in determining what went wrong. The name has been used since the Second World War. Originally it was RAF slang for a box containing intricate navigational equipment. Flight recorders are in fact *orange* so as to be more easily seen. The popular name arose probably because black is a more mysterious colour, appropriate for a box containing 'secret' equipment (Pye produced a record player with the name in the 1950s), and because of the alliteration.

> Absence of a 'black box' accident data recorder in the Chinook could mean the precise cause of the crash may never be known.
> *Evening Standard* (London) (3 June 1994)

Black Dwarf. *See under* POISON(ED) DWARF.

Black Friday. Originally this was a description of Good Friday, when clergymen wore dark vestments. However, there have been any number of specific 'Black Fridays', so designated. In Britain, on one such day (15 April 1921), certain trade unions withdrew support from the hard-pressed miners, a general strike was cancelled, and this is recalled in the Labour movement as a day of betrayal. In the US, the 'first' Black Friday was on 24 September 1929 when panic broke out on the stock market.

During the Wall Street crash there were similarly a **Black Wednesday**, a **Black Thursday** – the actual day of the crash – and a **Black Tuesday**. In 1988, on stock markets round the world, there was a **Black Monday** (19 October) and another Black Thursday (22 October).

Black Maria. An American explanation for this name as applied to a police van is that a brawny black woman called Maria Lee kept a lodging house in Boston and helped bundle arrested people into the police van. The term was known in the US by 1847 and in the UK by 1869.

blackball, to. To exclude from a club or society by voting against an application for membership. The origin is literal as black balls were used – often just one black ball placed as a vote would mean that the application was rejected. Known by 1770.

> I shall make a note to blackball him at the Athenaeum.
> Benjamin Disraeli, *Vivian Grey* (1826)

blackleg. One who works while others are on strike; a scab. Formerly used of a swindler in cards or in betting at the races. The reasons for the coinage are unclear, though 'black' anything signifies evil and wrongdoing. Known by 1889.

blacklist, to. To exclude someone from an activity because of unsuitability. Said to date from the Middle Ages when students who misbehaved at British universities had their names listed in black books. Then the lists were of poor credit risks, then of bankrupts. The modern sense, referring to employers keeping out undesirable employees, was known by the 1880s. In Hollywood during the

1940s/50s, the blacklist was of suspected Communist sympathizers who were denied the opportunity to work.

blarney.   Kissing the Blarney stone at Blarney Castle near Cork in Ireland is supposed to bestow the gift of the gab on the kisser, but the custom is of relatively recent origin, having not been mentioned in print until the late eighteenth century. The word 'blarney' seems, however, to have entered the language a little while before. The origin traditionally given is that in 1602, during the reign of Queen Elizabeth I, one Cormac Macarthy or Dermot McCarthy was required to surrender the castle as proof of his loyalty. He prevaricated and came up with so many excuses that (it is said) the Queen herself exclaimed: 'Odds bodikins, more Blarney talk'.

blimp.   When used to describe a type of stupid, reactionary, elderly gentleman this name derives from the cartoon character Colonel Blimp, created between the wars by David Low, and who reached a kind of apotheosis in the film *The Life and Death of Colonel Blimp* (1943). The character, in turn, took his name from an experimental airship/balloon developed during the First World War. Without frames, these were described as 'limp'. There was an 'A-limp' and a 'B-limp'. The aviator Horace Short may have been the man who dubbed them 'blimps'.
    Another suggestion is that the name is onomatopoeic. In 1915, a Lt Cunningham of the Royal Navy Air Service is said to have flicked his thumb against the surface of one of the airships and imitated the odd noise thus produced. Alternatively, J.R.R. Tolkien, writing in 1926, hazarded a guess that the name derived from a mixture of 'blister' and 'lump', both of which the balloons resembled.

blinking idiot.   A very stupid person (with twinkling or half-opened eyes). Apparently an original coinage by Shakespeare. In *The Merchant of Venice*, II.ix.53 (1596), Arragon opens the silver casket and says: 'What's here? the portrait of a blinking idiot/Presenting me a schedule!'

blonde bombshell.   A journalistic cliché now used to describe *any* (however vaguely) blonde woman but especially if a dynamic personality and usually a film star, show business figure, or model. In June 1975, Margo Macdonald complained of being described by the *Daily Mirror* as 'the blonde bombshell M.P.' who 'hits the House of Commons today'. The original was Jean Harlow who appeared in the 1933 film *Bombshell*. In Britain – presumably so as not to suggest that it was a war film – the title was changed to *Blonde Bombshell*.

bloody deed is/was done. Some appalling act has been accomplished. In Shakespeare, the phrase 'bloody deed' occurs several times and Macbeth's 'I have done the deed' and the almost immediate references to 'blood', not to mention Ross's 'Is't known who did this more than bloody deed?' (II.iv.22), might have produced this conflation. The nearest one gets is *Richard III* (IV.iii.1): 'The tyrannous and bloody act is done' – which is what Tyrrel says about the murder of the Princes in the Tower. As with 'the bloody dog is dead' from the end of the same play (V.v.2), the phrase is almost there but the exact words remain untraced.

Two quotations from minor poets of the early nineteenth century do contain the phrases, however, and lead one to suppose that an original coinage may never be found: the phrases sound like proverbial expressions.

Pallid grew every face; and man on man,
Speechless with horror, looked; for well they knew
The bloody deed was done.

from *The Fall of Nineveh*, the chief poem by Edwin Atherstone (1788–1875), who was born in Nottingham.

'Tis past! – the bloody deed is done,
A father's hand hath sealed the slaughter!
Yet in Grenada's many a one
Bewails the fate of Selim's daughter.

from 'Zara' by William Motherwell (1797–1835), a Scottish balladeer and editor of Robert Burns's poems.

Bloody Sunday. As with BLACK FRIDAY, there has been a number of these. On 13 November 1887, two men died during a baton charge on a prohibited socialist demonstration in Trafalgar Square, London. On 22 January 1905, hundreds of unarmed peasants were mown down when they marched to petition the Tsar in St Petersburg.

In Irish history, there was a Bloody Sunday on 21 November 1920 when, among other incidents, fourteen undercover British intelligence agents in Dublin were shot by Sinn Fein. More recently, the name was applied to Sunday 30 January 1972 when British troops killed thirteen Catholics after a protest rally in Londonderry, Northern Ireland. Perhaps the epithet sprang to mind readily on this occasion because of the film *Sunday Bloody Sunday* (1971). Later (1973) the UK/US group Black Sabbath released an album with the title *Sabbath Bloody Sabbath*.

Since the nineteenth century there has been the exclamation 'Sunday, *bloody* Sunday!' to reflect frustration at the inactivity and boredom traditionally associated with the Sabbath.

bloomers. Women's knickers. Originally, the name given to a female costume consisting of a close-fitting jacket and a skirt reaching to just below the knees, under which were worn wide trousers gathered at the ankles. The fashion was introduced in New York – though not invented – by Mrs Amelia Jenks Bloomer around 1851. It was soon adopted in England where it had a vogue for a time and delighted cartoonists. The trousers were especially suitable for younger ladies taking up bicycling and the word became a nickname for these undergarments. Later, applied to loose, knee-length knickers, then to any knickers at all.

blot on the landscape. Anything that spoils a view or, figuratively, is simply objectionable. T.E. Lawrence used it in a 1912 letter: 'His two Kufti people . . . will be a blot on the landscape.' Title of a Tom Sharpe novel (1975) in which 'Blott' is a character.

> Their makeshift shanties have always been a blot on the landscape (they creep right up to the hard shoulder of the motorway that brings visitors in from the airport) and they are now not only a blot on the conscience but a blot, too, on the immediate scrutiny of the immaculate dream to which some whites still subscribe.
> *The Times* (9 December 1995)

> It is a blot on the landscape – and it's lost its flavour. Now Wrigley, the chewing-gum manufacturer, is trying to teach Britain's estimated 22 million chewers where not to stick the gluey residue.
> *Sunday Telegraph* (11 February 1996)

blot one's copybook, to. To make an error, usually in a not totally serious context. To go out of favour with someone because of something you have done. From when children used to learn to write by using copybooks and their spoiling them with inkblots. Known by the 1930s.

> Now it was the College that had blotted its copy-book and had called her in as one calls in a specialist.
> Dorothy L. Sayers, *Gaudy Night* (1935)

blouse. *See* BIG GIRL'S ...

blow hot and cold, to. Meaning, 'to vacillate between enthusiasm and apathy', this expression has been known in English since 1577 and comes from one of Aesop's *Fables*. On a cold day, a satyr comes across a man blowing his fingers to make them warm. He takes the man home and gives him a bowl of hot soup. The man blows on the soup, to cool it. At this, the satyr throws him out, exclaiming that he wants nothing to do with a man who can 'blow hot and cold from the same mouth'.

blow the gaff, to. An earlier (eighteenth-century) form was 'to blow the gab' meaning 'to blab about something; to let the secret out; give the game away' and, conceivably, 'gaff' could have developed from that. 'Gaff' may here mean 'mouth' (like gab/gob) and, coupled with 'blow', this gives the idea of expelling air through it and letting things out. Known by 1812.

> As she invariably uses her travels with a friend as the basis for her pieces, I really do not see why there needed to be any hiatus. Or has she found someone else to travel with and does not want to blow the gaff?
> *Sunday Times* (29 October 1995)

blue stocking. Denoting 'a literary or studious woman', this phrase derived from the gatherings of cultivated females and a few eminent men at the home of Elizabeth Montagu in London around 1750. Boswell in his *Life of Johnson* (1791) explains that a certain Benjamin Stillingfleet was a popular guest, soberly dressed but wearing blue stockings: 'Such was the excellence of his conversation, that his absence was felt as so great a loss, that it used to be said, "We can do nothing without the blue stockings," and thus by degrees the title was established.'

blue-blooded. This phrase is used to mean 'aristocratic; socially superior'. Human blood is red, but during the fifteenth century many Spanish aristocrats had fair complexions which made their veins appear bluer than those of darker-skinned Moorish people. Thus they were said to have blue blood.

> The old blue-blooded inhabitants of Cranford.
> Mrs Gaskell, *Cranford* (1853)

blue-rinse set (or **brigade**).   Women, usually in their fifties and upwards, who use a blue rinse when washing their hair. Often employed to castigate middle-class elderly women who are thought to be a bit past it. 'Blue rinse' has been known since the 1940s, 'blue rinse set' since the 1960s.

> During his 16-year tenure with the Los Angeles Philharmonic, Mehta was at once a matinee idol of the blue-rinse brigade and a favorite target of critical barbs.
> *Los Angeles Times* (16 August 1986)

blurb.   This word refers to the promotional notes on the cover of a book, describing its contents and merits in encouraging tones. In 1907, Gelett Burgess, the US novelist, is said to have produced a comic book-jacket featuring an alluring female called Miss B[e]linda Blurb. Presumably she was intended to attract readers in the way that a publisher's written, descriptive notes are now meant to do. Seven years later, Burgess defined the word he had invented as 'to make a sound like a publisher'.

blush wine.   Rosé wine by another name. A marketing ploy originating in California in the second half of the 1980s. As the fashion for drinking white wines grew, producers of red wines dreamed up this way of passing off the blend. There was nothing really wrong with rosé as a name: it was the product that was out of fashion. The move was successful initially, although the name-change has not really endured.

> Last summer every London wine bar and a great many shops and restaurants were doing a roaring trade in so-called blush wines. A year before the same places could hardly give such wine away, because in 1986 it was still called rosé – and rosé had been distinctly démodé since the Seventies.
> *Sunday Times* Magazine (27 March 1988)

boat. *See* IN THE SAME ...

Bob's your uncle! An almost meaningless expression of the type that takes hold from time to time. It is another way of saying 'there you are; there you have it; simple as that'. It was current by the 1880s but doesn't appear to be of any hard and fast origin. It is basically a British expression – and somewhat baffling to Americans. There is the story of one such who went into a London shop, had it said to him, and exclaimed: 'But how did you know – I do have an Uncle Bob!?' In 1886, Arthur Balfour was appointed Chief Secretary for Ireland by his uncle, *Robert* Arthur Talbot Gascoyne-Cecil, 3rd Marquis of Salisbury, the Prime Minister. Could this be a possible source?

bocca del lupo. *See under* BREAK A LEG!

bodies are buried. *See* KNOW WHERE THE ...

boffin. Meaning a scientist and inventor, this term is probably of RAF origin in the Second World War but was adopted by the other services. Such men produced navigational aids, bomb-aiming and gunnery gadgetry. There was an eccentric gentleman called Mr Boffin in Charles Dickens, *Our Mutual Friend* (1864–5).

bolshoi. The Russian word for 'big' – as in the name of Moscow's principal theatre for opera and ballet, and especially the world-famous Bolshoi Ballet. The building was opened in 1856.

The same root can be found in the term **Bolshevik**, the name for a member of a radical faction of what became the Russian Communist Party in 1918. In 1903, a Bolshevik was a member of the 'big part', the majority, who favoured extreme measures. A **Menshevik**, on the other hand, was a member of the 'less', the minority who were non-Leninist.

bomb. *See* GO (DOWN) A ...

bones. *See* MAKE NO ...

bonk, to. A hugely popular euphemism for sexual intercourse in Britain around the summer of 1987, though McConville and Shearlaw had it in *The Slanguage of Sex* (1984) and *OED2* finds it in a magazine in 1975. Like 'bang', used in a similar way, the notion seems to be one of sex as a brutal, bashing matter. 'To bonk' used to mean, simply, 'to hit'. Perhaps the appeal of the word had something to do with its resemblance to 'conk' (nose – as in the expression: ' BIG CONK, BIG COCK!') and 'bunk' (as in the verb meaning 'to sleep'). Nicholas Fairbairn MP listed his hobbies in the 1977 edition of *Who's Who* as 'bunking and debunking', which undoubtedly conveyed this sense. Another theory is that 'bonk' is back-slang for 'knob', a well-established name for 'penis'.

boobs.   Slang term for the female breasts, derived from 'bubby' or 'booby', both of which words defy analysis. Can 'bubble' have come into it? A 'booby' is also a fool. Another suggestion is that it has to do with 'bubo', a *swelling* in the groin, a common symptom of the bubonic plague.

> I felt her sloshy boobs joggling me.
> Henry Miller, *Sexus* (1949)

book.   *See* TURN UP FOR THE . . .

boondocks/boonies.   Somewhere obscure, out of the way and 'in the sticks'. During the Second World War, US GIs stationed in the Philippines were sometimes sent to the mountain regions. *Bundok* means 'mountain' in Tagalog, the official language of the Philippines.

> We [mankind] are in the galactic boondocks where the action isn't it.
> Carl Sagan, *The Cosmic Connection* (1973)

boot.   *See* TO . . .

bootleg.   Originally applied to the illegal selling of liquor, in more recent times this term has been applied to such things as records and cassettes and means 'counterfeit'. The word arose in the American Far West during the mid-nineteenth century when illegal liquor sales were made to Indians on reservations. The thin bottles of alcohol are said to have been concealed in the vendor's long boots.

boots.   *See* DIE WITH ONE'S . . .

booze.   As a verb, to drink heavily. As a noun, in the US, hard liquor; in the UK, beer or ale. One derivation for this word for alcoholic drink is from the name of E.C. (*or* E.S. *or* E.G.) Booz, a Philadelphia whisky distiller (*c.*1840), but the word was current in the fourteenth century. Middle English *bousen* meant 'to drink deeply'. 'Booze' as a noun was known in English by 1732. Mr Booz seems merely to have helped popularize the word.

born-again.   Applied to evangelical and fundamentalist Christians in the Southern US since the 1960s, this adjective derives from the story of Jesus Christ and Nicodemus in John 3 ('Ye must be born again'). Originally suggesting a re-conversion or conversion to Christianity, the phrase took on a figurative sense of 'revitalized', 'zealous', 'newly converted' around the time when Jimmy Carter, from a born-again Baptist background in the South, was running for the US presidency in 1976. Hence, 'born-again automobiles' (for reconditioned ones) and such like.

> We believe that the first time we're born, as children, it's human life given to us; and when we accept Jesus as our Saviour, it's a new life. That's what 'born again' means.
> Jimmy Carter, in an interview with Robert L. Turner (16 March 1976)

bottle.   'Milk's gotta lotta bottle' was a slogan promoting milk consumption in Britain, *c.*1982. Milk comes in bottles, of course, but why was the word 'bottle' used to denote courage or guts in this major attempt to get rid of milk's wimpish image? Actually, the word 'bottle' has been used in this sense since the late 1940s at least. To 'bottle out' consequently means to shrink from, e.g. in *Private Eye* (17 December 1982): 'Cowed by the thought of six-figure legal bills and years in the courts, the Dirty Digger has "bottled out" of a confrontation with Sir Jams.'

One suggestion is that 'bottle' acquired the meaning through rhyming slang: either 'bottle and glass' = class (said to date from the 1920s); 'bottle and glass' = arse; or, 'bottle of beer' = fear. But the reason for the leap from 'class/arse' to 'courage', and from 'fear' to 'guts', is not clear, though it has been explained that 'arse' is what you would void your bowels through in an alarming situation. And 'class' is what a boxer has. If he loses it, he has 'lost his bottle'.

Other clues? Much earlier, in *Swell's Night Guide* (1846), there was: 'She thought it would be no bottle 'cos her rival could go in a buster', where 'no bottle' = 'no good'. In a play by Frank Norman

(1958), there occurs the line: 'What's the matter, Frank? Your bottle fallen out?' There is also an old-established brewers, Courage Ltd, whose products can, of course, be had in bottles.

The way forward for the 1982 advertising use was probably cleared by the ITV series *Minder* which introduced much south London slang to a more general audience.

bowdlerize, to. Meaning 'to expurgate', this verb derives from the name of Thomas Bowdler who published *The Family Shakespeare* (1818), a ten-volume edition of the dramatist's works with all the dirty bits left out (or, as he put it, those words 'which cannot be read aloud in a family'). 'Out damn'd spot' became 'Out crimson spot', and so on. Dr Bowdler, in consequence, has given his name to any form of literary expurgation. Possibly the word 'bowdlerize' caught on because of its resemblance to 'disembowel'. It was already current by 1836.

box. A slightly passé term for a TV set (having earlier been applied to wirelesses and gramophones), and one of several derogatory epithets which were applied during the medium's rise to mass popularity in the 1940s and 50s. Groucho Marx used the expression in a letter (1950). Maurice Richardson, sometime TV critic of the *Observer*, apparently coined the epithet **idiot's lantern** prior to 1957.

> I don't sleep here, but come out at 4.30 p.m.–9 p.m. nearly every evening, and dream, or write, or read by the fire, or play Beethoven and Mozart to myself on the box.
> T.E. Lawrence, in a 1924 letter

boy meets girl. Neat summary of what might seem to be the most popular plot in all fiction. Known by 1945 and possibly originating in discussion of Hollywood movies in the 1930s. Capable of various extensions: 'Boy meets girl, boy loses girl, boy wins her back', etc.

boycott. *See* MOUNT A . . .

bra burner. One who demonstrates solidarity with the feminist cause. In *c.*1970, women were encouraged to destroy an item of apparel quite clearly designed by a MALE CHAUVINIST PIG and likely to make a woman more of a sex object. It followed the example of burning draft-cards as a protest against the Vietnam War.

> The whole point of bra-burning seems to have vanished from some English liberationist minds.
> *Guardian* (18 January 1971)

brains trust. *The Brains Trust* was the title of a BBC radio discussion programme (1941 onwards), originating from the American term for a group of people who give advice or who comment on current issues. In his first presidential campaign in 1932, Franklin D. Roosevelt set up a circle of advisers which became known as his '*brain* trust'. In Britain, the term was borrowed and turned into '*brains* trust'. Curiously, the Roosevelt coinage, attributed to James Michael Kieran Jnr, was at first 'the *brains* trust' also.

brand new (sometimes **bran new**).   This expression for 'very new' comes from the old word meaning 'to burn' (just as a 'brand' is a form of torch). A metal that was brand (*or* bran) new had just been taken out of the flames, having just been forged. Shakespeare has the variation 'fire-new', which points more directly to the phrase's origin. Known by 1570.

brass knobs on.   *See* WITH KNOBS ON.

brass monkey.   *See* COLD ENOUGH TO FREEZE . . .

brass tacks.   *See* GET DOWN TO . . .

break a leg!   A traditional theatrical greeting given before a performance, especially a first night, because it is considered bad luck to wish anyone 'good luck' directly. Another version is **snap a wrist!** Partridge/*Slang* has 'to break a leg' as 'to give birth to a bastard', dating from the seventeenth century, but that is probably unconnected. As also is the fact that John Wilkes Booth, an actor, broke his leg after assassinating President Lincoln in a theatre. The *Morris Dictionary of Word and Phrase Origins* (1977) has it based on a German good luck expression, *Hals und Beinbruch* [May you break your neck and your leg]. Perhaps this entered theatrical speech (like several other expressions) via Yiddish.

Other theatrical good-luck expressions include *merde!* [French: 'shit!'], TOY! TOY! and *in bocca del lupo* [Italian: 'into the wolf's jaws'], although this last has also been heard in the form '*bocc' al lupo*'.

break the mould, to. To start afresh from fundamentals. When the Social Democratic Party was established in 1981, there was much talk of it 'breaking the mould of British politics' i.e. doing away with the traditional system of a government and one chief opposition party. But this was by no means a new way of describing political change and getting rid of an old system for good, in a way that prevents it being reconstituted. In *What Matters Now* (1972), Roy Jenkins, one of the new party's founders, had quoted Andrew Marvell's 'Horatian Ode Upon Cromwell's Return from Ireland' (1650):

And cast the kingdoms old,
Into another mould.

In a speech at a House of Commons Press Gallery lunch on 8 June 1960, Jenkins had also said: 'The politics of the left and centre of this country are frozen in an out-of-date mould which is bad for the political and economic health of Britain and increasingly inhibiting for those who live within the mould. Can it be broken?'

A.J.P. Taylor, in his *English History 1914–1945* (1965), had earlier written: 'Lloyd George needed a new crisis to break the mould of political and economic habit'. The image evoked, as in the days of the Luddites, is of breaking the mould from which iron machinery is cast – so completely that the machinery has to be re-cast from scratch.

breakfast. *See* LOOKING/DRESSED UP LIKE A DOG'S ...

bring home the bacon, to. Meaning, 'to be successful in a venture', this may have to do with the **Dunmow Flitch**, a tradition established in 1111 at Great Dunmow in Essex. Married couples who can prove they have lived for a year and a day without quarrelling or without wishing to be unmarried can claim a gammon of bacon. Also, country fairs used to have competitions which involved catching a greased pig. If you 'brought home the bacon', you won.

In 1910, when Jack Johnson, the American negro boxer, won the World Heavyweight boxing championship, his mother exlaimed: 'He said he'd bring home the bacon, and the honey boy has gone and done it.' The *Oxford Companion to American History* suggests that this 'added a new phrase to the vernacular'. Unlikely, given the Dunmow Flitch connection, and yet the *OED2*'s earliest citation is not until 1924 (in P.G. Wodehouse).

brinkmanship. Political policies which bring a country to the brink of war. The term was popularized by Adlai Stevenson during the 1956 US presidential campaign with reference to the Secretary of State, John Foster Dulles. He had said: 'If you are scared to go to the brink, you are lost.' Also used in competitive games and sports.

Bristols. Rhyming slang provides this word meaning 'breasts', the origin of which is otherwise far from obvious. The rhyme is 'Bristol Cities' [titties] – a use more or less restricted to the UK and since the 1950s. As Paul Beale suggests in his revision of Partridge/*Slang*, the football team Bristol City probably only gets invoked because of the initial similarity of the words 'Bristol' and 'breasts'.

> The main point (or should it be points?) of this programme is Miss Barbara Windsor's bristols which are ... well-developed.
> *Observer* (2 February 1969)

bromide. A trite remark or platitude. In *Are You a Bromide?* (1906), the American writer Gelett Burgess castigated people who spoke in clichés. He invented this word to describe someone so addicted and it gradually changed in meaning to become the thing so spoken by such a person.

Bronx cheer. A noise of derisive disapproval. *DOAS* suggests that this form of criticism (known by 1929) originated at the National Theater in the Bronx, New York City, although the Yankee baseball stadium is also in the same area. The UK equivalent is 'to blow a **raspberry**', from rhyming slang, 'raspberry tart' = fart.

brother of the more famous —. Phrase alluding to the intriguingly titled novel *Brother of the More Famous Jack* (1982) by Barbara Trapido. It refers neither to characters in the book nor to Robert and John F. Kennedy. No, Chapter 4 has: 'Yeats, William Butler ... Brother of the more famous Jack, of course.' The Irish poet W.B. Yeats did indeed have a brother, Jack, who was a leading artist.

The stars were Claude Hulbert, brother of the more famous Jack, his wife Delia Trevor, and another fine comedian called Sonny Hale.
Robert Stephens, *Knight Errant* (1995)

Bankside was, of course, theatreland in the seventeenth century. Edmund Shakespeare, brother of the more famous William, is buried here.
Michael Kerrigan, *Who Lies Where* (1995)

browned off. *See* CHEESED OFF.

brownie points. Originating in American business or the military, and certainly recorded before 1963, this has nothing to do with Brownies, the junior branch of the Girl Guides, and the points they might or might not gain for doing their 'good deed for the day'. Oh no! This has a scatological origin, not unconnected with brown-nosing, brown-tonguing, arse-licking and other unsavoury methods of sucking up to someone important.

Note also the American term 'Brownie', an award for doing something *wrong*. According to *DOAS*, 'I got a pair of Brownies for that one' (1942) refers to a system of disciplinary demerits on the railroads. The name was derived from the inventor of the system.

brush-off. Meaning 'a rebuff', this noun is said to derive from a habit of Pullman porters in the US who, if they thought you were a poor tipper, gave you a quick brush over the shoulders and passed on to the next customer. However, perhaps the mere action of brushing unwanted dirt off clothing is sufficient reason for the expression. Known by 1941.

Later when she began to hate her job at the *Evening Standard* and made plans to leave, she gave Robert Lutyens the brush-off. She no longer needed him.
Christopher Ogden, *Life of the Party* (1994)

buck. *See* PASS THE ...

bucket. *See* KICK THE ...

budget. *See under* CRY MUM.

buff. (1) An enthusiast, e.g. 'film buff', 'opera buff', etc. This use came from people who liked to watch fires being extinguished or who helped to extinguish them in an amateur capacity in New York

City. They were called 'buffs' (by 1903) either because of their buffalo uniforms or because the heavy buffalo robes they wore to keep them warm in winter (before the fires were started, presumably) somewhat hindered their usefulness. In which case, the term was used as a mild form of rebuke by the real fire-fighters.

(2) Naked, as in the phrase **in the buff**. This seems to derive from the buff-coloured leather shorts down to which people in the services were sometimes stripped. Although strictly speaking they were not naked, the term was extended to apply to those who were completely so. An English regiment has been known as 'The Buffs' for over three hundred years – not because it goes naked but because of the colour of its uniform.

Buggins's turn. This expression gives the reason for a job appointment having been made – when it is somebody's turn to get the job rather than because the chosen person is especially well qualified to do it. The name Buggins is used because it sounds suitably dull and humdrum ('Joseph Buggins, Esq. JP for the borough' appears in one of G.W.E. Russell's *Collections and Recollections*, 1898. Trollope gave the name to a civil servant in *Framley Parsonage*, 1861. The similar sounding 'Muggins', self-applied to a foolish person, goes back to 1855, at least).

The earliest recorded use of the phrase 'Buggins's turn' is by Admiral Fisher, later First Sea Lord, in a letter of 1901. Later, in a letter of 1917 (printed in his *Memories*, 1919), he said: 'Some day the Empire will go down because it is Buggins's turn.' It is impossible to say whether Fisher coined the phrase, though he always spoke and wrote in a colourful fashion.

bulge. *See under* BABY BOOMER.

bulldog breed. In 1857, Charles Kingsley wrote of: 'The original British bulldog breed, which, once stroked against the hair, shows his teeth at you for ever afterwards.' In 1897, the British were called 'boys of the bulldog breed' in a music-hall song, 'Sons of the Sea, All British Born' by Felix McGlennon. At the outbreak of the First World War in 1914, Winston Churchill spoke at a 'Call to Arms' meeting at the London Opera House. 'Mr Churchill has made a speech of tremendous voltage and carrying power,' the *Manchester Guardian* reported. 'His comparison of the British navy to a bulldog

– "the nose of the bulldog has been turned backwards so that he can breathe without letting go" – will live. At the moment of delivery, with extraordinary appositeness, it was particularly vivid, as the speaker was able by some histrionic gift to suggest quite the bulldog as he spoke.' Indeed, during the Second World War, small model bulldogs were manufactured bearing Churchill's facial pout and wearing a tin helmet.

John Bull as a symbol and personification of Britain (sometimes shown accompanied by a bulldog) dates from before John Arbuthnot's *The History of John Bull* (1712).

bum. The bottom, buttocks (or, as it used to say in one dictionary) the posteriors. The simplest origin for this old word would seem to be from 'bottom', but this is clearly ruled out by the *OED2* which fancies some 'echoic' source (i.e. one imitating a sound). Hence, bum would seem to come from the 'bump' which a person makes as he or she sits down.

bumf (sometimes **bumpf** or **bumph**). Paperwork containing (perhaps tiresome) details, instructions. 'If you'll give me your address, I'll send you all the bumf.' Undoubtedly derived from 'bumfodder', i.e. paper used for lavatorial purposes (hence the title of Alexander Brome's ballad *Bumm-foder: or waste-paper proper to wipe the nations rump with*, ?1660). The shorter word known since 1889.

Bunbury. An imaginary person whose name one invokes in order to furnish oneself with an excuse not to do something, from Oscar Wilde's *The Importance of Being Earnest* (1899): 'I have invented an invaluable permanent invalid called Bunbury, in order that I may be able to go down into the country whenever I choose.' Bunbury is the name of an actual village in Cheshire.

bunk. In 1820, Felix Walker, a Congressman from Buncombe County, North Carolina, made a totally worthless speech in the House of Representatives. He justified himself by saying he was not speaking to the House, 'but to Buncombe', and the name has come to mean 'worthless rubbish' ever since, though the spelling has been simplified and shortened.

Hence, also, **to debunk**, meaning 'to draw attention to nonsense' or 'to deflate a reputation'. This was the creation of William E.

Woodward in his book *Bunk* (*c.*1920), an exposé of Henry Ford (famous for saying: 'History is more or less bunk').

burn.   *See under* GO FOR IT!

burnsides.   *See* SIDEBURNS.

Burton.   *See* GONE FOR A . . .

business.   *See* DO THE . . .

butler did it!   A jokily suggested solution – especially for 1920s and 1930s detective stories where presumably it originated. Early use curiously undocumented, but a cartoon drawn by Norman Mansbridge appeared in the issue of *Punch* dated 14 September 1938. Two policemen are shown standing outside a cinema which is screening *The Mansion Murder* and on the posters it asks 'Who killed the duke?' One policeman is saying to the other: 'I guessed the butler did it.'

buttonhole, to.   In the sense, 'to detain a reluctant listener', this verb does not derive from 'buttonhole', the hole through which a button passes, nor from the flower, so called, worn in the slit on a coat lapel. The verb is really 'to button*hold*', to stop persons going away by holding on to one of their buttons. By 1716. An earlier form was 'to take by the button'.

buy British.   Alliterative but uninspired slogan, often revived under government influence when too much reliance is being placed by consumers on imported products. An early appearance is in a *Punch* cartoon on 2 December 1931, though in a book published in 1925 (*Second Essays on Advertising*), 'Buy British Goods' was discussed. The commentator wrote: 'The slogan has never from its birth rung like true metal. There is nothing satisfying about it. It savours of a cry of distress – an SOS – and does not begin to present the spirit of a commerce that is reconstructing and paying its debts simultaneously.'

'I'm Backing Britain' was a variant in 1968. The slogan 'Buy British' was revived by the troubled motor manufacturer British Leyland in 1980. In 1981, the British textile industry launched a 'Think British' campaign.

by and large. Meaning, 'generally speaking'. Originally this was a nautical term: to sail by and large meant to keep a ship on course so that it was sailing at a good speed even though the direction of the wind was changing. *Brewer* defines it thus: 'To sail slightly off the wind, making it easier for the helmsman to steer and less likely for the vessel to be taken aback.' The nautical sense was current by 1669, the general sense by 1706.

bygones. *See* LET BYGONES BE ...

C

cabal. This word for a group of plotters is from the Hebrew *qabbalah* meaning 'accepted by tradition', used in connection with a Jewish mystical system of theology and metaphysics. It is *not* true to say that it gained its modern meaning from the initial letters of Clifford, Ashley, Buckingham, Arlington and Lauderdale, ministers in the reign of Charles II who signed the Treaty of Alliance with France in 1672. Their initials merely conformed to a word already in existence (in fact, by 1646).

caddy. One who carries the clubs and other equipment for a golfer. Known by 1857. No more and no less than a shortened form of the word 'cadet' (from the French for the younger of two brothers). Such people were often used for running errands or providing ancillary services.

Caesar —. Julius Caesar has given his name to fewer things than you might expect. In recent times, a **Caesar haircut** was one like those seen on busts of Caesar (and popularized by Marlon Brando in the 1953 film of *Julius Caesar* – although, in fact, he was playing Mark Antony).

The **Caesarian section method** of childbirth is *not* so named because Caesar was born in that way. It was illegal under Roman law, except where the mother was dead. The part of the Caesarian

Laws dealing with this aspect was called the Caesarian Section. An even simpler derivation is from the Latin word *caesus*, part participle of *caedere*, to cut.

Which brings us to **Caesar salad**, beloved of Hollywood diners-out. It took its name from its creator, Caesar Gardini, who ran Caesar's Place restaurant in Tijuana, Mexico. In the great tradition of kitchen creativity, he had to improvise a salad when more people turned up to eat than he had prepared for. The ingredients included lettuce, garlic, olive oil, croûtons, cheese and eggs, all lightly tossed.

Cain. *See* RAISE . . .

Calamity Jane. The nickname for a female prophet of doom derives from that of Martha Jane Canary (1852–1903) of Deadwood, South Dakota. She behaved like a cowboy but was generally unlucky in nefarious activities and brought catastrophe on her associates. Eleven of her twelve husbands died untimely deaths. She dressed, swore, and shot like a man, eventually went into show business, and threatened 'calamity' to any man who offended her. Known in this sense since the 1920s.

call a spade a spade, to. To speak bluntly, to call things by their proper names without resorting to euphemisms. But why a spade? Said to have arisen when Erasmus mistranslated a passage in Plutarch's *Apophthegmata* where the object that 'Macedonians had not the wit to call a spade by any other name than a spade' was rather a trough, basin, bowl or boat in the original Greek. The phrase was into the language, however, by 1580.

call of nature/the great outdoors. *See under* ANSWER THE CALL OF NATURE.

Camelot. (1) The legendary location of King Arthur's court. (2) The nickname for President Kennedy's 'court'. In January 1961, the inauguration of a stylish young US President, with a glamorous wife at his side, aroused hopes of better things to come, following the sober Eisenhower years. But this in itself was not enough for people to apply the epithet to members (and hangers-on) of John F. Kennedy's administration. What triggered it was the fact that the Lerner-Loewe musical *Camelot* (about King Arthur and Queen Guinevere) had opened on Broadway in December 1960.

camp. A word used to refer to anyone, male or female, who ostentatiously, exaggeratedly, self-consciously, somewhat vulgarly and theatrically flaunts himself or herself, without necessarily being homosexual. It is probably derived from the word used of prostitutes (male and female) who used to trail along behind the military and were thus 'camp followers'. It entered popular speech in the 1960s, although its origin is older.

> Alfred has a new word he uses rather a lot, which is 'camp'. He uses it mainly when he is talking about the opera. He says it's got nothing to do with Boy Scouts but just means anything outrageous, or over the top – camp in fact! He thinks Basil's new tie is camp.
> Joan Wyndham, *Love Lessons* (1985) (diary entry for 27 April 1940)

can. *See* CARRY THE . . .

can I have a P, please, Bob? On *Blockbusters*, the British ITV quiz (1983–93), the teenage contestants were asked questions according to their choice of letters on a honeycomb grid. The host was Bob Holness. Infantile humour dictated that they put this question to him when they were not asking, 'I'll have an E please, Bob' (referring to the rave culture's drug of choice) or (from the girls) 'I'll have U please, Bob.'

candle. *See* HOLD A . . .

cannon. *See* LOOSE . . .

canoe. *See* PADDLE ONE'S OWN . . .

cap. *See* HAVE A FEATHER IN ONE'S . . .; SET ONE'S . . .

carborundum. *See* FILLEGITIMI NON . . .

cardigan. A woollen sweater that buttons down the front. So called after the 7th Earl of Cardigan (1797–1868) who wore one during his service in the Crimean War to protect himself from the severe cold. He also led the charge of the Light Brigade at Balaclava. Known as such by 1868.

career. *See* GOOD ...

carry the can, to. Meaning 'to bear responsibility; take the blame; become a scapegoat', this is possibly a military term, referring to the duties of the man chosen to get beer for a group. He would have to carry a container of beer to the group and then carry it back when it was empty. Some consider it to be precisely naval in origin; no example before 1936. Alternatively, it could refer to the man who had to remove 'night soil' from earth closets – literally, carrying the can – and leaving an empty can in its place. Or then again, it could have to do with the 'custom of miners carrying explosives to the coal face in a tin can (hence everyone's reluctance to "carry the can")' – *Street Talk, the Language of* Coronation Street (1986).

cart. *See* IN THE ...

Case is Altered, the. Name given to a number of public houses in Britain and sometimes erroneously said to be a corruption of the Spanish *casa alta* (high house). Rather is it from the proverb, 'The case is altered, quoth Plowden', where the person mentioned is Edmund Plowden (1518–85). A Roman Catholic, he was arrested after 1570 for the treasonable offence of attending a surreptitious mass. He defended himself and was able to prove that the priest who had presided over the mass in question was an agent provacateur. He argued that a true mass could not be celebrated by an impostor – 'the case is altered' – and was acquitted. The phrase was subsequently much quoted. In Shakespeare's *King Henry VI, Part 3*, IV.iii.30 (1590–1) there occurs the following exchange:

King Edward: Why, Warwick, when we parted,
Thou call'dst me King.
Warwick: Ay, but the case is alter'd:
When you disgrac'd me in my embassade,
Then I degraded you from being King,
And come now to create you Duke of York.

In Mieder & Kingsbury *Dictionary of Wellerisms* (1994), Plowden is described as an eminent English jurist who while 'giving advice on trespassing ... was told that that the animals that had trespassed were his.' Can this be so?

cast. *See* DIE IS . . .

cat. *See* GRIN LIKE A CHESHIRE . . .; HAVE A . . . IN HELL'S CHANCE; LET THE . . .; NO ROOM TO SWING A . . .

cat has nine lives. A proverbial saying (known by 1546). But why so many? While cats have an obvious capacity for getting out of scrapes – literally 'landing on their feet' in most cases – in ancient Egypt, they were venerated for ridding the country of a plague of rats and were linked to the trinity of Mother, Father and Son. 'To figure out how many extra lives the cat had, the Egyptians multiplied the sacred number three, three times, and arrived at nine' – Robert L. Shook, *The Book of Why* (1983).

cat's breakfast. *See under* LOOKING/DRESSED UP LIKE A DOG'S BREAKFAST.

cat's pyjamas/whiskers. *See under* BEE'S KNEES.

catgut. Sheep, horse, ass, but *not* cat intestines are used in the making of strings for musical instruments. Shakespeare got it right in *Much Ado About Nothing*, II.iii.59 (1598): 'Is it not strange, that sheeps' guts should hale souls out of men's bodies?' Cats' intestines are never used – though they were for tennis racquets. Possibly the word was introduced as a pejorative way of describing the sound made by badly played violin strings, whatever their actual source.

cathouse. In *Catwatching* (1986), Desmond Morris traces this term for a brothel (mostly US use, by 1931) from the fact that prostitutes have been called 'cats' since the fifteenth century, 'for the simple reason that the urban female cat attracts many toms when it is on heat and mates with them one after the other'. As early as 1401, men were warned, Morris says, of the risk of chasing 'cat's tail' – women. Hence the slang word **tail** to denote the female genitals (compare 'pussy').

cats and dogs. *See* RAIN . . .

Caudle lecture. *See* CURTAIN LECTURE.

caught in the act. Caught in the very act for which retribution will be forthcoming. Known by 1655. In Jane Austen's novel

Persuasion (1818), there is rather 'caught in the *fact*'. Compare **caught red-handed**, where a murderer still has blood on his hands.

caviare to the general.   A famously misunderstood phrase meaning 'of no interest to common folk', this has nothing to do with giving expensive presents of caviare to unappreciative military gentlemen. In Shakespeare's *Hamlet*, II.ii.434 (1600–1), the Prince refers to a play which, he recalls: 'pleased not the million, 'twas caviare to the general' (the general public, in other words). The Arden edition notes that in *c*.1600, when the play was written, caviare was a novel delicacy. It was probably inedible to those who had not yet acquired a taste for it.

CE.   *See under* BCE.

Celsius.   Another way of referring to temperatures measured in centigrade. So called after Anders Celsius, a Swede, who proposed the first centigrade scale in 1742. British weather forecasters in the early 1970s, when the country was becoming metric-conscious, attempted to introduce the word Celsius when drawing comparisons with Fahrenheit temperatures (i.e. those measured on a scale where freezing is 32° and boiling point 212°). The logic was supposed to be that since Daniel Gabriel Fahrenheit, the German physicist, had given his surname to the scale he established in 1715, it would be more consistent to call the centigrade scale after Celsius. The idea barely caught on.

chalk.   *See* AS LIKE/DIFFERENT AS . . .; NOT BY A LONG . . .

Charlie Farnsbarns.   A foolish person whose name one cannot remember or does not care to. Noting that this moderately well-known expression had escaped Eric Partridge, his reviser, Paul Beale came back (1985) with: 'Charlie Farnsbarns was a very popular equivalent of e.g. "Mrs Thing" or "Old Ooja", i.e. "Old whats-isname". Much play was made with the name in [BBC radio series] *Much Binding In The Marsh*, but whether Murdoch and Horne actually invented it, or whether they borrowed it "out of the air", I'm afraid I don't know. They would mention especially, I remember, a magnificent motorcar called a "Farnsbarns Special" or something like, say, a "Farnsbarns Straight Eight". This was in the period, roughly, 1945–50, while I was at school – I recall a very jolly aunt of mine who was vastly amused by the name and used it a lot.'

'Charlie' is a name given to an ordinary bloke; 'Farnsbarns' has the numbing assonance needed to describe a bit of a nonentity. The phrase probably came out of the services in the Second World War.

chauffeur.   The first motor cars ran on a steam-operated principle, so the drivers had to heat up (French *chauffer*) the vehicles before they would start. 'Chauffeur', the name for these warmer-uppers (also used in French to describe the firemen on steam engines) has since been applied in English to the person paid to drive a vehicle for an employer. Since 1899.

chauvinism.   *See under* MALE CHAUVINIST.

che sera sera.   The proverbial saying 'What must be, must be' can be found as far back as Chaucer's 'Knight's Tale' (*c.*1390): 'When a thyng is shapen, it shal be.' But what of this foreign version, as sung, for example, by Doris Day in her 1956 hit song 'Whatever Will Be Will Be'? She also sang it in the remake of Alfred Hitchcock's *The Man Who Knew Too Much* in the same year. Ten years later, Geno Washington and the Ram Jam Band had a hit with a song entitled '*Que Sera Sera*'.

Is it *che* or *que*? There is no such phrase as *che sera sera* in modern Spanish or Italian, though *che* is an Italian word and *será* is a Spanish one. What we have is an Old French or Old Italian spelling of what would be, in modern Italian, *che sara, sara*. This is the form in which the Duke of Bedford's motto has always been written.

cheesed/browned off, to be.   To be fed up – both terms known since 1941. 'Cheese' and 'off-ness' rather go together, so one might think of cheese as having an undesirable quality. Also, when cheese is subjected to heat, it goes brown, or gets 'browned off'. On the other hand, the phrase could derive from 'cheese off', an expression like 'f*** off', designed to make a person go away. 'Cheesed off' may just be a state of rejection, like 'pissed off'.

cherries.   *See* LIFE IS JUST A BOWL OF ...

cherry-picking.   The choosing of ripest and best fruits – with the implication that the picker has got in before anyone else to do so.

Used figuratively in connection with business by 1984, possibly American in origin. Compare the picking of plums, celebrated notably in the nursery rhyme 'Little Jack Horner' (known since 1725).

> Whatever the justification for it, the fact is that major foreign buyers have been emerging for US property ... In the past 18 months you can't open a paper without seeing a Japanese deal – cherrypicking the Americans. *Financial Times* (25 April 1987)

> Insurers are also grumbling. Smaller companies say they cannot compete with firms that engage in 'redlining', the practice of refusing to cover people likely to be major users of medical care and 'cherrypicking', or seeking out low-risk young and healthy people to insure. *Guardian* (10 June 1991)

Cheshire Cat. *See* GRIN LIKE A ...

Chevy Chase. Assumed name of the US comedy actor who came to the fore in the 1970s. He appeared on *Saturday Night Live* on TV and in films such as *Foul Play*. He was born Cornelius Crane Chase in 1943, so why did he adopt the name 'Chevy' – except to get away from Cornelius? Could it be that he wanted to allude to Chevy as in the abbreviated form of Chevrolet, the US motor car which derives its name from Louis Chevrolet, a Swiss engineer? Or could he have wanted to allude to the fifteenth-century ballad 'Chevy Chase' which describes an old dispute between the Percy and Douglas families on the Scottish border, arising from a hunting accident? ('Chevy' or 'chivvy' is a huntsman's call meaning 'chase or harass the fox'.) More likely it comes from the suburb of Washington DC known as Chevy Chase, though this was probably named after the fifteenth-century ballad by colonists who settled there.

'Chevy Chase' is also rhyming slang for 'face' (recorded by 1857).

chew the cud, to. Meaning 'to think deeply about something, especially the past'. This figurative expression (in use by 1382) refers to the ruminative look cows have when they chew their 'cud' – that is, bring back food from their first stomachs and chew it in their mouths again. 'Cud' comes from Old English *cwidu*, meaning 'what is chewed'.

chew the rag, to. 'To chew something over; to grouse or grumble over something at length, to discuss matters with a degree of thoroughness' (compare 'to chew the fat'). Known by 1885. As in the expression 'to chew something over', the word 'chew' here means simply 'to say' – that is, it is something that is carried on in the mouth like eating. The 'rag' part relates to an old meaning of that word, in the sense 'to scold' or 'reprove severely'. 'Rag' was also once a slang word for 'the tongue' (from 'red rag', probably).

Compare CHEW THE CUD.

chicken à la King.   Cooked chicken breast served in a cream sauce with mushrooms and peppers does not have a royal origin. Rather, it is said to have been named after E. Clark King, a hotel proprietor in New York, when the dish was introduced in the 1880s (*OED2*).

Another story is that it was dreamed up at Delmonico's restaurant by Foxhall Keene, son of the Wall Street operator and sportsman J.R. Keene, and served as *chicken à la Keene*. Yet another version is that the dish was created at Claridge's in London for J.R. Keene himself after his horse won the Grand Prix.

Chinese wall.   Term for the artificial division in a financial institution (or other large business organization) preventing the exchange of sensitive information which otherwise might lead to charges of conflict of interest. Became popular in the 1980s.

> A dozen leading Japanese commercial banks asked the government to knock holes in the Chinese wall between banking and securities business. *Economist* (12 April 1986)

chip(s).   *See* HAVE A . . .; WHEN THE . . .

chop suey.   Robert L. Shook in *The Book of Why* (1983) says, 'In New York, on August 29 1896, the Chinese statesman Li Hung-Chang had his chef create *chop suey* which was unknown in China. It was an attempt to create a dish that would appeal to both American and Oriental tastes.' But *OED2* turns up a reference in 1888 (from an American source): 'A staple dish for the Chinese gourmet is now chow chop svey [*sic*], a mixture of chickens' livers and gizzards, fungi, bamboo buds, pigs' tripe, and bean sprouts stewed with spices.'

Whatever the case, the dish seems probably to owe more to origins in America than China, though the meaning of the words *shap sui* in Cantonese is clear enough: 'mixed bits'.

chow. If 'chow' is a breed of dog and 'chow mein' is the name of a Chinese dish (known in English by 1903), could a diner's worst fears be justified? Well, 'chow' in Mandarin means to cook or fry (and so 'chow mein', from *chao mian*, means 'fried flour').

In Cantonese, 'chow' means food and Chow dogs were, it is true, originally bred to be eaten and were clearly labelled as such (*chow-chow*, in full).

chuff. *See* HONK ONE'S ...

chuffed, to be. (1) To be pleased. (2) To be fed up. This is called a Janus word because it has two opposite meanings. The first meaning possibly predominates and was known by the 1860s. When Paul McCartney of the Beatles returned to Liverpool to receive the Freedom of the City in November 1984, he declared that he was 'well chuffed'. Paul Beale in Partridge/*Slang* suggests a development (in military circles) from the word 'chow' (meaning food in general). This might indeed account for the pleased or well-sated meaning. The opposite 'fed up' may derive from a dialect use of 'chuff' (dating from 1832) meaning 'churlish, gruff, morose'.

chunder, to. To be sick. This Australian word is of uncertain origin, according to the *Macquarie Dictionary* (1981). According to the *Dictionary of Australian Quotations* (1984), 'Barry Humphries states that, to the best of his knowledge, he introduced the words "chunder" and "chundrous" to the Australian language [by 1964 at least]. Previously "chunder" was known to him only as a piece of Geelong Grammar School slang.' But this ignores the fact that 'chunda' appears in Neville Shute's novel *A Town Like Alice* (1950).

The usual derivation concerns the cry 'Watch under!' made by those about to be sick over the side of a ship to those on lower decks. Partridge/*Slang* has that it is rhyming slang for Chunder Loo ('spew'), from Chunder Loo of Akin Foo, 'a cartoon figure in a long-running series of advertisements for Cobra boot polish in the *Bulletin* [Australia] from 8 April 1909'.

Cinderella.   Describing a young woman (usually) who is neglected or whose merit or beauty goes unrecognized, the name derives from the heroine of Perrault's famous fairytale from *Histoires ou Contes du Temps Passé* (Paris, 1697). In it, a 'cinder-girl' is able to go to a ball through the intervention of a fairy godmother provided she returns before midnight. Her eventual marriage to a prince concludes the archetypal 'rags-to-riches' story. Known in English in this sense by 1840.

Clapham omnibus.   *See* MAN ON THE . . .

clean.   *See* MR . . .

clerihew.   A four-line, amusing, biographical poem, named after E. Clerihew Bentley (1875–1956) who pioneered the genre. An example of Bentley's own:

George the Third
Ought never to have occurred.
One can only wonder
At so grotesque a blunder.

According to Peter Jeffrey:

When questioned, E. Clerihew Bentley
Smiled gently,
And said, 'Those who can write a good clerihew
Are very few.'

The form first appeared in *Biography for Beginners* (1906) published under the name 'E. Clerihew' and became known as that shortly after (rather than as a 'bentley').

clever-clogs.   Alliterative phrase used to put down a person who is showing off his or her cleverness. Known by at least 1983.

climb aboard the gravy train, to.   To obtain access to a money-spinning scheme. This was an American expression originally – *DOAS* suggests that it started in sporting circles. An alternative version is 'to climb aboard the gravy *boat*', which is a bit easier to understand. Gravy boats exist for holding gravy in and take their name from their shape. So, if money is perceived as being like gravy, it is not hard to see how the expression arose.

According to *Webster's Dictionary*, the 'train' and 'boat' forms are equally popular in the US (and have been since the 1920s). 'Boat' is probably less popular in the UK.

cloth-eared. Phrase used to describe someone who is somewhat deaf and thus, in a transferred sense, perhaps has no taste in matters musical. Known by 1912. It is not completely obvious why 'cloth' is used in this phrase – maybe in contrast with a richer material.

cloud nine/seven. *See* ON . . .

club. *See* IN THE . . .

clue. A fact or discovery that helps solve a problem or leads to the completion of an investigation. The original was the 'clew' or ball of thread which Theseus took into the labyrinth at Knossos and which enabled him to find his way out again after encountering the Minotaur. A word in its own right by 1596.

cobblers. *See under* CODSWALLOP.

cock a snook, to. A snook is the derisive gesture made with thumb and hand held out from the nose. 'To take a sight' is a variation. Both were known by the mid-nineteenth century, indeed *OED2* has 'cock snooks' in 1791. The game of **snooker** derives its name not from this, but rather from the military nickname for a raw recruit.

cockroach. A voracious beetle infesting kitchens. The name has nothing to do with cocks or roaches (fish) but derives from the Spanish *cucaracha*. Known in the English form since the seventeenth century.

The **tarantula** spider, meanwhile, derives its name from Taranto in southern Italy. Those bitten by the spider were said to suffer from tarantism (dancing mania), the effect being that they danced a tarantella.

cocoa. *See* I SHOULD . . .

codswallop. Nonsense. Known since the 1960s. One suggested derivation is from 'cods', a nickname for testicles. Compare the similar expression, **load of old cobblers**, rhyming slang where cobbler's awls = balls. Known by 1955. According to *Street Talk: The Language of* Coronation Street (1986): 'Another suggested etymology is Codd's ginger beer (Codd invented the pressurized beverage bottle) and wallop, an old term for beer – "fool's beer", or something patently full of froth or fizz and not to be taken seriously.' Whilst original this may be a little too neat an explanation.

cold blood. *See* IN . . .

cold enough to freeze the balls off a brass monkey. The derivation of this phrase meaning 'extremely cold' (known by 1835) probably has nothing to do with any animal. A brass monkey was the name given to the plate on a warship's deck on which cannon balls (or other ammunition) were stacked. In cold weather the brass would contract, tending to cause the stack to fall down. 'Monkey' appears to have been a common slang word in gunnery days (and not just at sea) – there was a type of gun or cannon known as a 'monkey' and a 'powder monkey' was the name for a boy who carried powder to the guns.

cold shoulder. *See* GIVE SOMEONE THE . . .

Collins. A thank-you letter for having stayed in another person's house, possibly written more out of duty than pleasure. It may differ from an ordinary 'bread-and-butter' thank-you letter by being too studied. Named after Mr Collins, the clergyman, in Jane Austen's *Pride and Prejudice* (1813) who threatens to send one of his obsequious missives to the Bennett family following his visit to them.

collywobbles. A state of extreme nervousness; the stomach ache. The second (original) meaning is, more fully, a 'disordered state of the stomach characterized by rumbling in the intestines' and has been known since 1841.

colour. *See* HORSE OF A DIFFERENT . . .

colour bar. Name given to the divisions, legal and social, between white people and 'people of colour' in the first half of the twentieth century. Known by 1913.

colours. *See* WITH FLYING . . .

comb. *See* GO THROUGH (SOMETHING) WITH A FINE-TOOTH . . .

come a cropper, to. To have a bad fall (physically) or, in a transferred sense, to run into major misfortune particularly when things seem to be going well. Possibly from a horse-riding accident where the rider might fall with a crop (handle of a whip) in the hand. Also the phrase 'neck and crop' means 'completely'. Known by the mid-nineteenth century.

come Hell and/or high water. Meaning 'come what may', this phrase is mentioned in Partridge/*Slang* as a cliché but, as such phrases go, is curiously lacking in citations. *OED2* finds no examples earlier than the twentieth century. *Come Hell or High Water* was used as the title of a book by yachtswoman Clare Francis in 1977. She followed it in 1978 with *Come Wind or Weather. Hell and High Water* was the title of a US film in 1954.

Graeme Donald in *Today* (26 April 1986) linked it to punishments meted out to witches in the Middle Ages: 'Lesser transgressions only warranted the miscreant being obliged to stand in boiling water, the depth of which was directly proportional to the crime. Hence the expression "From Hell and high water, may the good Lord deliver us".' This is rather fanciful. Perhaps he was thinking of the so-called Thieves' Litany – 'from Hull, Hell and Halifax, good Lord deliver us' (known by 1653, because the gibbet was much used in these places in the sixteenth and seventeenth centuries).

comment. *See* NO . . .

compassion fatigue. Reluctance to contribute further to charities and good causes because of the many demands made on one's compassion. A coinage of the 1980s when numerous fund-raising events such as Live Aid for famine relief led to instances of public withdrawal from giving. Originally used in the US regarding refugee appeals. Derived from 'metal fatigue'. A variant was **donor fatigue**.

> Geldof, the Irish rock musician who conceived the event and spearheaded its hasty implementation, said that he 'wanted to get this done before compassion fatigue set in.'
> *New York Times* (22 September 1985)

> What the refugee workers call 'compassion fatigue' has set in. Back in the 1970s, when the boat people were on the front page, the world was eager to help. But now the boat people are old news.
> *Listener* (29 October 1987)

condom. This name for a prophylactic sheath does not derive from the town of Condom in south-western France. Indeed, early eighteenth-century use of the term tended to be in the form 'cundum' (*or* 'condon'), suggesting a different source. No 'Dr Condom' who prescribed this method of contraception has been discovered either. A Colonel Cundum, while courtier to King Charles II, is also said to have introduced the sheath into Britain.

conduct unbecoming. The full phrase is 'conduct unbecoming the character of an officer and a gentleman' and seems to have appeared first in the (British) Naval Discipline Act (10 August 1860), Article 24, though the notion has also been included in disciplinary regulations of other services, and in other countries, if not in quite these words.

Conduct Unbecoming is the title of a play by Barry England (1969; film UK, 1975) and, accordingly, came from the same source as the title of the film *An Officer and a Gentleman* (US, 1982).

conk. The nose. Known by 1812. Possibly from the word 'conch'. *See also* BIG CONK, BIG COCK!

conspiracy theory. The belief that a happening (usually political) is the result of a group of people conspiring together rather than the activity of a lone individual (or is the result of sheer chance or accident). The phrase arose in the mid-1960s when arguments raged over whether the 1963 assassination of President John F. Kennedy was the work of one man – Lee Harvey Oswald – working on his own, or was the result of a plot by organized crime, the Soviet Union, the FBI, or any number of bodies. Now inevitably invoked whenever causes of events are being investigated. Sometimes people say that they prefer the 'cock-up theory' of history rather than conspiracies.

> Conspiracy theories are often framed after the deaths of famous people. Like a kaleidoscope, the conspiracy theory can create satisfying shapes and patterns from even the most random details ... Others said Lincoln had been killed on the orders of his cabinet, or by Roman Catholics or Southerners.
>
> *The Times* (12 November 1991)

Cook's tour. *See* GO ON A ...

cool as a cucumber. (Of a person) very calm and collected, not nervous. First recorded use in a poem (1732) by John Gay: 'I, cool as a cucumber, could see the rest of womankind.'

cool hundred/thousand/million. *OED2* says drily that the 'cool' 'gives emphasis' to the (large) amount. Is this because a large amount of money is rather chilling, lacking in warmth, or because of the calm way the money is paid out? Perhaps the word 'cool' in this context anticipates its more modern connection with jazz, as something thrilling, to be admired and approved of. In Henry Fielding's *Tom Jones* (1749) we read: 'Watson rose from the table in some heat and declared he had lost a cool hundred ...' In Charles Dickens's *Great Expectations* (1861): 'She had wrote a little [codicil] ... leaving a cool four thousand to Mr Mathew Pocket.' *A Cool Million* is the title of a satire by Nathaniel West (1934), and in Anthony Powell's *Hearing Secret Harmonies* (1975), Lord Widmerpool comments on a smoke bomb let off at a literary prize-giving: 'I wouldn't have missed that for a cool million.'

cop. A policeman. Two explanations have been advanced for this term. Either it is because when Sir Robert Peel organized the Metropolitan Police in London in 1829, he dressed the men in blue uniforms with conspicuous copper buttons. Coppers were known as such by 1846. Or, the word comes from the verb 'to cop' meaning to catch or apprehend. Probably the latter.

copybook. *See* BLOT ONE'S ...

copycat. One who copies another's work. Known by 1896 and North American in origin. But why a cat? There is no very convincing explanation. Another case of fairly irrelevant animal involvement (compare 'dirty dog', 'cheeky monkey', 'cat's whiskers'), purely dictated here by the requirements of alliteration.

corned beef.   Beef which has been preserved with salt. Known as such since the seventeenth century. But why *corned*?

corpse, to.   When actors 'corpse', it means that they are overtaken by such involuntary laughter that they are unable to go on speaking their lines – or, if they are supposed to be lying dead on the stage, they are unable to stop shaking with mirth. Alternatively, the origin of the word lies in the actors being rendered as incapable as a dead body, or, when another actor has made them forget their lines, it is the equivalent of killing them by stopping their performance. Known by 1873.

couch potato.   A pejorative term for an addictive, uncritical (and possibly fat) TV viewer. Said to have been coined in the late 1970s by Tom Iacino in southern California. *Sunday Today* was only getting round to explaining the word to British readers on 27 July 1986. But why potato? Is it because of the shape of a fat person slouched on a couch? Or does it allude to the consumption of potato crisps, or to behaviour like that of a 'vegetable'? It seems the phrase is a complicated pun on the phrase 'boob-tube' (US slang for TV, not an article of clothing) and 'tuber', meaning a root vegetable.

couldn't run a whelkstall.   A way of describing incompetence, this appears to have originated with John Burns, the Labour MP: 'From whom am I to take my marching orders? From men who fancy they are Admirable Crichtons ... but who have not got sufficient brains and ability to run a whelk-stall?' (*South-Western Star*, 13 January 1894). Partridge/*Slang* has 'no way to run a whelk-stall' as the UK equivalent of the US '[that's] a hell of a way to run a railroad', and dates it from later, in the twentieth century. The phrases 'couldn't organize a piss-up in a brewery' and 'couldn't fight his/her way out of a paper bag' are more likely to be employed nowadays.

countdown.   It is said that the backward countdown to a rocket launch was first thought of by the German film director Fritz Lang. He thought it would make things more suspenseful if the count was reversed – 5–4–3–2–1 – so, in his 1928 film *By Rocket to the Moon* (sometimes known as *Frau im Mond* or 'The Woman in the Moon', from the German title) he established the routine for future real-life space shots.

Coventry.   *See* SEND SOMEONE TO . . .

cradle to the grave.   *See* FROM THE . . .

crapper.   A privy, lavatory, toilet, restroom. In 1979, the Greater London Council, after earnest consideration, declined to erect a blue plaque to commemorate the former home of the Victorian sanitary engineer, Thomas Crapper. The council's historic buildings committee decided that 'memorable though Crapper's name might be in popular terms', evidence from the Patent Office showed that he was not a notable inventor or pioneer in his field.

But did Thomas Crapper give part of his name to 'crap', meaning 'defecation, faeces, excretion' and, by extension, to 'rubbish, bad work'? Or did his surname become another word for 'privy'?

Well, he invented a *refinement* of the lavatory – a valve-and-syphon system which automatically shut off the water after its flushing job had been done. Mr Crapper was born in 1837 and died in 1910. And yet the *OED2* finds this in 1846: '"Fenced, in a dunniken". . ."What? Fenced in a crapping ken?"' In the same year, the *OED2* also finds in *The Swell's Night Guide*: 'Which of us had hold of the crappy (sh-ten) end of the stick?' (making a direct link between crap and shit). Both these examples prove that the noun 'crap' and its derivatives were being used in this situation when Crapper was a mere thirteen years old and presumably had not yet made his mark in the lavatory.

Surely, 'crapper' as the name for a 'privy' derives (as you would expect) from the noun or verb 'crap' and that word comes from Middle English *crappe* (residue, rubbish – used originally in connection with grain). By way of compensation, however, it may be that the use of the words 'crap-house' and 'crapper' were reinforced because of the existence of the British sanitary engineer with the wonderfully appropriate name.

There are those who still argue that Mr Crapper really did lead to the coinage of the term for a house of easement, denying that it derived from terms like 'crapping-ken' or 'crapping-case', in the way I have suggested. The best that I can say is that the case either way is not proven with any great finality. It would be of great assistance if a precise use of the word 'crapper' could be found earlier than the 1932 citation (from *American Speech*) which is the best the *OED2* can do.

craps. The American term for a game of dice. One theory for the name is that Bernard Marigny, a Creole gambler nicknamed 'Johnny Crapaud', introduced the game to New Orleans. From 'Crapaud's game' it became shortened to 'craps'. Another theory is that in the old dice game called Hazard, 'crabs' or 'craps' was the lowest possible throw. Known by 1843.

crazy like a fox. 'Apparently crazy but with far more method than madness' (Partridge/*Catch Phrases*). Craziness is hardly a quality one associates with foxes, so the expression was perhaps merely formed in parallel with the older 'cunning as a fox'. The similar 'crazy *as* a fox', also of US origin, was known by the mid-1930s.

Foxes always seem to get into expressions like these. In a 1980 radio interview, the actress Judy Carne was asked about Goldie Hawn, her one-time colleague on *Laugh-In*. Carne said: 'She's not a dizzy blonde. She's about as *dumb* as a fox. She's incredibly bright.'

Crazy Like a Fox was the title of a US TV series about a sloppy old private eye and his smart lawyer son (from 1984). Before that, it was used as the title of a book by S.J. Perelman (1945).

crazy, man, crazy! *See under* GO, MAN, GO!

crazy name, crazy guy! Comment (often journalistic) after an unusual name. Presumably of American origin.

> The delectable Peter Coyote – crazy name, crazy guy – plays top screen Method actor Steve Elliot ensconced in Italy to play the life of Communist poet Cesare Pavesi.
> *Today* (29 July 1988)

> Lord Owen, aghast, called out to his researcher, Norbert Both – crazy name, crazy guy –: 'Norbert, this chap's fucked up the CD-Rom.'
> *Observer* (5 November 1995)

Also used allusively:

> According to the AAAS's session on zoopharmacognosy – crazy name, enthralling discipline – they agree with their human cousins about what is useful.
> *Economist* (15 February 1992)

credibility gap. The difference between what is claimed as fact and what is actually fact. It dates from the time in the Vietnam war when, despite claims to the contrary by the Johnson administration, an escalation in US participation was taking place. 'Dilemma in "Credibility Gap"' was the headline over a report on the matter in the *Washington Post* (13 May 1965) and may have been the phrase's first outing.

crew cut. Brush-like short haircut popular with the US military but apparently first adopted by oarsmen at Harvard and Yale Universities (hence the 'crew') and athletes who no doubt appreciated its aerodynamic qualities. Known since 1942.

crime doesn't pay. Slogan used variously by the FBI and the cartoon character Dick Tracy. Of American origin and known since 1927.

> Crime never pays, not even life insurance benefits.
> Zelda Popkin, *No Crime For a Lady* (1942)

crisis. *See* MID-LIFE ...

crisis management. A corporate discipline dedicated to handling the aftermath of events which might otherwise prove detrimental. A form of higher public relations intended to forestall bad publicity or to turn it into something positive. Of American origin, the phrase has been known since 1965 but became something of a buzzword in the 1980s.

> Crisis management has become a growth industry ... Some firms have people around the country who can move on a 24-hour basis to handle a corporate crisis.
> *Time* Magazine (24 February 1986)

cropper. *See* COME A ...

cross the Rubicon, to. To make a significant decision from which there is no turning back, after Julius Caesar's crossing the stream of that name in 49 BC, which meant that he passed from Cisalpine Gaul into Italy and thus became an invader. Known by 1626. Hence also this limited application:

'I've been to Paris with Fulke Warwick ...' 'Talk about crossing the Rubicon.' 'Crossing the Rubicon' was deb talk for going all the way.
Christopher Ogden, *Life of the Party* (1994)

crow. *See* EAT ...

crown jewels. Anything of great value, so named after the British Crown Jewels stored in the Tower of London.

The male genitals.
Julia P. Stanley, 'Homosexual Slang', *American Speech*, xlv (1970)

Material so sensitive that national security demands that the material is not exposed to the public ... It was necessary for the jury to examine in detail the material – called 'the Crown Jewels' – in order that it might understand the full facts.
Guardian (29 January 1985)

Move to safeguard TV 'crown jewels'.
Headline, *Guardian* (17 January 1996)

crud. *See under* CURD.

cry mum. Keep quiet. Compare the more common 'keep mum'. In Ngaio Marsh's *A Wreath for Riviera* (1949), Inspector Alleyn whispers, 'You cry mum and I'll cry budget' when hiding from a villain. The allusion is to Shakespeare, *The Merry Wives of Windsor*, V.ii.6 (1600–1) in which Slender's ludicrous planned elopement with Anne Page is to be carried out by their finding each other in the crowd with the greeting 'Mum' to be answered by 'Budget' – 'and by that we know one another'. The Arden edition of Shakespeare adds the gloss: 'An appropriately childish greeting. "Mumbudget"... was used of an inability or a refusal to speak ... *OED* conjectures, with convincing citations, that it was "the name of some children's game in which silence was required". Thomas Hardy later uses "to come mumbudgeting" in the sense of "to come secretly".'

Crystal Palace. Name given to the huge structure of glass and iron originally erected in Hyde Park, London, to house the Great Exhibition of 1851. Subsequently moved to Sydenham it was destroyed by a fire in 1936. According to *Punch* (9 December 1936), the name was bestowed on the building by the humorous magazine in 1850 before it was built.

cucumber. *See* COOL AS A . . .

cud. *See* CHEW THE . . .

cupboard love. Devotion to people because of the material things, notably food, that they can provide. Originally, perhaps, from the display of love by children towards the cook in a household – love which is based on this kind of self-interest. From the middle of the eighteenth century. Later also known as **lump-love**, where the real object of affection is a lump of food.

curd. Lumps of coagulated milk which can be turned into cheese. Like the word 'crowd', this derives from the Old English *creodan*, meaning 'to press together'. Indeed, the original form of the word was 'crud' but, through metathesis, the more familiar form emerged. Much more recently, **crud** somehow resurfaced, meaning lumps of disgusting matter.

currant. A type of small berry. The name derives from Corinth, the Greek city, which in ancient times used to export dried grapes. These became known in French as *raisins de Corinthe* and so passed into English as 'raisins of Corauntz'. Eventually, in the sixteenth century, the word 'currant' was applied to a shrub which had nothing to do with dried grapes at all.

curtain lecture (or **Caudle lecture**). Meaning 'a private reproof given by a wife to her husband', it refers to the scolding that took place after the curtains round the bed (as on a four-poster) had been closed. It was known as such by 1633.

The 'Caudle' variation derives from Douglas Jerrold's *Mrs Caudle's Curtain Lectures*, a series published by *Punch* in 1846 in which Mr Caudle suffered the naggings of his wife after they had gone to bed. Another early version of the idea is 'boulster lecture' (1640).

Lady Diana Cooper in a letter of 12 January 1944 wrote: 'Clemmie has given him [Winston Churchill] a Caudle curtain lecture on the importance of not quarrelling with Wormwood.'

custom(s). *See* IT'S AN OLD . . .; OLD SPANISH . . .

cut and run, to. Meaning 'to escape; run away', the phrase has a nautical origin (recorded in 1704). In order to make a quick getaway, instead of the lengthy process of hauling up a ship's anchor, the ship's cable was simply cut. This was easy to do when the anchor

was attached to a hemp rope rather than a chain. The figurative use
was established by 1861.

cut no ice with someone, to.   To make no impression whatsoever.
Of self-explanatory American origin. Known by 1895.

> Such speeches! Eloquence cut no ice at *that* dinner.
> J.S. Wood, *Yale Yarns* (1895)

cut of someone's jib.   *See* LIKE THE . . .

cut the mustard, to.   To succeed, to have the ability to do what's
necessary. One might say of someone, 'He didn't cut much mustard.'
An American phrase dating from the turn of the century when
'mustard' was slang for the 'real thing' or the 'genuine article', and
this may have contributed to the coinage.

> Boss Finley's too old to cut the mustard [i.e. perform sexually].
> Tennessee Williams, *Sweet Bird of Youth* (1959)

D

dagmars.   Motor-car bumpers (fenders in the US) – so dubbed in
the US during the 1950s after a well-endowed actress, Virginia Ruth
Egnor, known as 'Dagmar', who appeared on a TV show called
Broadway Open House. One might compare the expression 'the bird
with the big headlights', to describe the same sort of features.

Dalek.   This is the name given to the robotic characters in BBC
TV's science-fiction series since 1963. They resemble pepper-pots
and go around screeching 'Exterminate! Exterminate!' The explanation given by writer Terry Nation in 1971 (and quoted in
OED2) that he took the name from the spine of an encyclopedia
volume covering DAL-LEK was withdrawn by him in 1973.

damage limitation exercise.   A measure akin to CRISIS MAN-
AGEMENT but more usually to be found in politics than industry or

business. Known since 1965 – in connection with planning for the disaster of a nuclear war – but especially current in the 1980s when politicians required the treatment after a whole series of mistakes and scandals. Ronald Reagan was US President at the time.

> The meeting decided to put Lord Whitelaw in charge of a 'damage limitation exercise'. Part of this would be a speech by Mrs Thatcher distancing the government from the [Channel] tunnel.
> *Economist* (14 February 1987)

Damascus. *See* ROAD TO . . .

dandelion. The plant's name comes from the French *dent de lion* [lion's tooth], from the supposed resemblance of the outline of the widely toothed leaves (in Medieval Latin, *dens leonis*). The Italians call it, similarly, *dente di leone* and the Spanish, *diente de león*. The French themselves, however, call it *pissenlit* – drinks made from dandelion are a powerful diuretic and could make you wet the bed.

dander. *See* GET ONE'S . . .

dark. *See* LEAP IN THE . . .

Datsun. Name of a make of Japanese motor car. It was in 1911 that the first small 'Dat' car was made by the Kwaishinsha Company – 'dat' supposedly meaning 'as fast as a rabbit'. After a merger with the Jitsuyo Jidosha Seizo Company, the first 'Datsun' (literally, 'son of Dat') was produced in 1932. Adrian Room in *The Dictionary of Trade Name Origins* (1982) states, however, that the original car was manufactured in 1913 and took its name – DAT – from the initials of the company's financial backers.

dawn raid. (1) Name given to a surprise attack or search launched by the police or the military in order to catch drug smugglers or other criminals or the enemy unawares. Known since the nineteenth century. (2) Adopted into financial jargon since 1980 to describe a swift buying operation at the start of the day's trading. The aim is to acquire a substantially increased shareholding for a client prior to a takeover.

> Market lethargy has brought out the dawn raiders again, despite the recent stock exchange report on such practices.
> *Economist* (26 July 1980)

day job. *See* DON'T GIVE UP THE ...

D-Day. Meaning 'an important day when something is due to begin', the most frequent allusion is to 6 June 1944, the day on which the Allies began their landings in northern France in order to push back German forces. Like H-Hour, D-Day is a military way of detailing elements in an operation. The 'D' just reinforces the 'Day' on which the plan is to be put into effect and enables successive days to be labelled 'D-Day plus one', etc.

dead ringer. Meaning 'one person closely resembling another', the expression derives from horse-racing in the US, where 'ringer' has been used since the nineteenth century to describe a horse fraudulently substituted for another in a race. 'Dead' here means 'exact', as in 'dead heat'.

deadlock. A stalemate incapable of resolution. From a lock that has no spring catch and can only be opened or shut with a key. Known since 1779.

> I have them all at a dead lock! for every one of them is afraid to let go first.
> R.B. Sheridan, *The Critic* (1779)

> In the detestable slang of the day, we were now both 'at a deadlock', and nothing was left for it but to refer to our clients on either side.
> Wilkie Collins, *The Woman in White*, II.iii (1860)

debunk. *See under* BUNK.

deed. *See* BLOODY ...

deep (blue) sea. *See* BETWEEN THE DEVIL AND ...

deep throat. A person within an organization who supplies information anonymously about wrong-doing by his colleagues. The phrase comes from the nickname given to the source within the Nixon White House who fed *Washington Post* journalists Carl Bernstein and Bob Woodward with information which helped in their Watergate investigations (1972–4). It has been suggested that 'Deep Throat' never existed but was a cover for unjustified suppositions. *Deep Throat*, a notorious porno movie (US, 1972), concerned a woman, played by Linda Lovelace, whose clitoris was placed in the back of her throat.

deep-six, to.   Meaning 'to dispose of; destroy', the expression is of nautical origin – from men who took soundings. When they said 'by the deep six', they meant six fathoms (11 m or 36 ft). In naval circles, 'to deep-six' equally means 'to jettison overboard'. *DOAS* notes an extension to this meaning in jive and jazz use since the 1940s where 'the deep six' means 'the grave'. During Watergate, former presidential counsel John Dean told of a conversation he had had with another Nixon henchman, John Erlichman: 'He told me to shred the documents and "deep-six" the briefcase. I asked him what he meant by "deep-six". He leaned back in his chair and said, "You drive across the river on your way home tonight, don't you? Well, when you cross over the bridge . . . just toss the briefcase into the river."' (Erlichman, before going to prison, denied this conversation ever took place.)

degree.   *See* TO THE NTH . . .

denim.   Material from which jeans are made, hence 'denims'. The cloth takes its name from Nîmes, the town in southern France where it was originally manufactured, and called *serge de Nîm* or *Nîmes*. As denim or denims (originally of a serge material), the word has been known since 1695.

Derby.   The original of Derbys run all over the world was started in 1780 by the 12th Earl of Derby, who is said to have discussed the idea of a flat race for three-year-old fillies, over dinner with his friend, Sir Charles Bunbury. Tradition has it that they tossed a coin over which of them the race should be named after and Derby won. The idea of a race called the 'Kentucky Bunbury' would have been a little hard to take seriously.

deserts.   *See* GET ONE'S JUST . . .

design for living.   Phrase often used in magazine journalism for headlines when the practical aspects of furniture and even clothes design are being discussed. The Flanders & Swann song 'Design for Living' in *At The Drop of a Hat* (1957) concerned trendy interior decorating and furnishing. The source for all this appears to be *Design for Living* as the title of Noël Coward's play of 1932. This, although dealing with what would now be called 'trendy' people, had nothing to do with fashion. It was about a *ménage-à-trois*, so the 'living' was in that sense.

deuce. *See under* LOVE.

devil. *See* BETWEEN THE ...

devil's dozen. *See under* BAKER'S DOZEN.

die for, to. As a verb meaning 'to desire keenly or excessively', this has been around since 1591 at least. But as an adjectival expression meaning 'something of great worth', it has been a popular colloquial usage since the early eighties ('A tad overweight, but violet eyes to die for', G.B. Trudeau, 1980). In the film *Splash* (US, 1984), a character says: 'That outfit is to die for.' Michelle Pfeiffer gets to breathe the words in *Batman Returns* (1992). A US film with the title *To Die For* appeared in 1995. However, there is a much earlier isolated instance from E.N. Westcott (*David Harum*, 1898) – 'Oh! and to "top off" with, a mince-pie to die for.'

die is cast. The fateful decision has been made, there is no turning back now. Here 'die' is the singular of 'dice' and the expression has been known in English since at least 1634. When Julius Caesar crossed the Rubicon, after coming from Gaul and advancing into Italy against Pompey (49 BC), he is supposed to have said '*Jacta alea est*' – 'the dice have been thrown' (although he actually said it in Greek).

> At 4 a.m. on June 5 the die was irrevocably cast: the invasion would be launched on June 6 [1944: the D-Day landings in Normandy].
> Winston S. Churchill, *The Second World War* (Vol. 5, 1952)

die with one's boots on, to (sometimes **to die in one's boots/ shoes**). Meaning to die violently, or to be hanged summarily. *OED2* finds this in England by the eighteenth century, and in the American West by 1873. It was firmly ensconced in the language by the time of the 1941 Errol Flynn film *They Died With Their Boots On*, about General Custer and his death at Little Big Horn, and a porn film with Vivien Neves, *She Died With Her Boots On* (UK, 1970s). In one sense, the phrase can suggest an ignominious death (say, by hanging) but in a general way it can refer to someone who dies 'in harness', going about his work, like a soldier in the course of duty.

'To die with one's boots *off*' suggests, rather, that one dies in bed.

died. *See* LAUGH? I THOUGHT I SHOULD HAVE . . .

died and gone to Heaven. *See* I'VE . . .

dim sum. Name of a Chinese food dish – bite-sized dumplings filled with meat or fish. Known in English since 1948. The word means 'speck heart' or, more helpfully, the sort of food that would touch one's heart and invigorate it.

dinner. *See* LOOKING/DRESSED UP LIKE A DOG'S BREAKFAST . . .

dirtwater. *See under* JERKWATER.

disco. Meaning 'a place for dancing to records', the name is a contraction of the French word *discothèque*, which dates from the early 1950s. That in turn was an adaptation of *bibliothèque*, 'a library' (from the Greek word for 'book repository'), conveying the idea of a 'record library' initially, rather than a dancing place.

disgusted, Tunbridge Wells. The archetypal holder of reactionary, blimpish views who might sign himself or herself thus if writing to a newspaper – Royal Tunbridge Wells in Kent having acquired the reputation of being where such stuffy views might normally be held. Used as the title of a BBC Radio 4 programme providing a platform for listeners' views on broadcasting in 1978, it was intended to evoke the sort of letter fired off to the press between the two world wars when the writer did not want to give his or her name and so signed 'Mother of Three', 'Angry Ratepayer', 'Serving Policeman', etc.

The *Kent Courier* (24 February 1978) reported the 'disgust' that the 'Disgusted' label had stirred up in the town. Some people interviewed thought the tag had originated with Richard Murdoch of the 1940s radio show *Much Binding in the Marsh* in which 'he made much use of his connections with the town' and was always mentioning it. Can the phrase ever have been seriously used, however? Earlier citations are lacking.

Obviously, there is no disgusted of Tunbridge Wells, but there is Mr Tsurkan of Kishinev. 'I have been reading the paper for 10 years,' he is reported as saying, 'but you can't see the people and the problems in the paper behind the technology. My comrades are cancelling their order . . .' *Guardian* (8 October 1984)

A paper must surely have the right to an editorial opinion. So must a columnist. If the columnist becomes too eccentric his editor will remove him. If a paper gets too far out of touch with disgusted of Tunbridge Wells or Dave Spart of Islington he will take his 23 pence a day elsewhere. *Guardian* (4 March 1985)

Dixie. Name for the American South. Possibly derived from the Mason-Dixon line which before the Civil War came to be the boundary between the free and slave states (after Charles Mason and Jeremiah Dixon, English surveyors, who surveyed a disputed boundary between Pennsylvania and Maryland in the 1760s). But a 'dixie' was also the name given to a ten-dollar bill issued by a bank in New Orleans (where *dix* was French for ten), and this seems the more likely explanation. The name for the South seems to have caught on by 1859 when Daniel Emmet's song 'Dixie' became popular. There are other explanations.

do. *See* I . . .

do the business, to. (1) Teenage slang for anything that is particularly good – an early 1980s phrase, in Britain at least. Paul Beale's *Concise Dictionary of Slang* (1989) gives an example: '"They did the business" was about the highest praise you could get from fellow hooligans for a really spectacular display of violence, such as that by the Millwall [football] "fans" at Luton, Spring 1985.' (2) Accomplish what needs to be done, do the trick. Much older, this. In a letter by Laurence Sterne (conjecturally dated September 1758), he mentions someone being 'ready to be call'd in to do his part either to frighten or outwit You, in case the Terror of Grand Mama should not do the Business without him' (L.P. Curtis, ed., *The Letters of Laurence Sterne*, 1965).

It would have taken me all my life to perform it, if I had not luckily thought of turning the channel of a river through the stable-door. That did the business in a very short time!
Nathaniel Hawthorne, *A Wonder Book for Girls and Boys* (1892)

I [Tony Sibson] can't even contemplate it [defeat]. I have great respect for Kaylor but, on the night, I'm going out there to do the business. *Sunday Express* (25 November 1984)

(3) To be engaged in the sexual act, especially where a prostitute is involved. Late twentieth-century use.

Why do nice men go whoring? ... There was, I thought, lurking in all this, a slight distaste both for male weakness and for 'doing the business'. *Sunday Times* (2 November 1986)

dog. *See* GIVE A ...; HAIR OF THE ...; LOOKING/DRESSED UP LIKE A ...; LOVE ME, LOVE MY ...; PUT ON THE ...

dog days. Nothing to do with dogs getting hot under the collar, contracting rabies, or anything like that. The ancients applied this label to the period between 3 July and 11 August when the dog star, Sirius, rises at the same time as the sun. At one time, this seemed to coincide with the overwhelmingly hot days of high summer. Known as such from ancient times but in English from 1597.

dog's breakfast/dinner. *See* LOOKING/DRESSED UP LIKE A ...

dolce vita. Literally, 'the sweet life', but when used as the title of Federico Fellini's 1960 Italian film *La Dolce Vita* it passed into English as a phrase suggesting a high-society life of luxury, pleasure, and self-indulgence. It is not clear how much of a set phrase it was in Italian (compare ***dolce far niente*** [sweet idleness]) before it was taken up by everybody else.

dollop. Possibly originating with the Norwegian word *dolp*, meaning 'lump', this word first appears to have meant a clump of grass in a field (known by the mid-sixteenth century). The culinary, rough-measuring, large quantity sense only emerged in the early nineteenth century. It has been defined as 'roughly the amount of warm butter that you can scoop on to the end of a spatula before dropping it into your frying pan' – Mark Morton, *Cupboard Love: A Dictionary of Culinary Curiosities* (1996).

donkey's years. As in, 'I haven't seen her for donkey's years' – i.e. for a very long time (current by 1916). It is not very hard to see that what we have here is a distortion of the phrase 'donkey's *ears*' (which are, indeed, long). As such, what we have is a form of rhyming slang: donkey's = donkey's ears = years.

This also helps to explain the alternative expression, 'I haven't seen her **for yonks**', where 'yonks' may well be a distortion of year and donk(ey)s. There is also the less enjoyable explanation that 'donkey's years' is an allusion to the 'old tradition' that one never sees a dead donkey.

donor fatigue.   *See* COMPASSION FATIGUE.

don't eat oysters unless there's an R in the month.   This is an old belief, hard to dispose of, but no longer tenable. Before modern refrigeration came along, oysters did 'go off' in the warmer months from May to August which, as it happens, do not have an R in them. Now oysters may be eaten at any time. As it was, some people allowed themselves to eat oysters in August by spelling it 'Orgust'.

> The oyster is unseasonable and unwholesome in all months that have not the letter R in their name.
> Richard Buttes, *Diet's Dry Dinner* (1599)

> Though politics, like oysters, are only good in the R months ...
> *Lord Chesterfield's Letters to Lord Huntingdon* (for 30 August 1769) (1923)

don't get your knickers in a twist.   *See under* KNICKERS.

don't give up the day job.   Advice ostensibly given to, say, a part-time actor or entertainer on experiencing their talents and not finding them good. In other words, you would be unwise to risk trying to do this professionally because you probably won't succeed, so hold on to the security you have got. Suddenly popular in the early 1990s. In 1995, a BBC2 TV talent show was called *Don't Give Up the Day Job* and, at the same time, advertisements for Kenwood audio equipment featured members of its workforce who had interesting spare-time activities (judo, magic, whatever). The headline to these was, 'Don't give up the day job, [name of employee].'

> Books: Don't give up the day job, Britt.
> Headline, *Daily Mail* (16 April 1994)

> Father Norbert Bethune, of Tielt in Belgium, wants to get married. He wants to be made an honest man. And, he says, he won't give up his day job or relinquish his frock.
> *Guardian* (26 May 1993)

don't teach your grandmother to suck eggs.   Meaning, 'don't try to tell people things which, given their age and experience, they might be expected to know anyway'. According to Partridge/*Slang*, variations on this very old expression include advice against instructing grandmothers to 'grope ducks', 'grope a goose', 'sup sour milk', 'spin', and 'roast eggs'. Known by 1707. In 1738, Jonathan Swift's *Polite Conversation* had 'Go teach your grannam to suck eggs'.

It has been suggested that, in olden days, sucking eggs would be a particularly important thing for a grandmother to be able to do because, having no teeth, it would be all she was capable of.

> We have concern over appointment procedures in councils. Some authorities, we feel, still have to be taught how to suck eggs – how to do the job properly – and it is good there is an agreed procedure on that.
> *Herald* (Glasgow) (30 January 1996)

doobry.   A 'thingy', a 'thingamy', a 'thingumajig', a 'thingumabob', a 'whatsit' – a word for when you can't think what to call an object. Paul Beale in Partridge/*Slang* has it as **doobri**, 'an elaboration of *doofah*, a gadget' or, applied to a person, as the short form of 'doobrifirkin'. A correspondent (1996) who was in the Royal Navy (1948–55) recalls that people with the surname Perkins were given the nickname 'Dooberry Perkins' (a corruption of Dorothy Perkins, the name of a British store). 'Doobry' was certainly in general use in Britain by the 1980s. It is ignored by the *OED2*.

doolally (or **doolally tap**).   Crazy, mad. From Deolali, a Bombay sanatorium *c.*1900 where many British soldiers were detained before being shipped home. Recorded as military slang in 1925.

double cross, to.   To cheat (someone), particularly over a plan which has been agreed upon in advance. Known by 1834 in Britain. Possibly from a double cheat in certain games and sports – as where a player was being paid to lose but then allowed himself to win.

down.   *See* WHEN THE CHIPS ARE . . .

down in the dumps.   Depressed. Often at one time 'in the doleful dumps'. But apart from being an appropriate sounding word, what is/are 'dumps'? Probably, in this context, 'haze or mist', after the

Dutch word *domp*. Known as such since the sixteenth century, presumably suggesting that the mind is befogged.

draconian.   As in expressions like 'draconian measures'. Sweeping, drastic, harsh or severe powers, chiefly legal ones. Named after Drakon, the seventh-century BC Athenian legislator. Known in English since 1876. A cliché by the mid-twentieth century.

> Dean Marsh, solicitor (advises on music licences): 'It's a further infringement of civil liberties. It gives the police draconian powers to seize equipment they consider to be involved and there seems to be no provision for these to be returned.'
> *Independent* (3 November 1994)

> In a speech yesterday, Mr Mandela made an apparently veiled threat that he might be forced to use draconian powers to clamp down on violence in the troubled province of KwaZulu/Natal.
> *The Times* (25 February 1995)

drag.   Slang word for transvestism, or at least the dressing up in the opposite sex's clothes, though usually women's clothes worn by men. Known by 1870 – because the clothes were 'dragged' on?

> I remember men dressed as women – Beaton, Byron etc – at parties in 1927 but they did not call it 'drag'. What an odd name. Dragging the skirts?
> *The Letters of Evelyn Waugh* (letter of 5 September 1965) (1980)

drains.   *See* LAUGH LIKE ...

Dreadnought.   Name given to the class of British big-gun destroyer developed in the years prior to the First World War. Admiral Lord Fisher was sufficiently identified with the strategy which proved correct in defeating German seapower that when he was elevated to the peerage he took as his motto 'Fear God and Dread Nought'. Presumably it was the sailors on board who were to dread nought: the enemy was supposed to dread the battleship. The first destroyer of this class was so named in 1906 but there had been a tradition in the British navy of giving the name *Dreadnought* to battleships which went back to the reign of Queen Elizabeth I. A 'dreadnought' was also the name given to a stout outer garment worn in bad weather (known by 1806).

dream ticket. An ideal pairing of politicians taking part in an election. Of American origin and used in connection with presidential and vice-presidential contenders whose qualities – age/youth, North/South affiliations, right-wing/liberal views, religious leanings – will, it is hoped, appeal to the largest number of electors, in order to ensure their victory. In use by 1960.

In British politics, the term was introduced when the Labour Party was choosing its leader and deputy leader in 1983.

> Mr Kinnock, a leading left-winger, and Mr Hattersley, an outspoken figure on Labour's Centre-Right, have been described as the dream ticket because they would form a team uniting both wings of the Labour Party.
> *Sunday Telegraph* (2 October 1983)

> Staring down at Bill [Clinton] and Al [Gore] on the Madison Square Garden podium, she could see how they complemented one another. Suddenly, the two looked like a dream ticket.
> Christopher Ogden, *Life of the Party* (1994)

dress. *See* LITTLE BLACK . . .

dressed to kill. Dressed extremely smartly, very fashionably, so that you are capable of making a 'kill' or conquest of a member of the opposite sex. A film *Dressed to Kill* (US, 1980), being a thriller, took the phrase literally. The murderer wore the clothes of the opposite sex.

> One chap was dressed to kill for the King in Bombastes.
> John Keats, letter of 23 January 1818

> 'I am dressed to kill,' as the recruit said when he donned his uniform.
> *Cambridge Tribune* (US newspaper, 10 November 1881)

dressed up to the nines. Very smartly dressed. This may have come to us via a pronunciation shift. If you were to say dressed up 'to then eyne', that would mean, in Old English, 'dressed up to the eyes' (*eyne* being the old plural of 'eye'). The snag with this is that no examples of the phrase occur before the eighteenth century.

There are also suggestions that it refers to the setting of a standard with ten as the highest point one can reach; or it has something to do with setting oneself up to match the Nine Muses of classical mythology; or with the mystic number nine; or with the 99th Regiment of Foot's renowned smartness of dress (so anyone well turned out was 'dressed up [to equal] the nines').

drummed out of. *See under* FACE THE MUSIC.

dukes/dooks. *See* PUT ONE'S ...

dumps. *See* DOWN IN THE ...

Dunmow Flitch. *See under* BRING HOME THE BACON.

dunny. *See under* NETTY.

dust. *See* KICK THE BUCKET.

Dutch uncle. A stern disciplinarian – one who criticizes severely. Of American origin and probably inspired by the unbending colonists who settled in Pennsylvania and New York. Known since 1838. More recently, the phrase has acquired a kinder meaning: a Dutch uncle is one who takes an interest in or watches over a person.

dyed in the wool. Rigid in opinions, not susceptible to persuasion. Wool that is dyed before it is treated or made up into a garment retains the dye more thoroughly. Known since 1830 in the US but the idea was written down in England in 1579.

E

eat crow, to. Meaning 'to recant, to have to do something distasteful', it refers to an incident in the British-American War of 1812–14. During a ceasefire, a New England soldier went hunting and crossed over into British lines where, finding no better game, he shot a crow. An unarmed British officer encountered the American and, by way of admiring his gun, took hold of it. He then turned it on the American and forced him to eat part of the crow. Expression known since 1851.

eat humble pie, to. Meaning 'to submit to humiliation'. The 'humbles' or 'umbles' were those less appealing parts of a deer (or other animal) which had been killed in a hunt. They would be given to those of lower rank and perhaps served as 'humble pie' or 'umble pie'. A coincidence then that 'humble pie' should have anything to do with being humble. Recorded in 1830. Appropriately, it is Uriah Heep in Charles Dickens, *David Copperfield*, Chap. 39 (1849–50), who says: 'I got to know what umbleness did, and I took to it. I ate umble pie with an appetite.'

eat someone out of house and home, to. To eat so much that the houseowner who has provided the fare for the guest(s) is in a seriously depleted state as a result. Never said in complete seriousness. Parents might say to their children, 'You would eat us out of house and home you would.' Apparently it was a proverbial expression by the time Shakespeare used it in *Henry IV, Part II* (II.i.72) (1597). Mistress Quickly says of Falstaff: 'He hath eaten me out of house and home; he hath put all my substance into that fat belly of his.'

—, eat your heart out! A minor singer having just finished a powerful ballad might exult defiantly, 'Frank Sinatra, eat your heart out!' Partridge/*Catch Phrases* glosses it as: 'Doesn't *that* make you jealous, fella!' As something said *to* another person, this expression acquired popularity in the mid-twentieth century largely through its American show business use.

As such, it is probably another of those Jewish expressions popularized by show biz. Originally, 'to eat one's (own) heart out', simply meant 'to pine', was current in English by the sixteenth century, and Leo Rosten in *Hooray for Yiddish* (1983) finds it in the Yiddish *Es dir oys s'harts*. Apparently, Diogenes Laertius ascribed to Pythagoras the saying 'Do not eat your heart' meaning 'do not waste your life in worrying'.

egg. *See* LAY AN . . .

eggs. *See* SURE AS . . .

eggs Benedict. Poached eggs, toasted English muffin, slice of ham – with hollandaise sauce all over it. A high-calorie breakfast dish devised by Samuel Benedict and Oscar, the maître d' at the Waldorf-Astoria Hotel in New York, sometime in the 1880s? Others give the credit to Mr and Mrs LeGrand Benedict at Delmonico's Restaurant in New York City.

eight.   *See* ONE OVER THE . . .

eleventh hour.   *See* AT THE . . .

Emmy.   American TV's equivalent of the film Oscar has a most obscure origin. The image orthicon tube is an important part of the television camera, and, if you can believe it, 'image' became 'immy' became 'emmy'. The statuettes so called were first awarded by the American Academy of Television Arts and Sciences in the 1940s.

end.   *See* BITTER . . .

enemies list.   *See* HIT LIST.

envelope.   *See* PUSH THE . . .

equerry.   An officer in charge of the horses of a king or similar exalted person (now an officer of the British Royal household who attends a member of the Royal family). Oddly, this name has nothing to do with Latin *equus*, meaning 'horse', but is derived from the French *écurie*, meaning 'stable' which (although having to do with horses) leads to a meaning more akin to the title 'esquire' (which is derived from the Latin *scutarius*, meaning shield-bearer). Known in this form by 1600.

Essex Girl.   There was a craze for jokes on this theme in Britain in the autumn of 1991 – sample: 'How does an Essex Girl turn on the light afterwards? She kicks open the car door.' As such, they were a straight lift of the 'Blonde Jokes' that had been popular in the United States shortly before and really reflected very little that was unique to the county of Essex.

The British type was probably so named on the model of **Essex Man** – a term describing a prosperous, uncouth, uneducated person who did well out of the Thatcher years and was identified in the late 1980s as likely to be found dwelling in Essex.

Not long ago, I worked very briefly at [BBC] Radio 4, which is a terrifically politically correct sort of place, and one day in the office I told an Essex Girl joke. A young woman there turned on me as if I came from another,

less advanced planet, and, more in sorrow than in anger, said she didn't
think what I'd said was frightfully right-on.
Independent (23 April 1992)

eternal triangle. The traditional struggle and rivalry in a relationship between two persons of one sex and one of the other – often where a couple, married or not, has to relate to a third party. One of the most common situations in fiction and in fact. Known since 1907, though one would think it older.

Mrs Dudeney's novel ... deals with the eternal triangle, which, in this case, consists of two men and one woman.
Daily Chronicle (5 December 1907)

Exocet. Name of a deadly short-range guided missile, of French manufacture, since 1970. It is used in sea warfare and became widely known during the Falklands conflict of 1982. Taken from *exocet*, the French for flying fish, the word has also had a certain amount of allusive use. Delivering a devastating verbal attack in parliament might be described as 'launching an Exocet'.

extracting the Michael. *See under* TAKE THE MICKEY.

extreme prejudice. *See* TERMINATE WITH ...

eye. *See* APPLE OF ONE'S ...

eyeball to eyeball. Meaning 'in close confrontation'. Use of this expression is of comparatively recent origin. In the missile crisis of October 1962, the US took a tough line when the Soviet Union placed missiles on Cuban soil. After a tense few days, the Soviets withdrew. William Safire in *Safire's Political Dictionary* (1978) records that Secretary of State Dean Rusk (1909–94) was speaking to an ABC news correspondent, John Scali, on 24 October and said: 'Remember, when you report this, that, eyeball to eyeball, they blinked first.' Columnists Charles Bartlett and Stewart Alsop then helped to popularize this as, 'We're eyeball to eyeball and the other fellow just blinked.'

Before this, 'eyeball to eyeball' was a Black American serviceman's idiom. Safire quotes a reply given by the all-black 24th Infantry Regiment to an inquiry from General MacArthur's HQ in Korea

(November 1950): 'Do you have contact with the enemy?' 'We is eyeball to eyeball.'

F

face the music, to.   Meaning 'to face whatever punishment is coming' and known by 1850, this saying has two possible origins. An actor or entertainer must not only accept the judgement of the audience but also of the (often hard-to-impress) musicians in the orchestra in front of him. He literally faces the music. More likely is the second explanation, that it is akin to the expression 'to be **drummed out of**' something. At one time, if a soldier was dismissed from the army for dishonourable conduct, he would be drummed out in a ceremony which included having a description of his crime read out and his insignia stripped from his uniform.

Fagin.   Meaning 'a receiver of stolen goods; a trainer of thieves', the name derives from the character in *Oliver Twist* (1838–41) by Charles Dickens. That he was portrayed as 'a very shrivelled old jew ... villainous-looking and repulsive' led to allegations of anti-semitism. Dickens sought to make amends by introducing a kindly Jew, Mr Riah, in *Our Mutual Friend* (1864–5).

Falstaffian.   Fat and jolly, after Sir John Falstaff, the fat, jovial, likeable rogue in the first and second parts of Shakespeare's *King Henry IV* and *The Merry Wives of Windsor*. Shakespeare's original may have been Sir John Oldcastle (*d* 1417), High Sheriff of Herefordshire. In the history plays, he befriends Prince Hal, plans an abortive robbery at Gad's Hill, but is rejected when the prince becomes king. Tradition has it that Elizabeth I requested Shakespeare to revive him for *The Merry Wives of Windsor*, a light-hearted romantic romp.

family.   *See* ALL IN THE ...

family jewels.   (1) A 'jocular CIA phrase for its own most em-barrassing secrets', according to William Safire in *Safire's Political*

Dictionary (1978). Director of Central Intelligence William Colby reflecting on his predecessor's attempts to unearth CIA activities which were outside its charter, noted in his book *Honorable Men* (1978): 'They were promptly dubbed by a wag the "family jewels"; I referred to them as "our skeletons in the closet".' (2) The testicles or the whole 'male sexual apparatus'. Partridge/*Slang* finds this in services use in the Second World War and probably earlier, back to the 1920s.

family that prays together stays together. A slogan devised by Al Scalpone, a professional commercial writer, for the Roman Catholic Rosary Crusade in the US. The crusade began in 1942 and the slogan was first used in a radio broadcast on 6 March 1947 by Father Patrick Peyton. It is quoted in Joseph Heller's novel *Catch-22*, possibly anachronistically, as that story is set in 1944–5. There have been many variations: 'The family that shoots together loots together', 'the family that flays together stays together' – graffiti, quoted by 1974.

fan. A devoted admirer of a particular entertainer or of a sporting team or of any kind of pursuit. This is a contraction of 'fanatic' and may have originated in the US in the 1880s when avid followers of baseball were dubbed 'baseball fanatics' and, in time, by the shorter term. Earlier, in 1682, the same meaning had been expressed in such phrases as 'loyal Phans' and 'loyal Fanns'.

fancy-free. Not in love with anyone, without commitments. Apparently appears first in Shakespeare, *A Midsummer Night's Dream*, II.i.163 (1595): 'And the imperial votress passed on,/In maiden meditation, fancy-free.'

Fanny Adams. *See* SWEET . . .

fashion victim. A person (usually female) who wears clothes solely to be fashionable and without any reference to whether the particular items are suitable for her figure. Possibly a coinage of the American journal *Women's Wear Daily* and current by the early 1970s.

There is also the phrase **martyr to be smarter** which Partridge/*Slang* locates mid-century and which seems to be describing the same affliction.

fast and loose. *See* PLAY . . .

Faustian. Having the characteristics of Johann Faust(us), or 'one who sells his soul to the devil'. So named after a German astrologer and necromancer (*d* 1541) who was reputed to have practised the black arts and was later celebrated in several plays including Christopher Marlowe's *The Tragical History of Dr Faustus* (*c*.1592) and Goethe's *Faust* (1772–1831). In these plays Faust exchanges his soul for a longer life in which all pleasure and knowledge is his for the asking.

feather in one's cap. *See* HAVE A . . .

feel one's oats, to. To act in an important way as though pleased with oneself, to be lively. Seems to have originated in the US in about 1830. It referred, literally at first, to the way a horse was thought to feel friskier and more energetic after it had eaten oats.

feet under the table. *See* HAVE ONE'S . . .

fiddle. *See* FIT AS A . . .

Fifth Beatle. Someone who by association with The Beatles pop group in the 1960s was considered to have earned honorary membership status. Murray the K, the American disc jockey, applied this term to himself, on the basis of his presumed friendship with The Beatles during the group's visit to the US in 1964 – much to the annoyance of Brian Epstein, their manager. The tale is recounted in an essay entitled 'The Fifth Beatle' in Tom Wolfe's *The Kandy-Kolored Tangerine-Flake Streamline Baby* (1966).

Others could more fittingly have merited the title – Stu Sutcliffe, an early member of the group who was eased out and died before fame struck; Pete Best, who was replaced as drummer by Ringo Starr; Neil Aspinall, road manager, aide and friend; and George Martin, the group's arranger and record producer. And others have had it applied to them with less reason.

Stitched-together . . . scrambled, incoherent . . . All this is the doing of Richard Lester, who still has 'Help!' and 'A Hard Day's Night' to his credit but hereby forefeits any claim he ever had to being the Fifth Beatle.
Review of the Paul McCartney concert movie *Get Back*, directed by Richard Lester, *New York Times* (25 October 1991)

There is a secondary meaning, referring to someone who has missed out on the success of something he was once a part of. This was certainly true in the case of Stu Sutcliffe and Pete Best. I can recall it being applied, for example, by a former *Observer* TV critic to Robert Hewison, the writer, who could be said to have missed out on the success of the Monty Python TV comedy team. At one time, Hewison worked closely at developing the Python type of humour with some of the other members of the group, though he never profited from it himself. Similarly, both Michael Bentine and Graham Stark have been referred to as 'the Fourth Goon' of the BBC radio *Goon Show* – and with some justification.

fifth column.   A group of traitors, infiltrators. In October 1936, during the Spanish Civil War, the Nationalist General, Emilio Mola, was besieging the Republican-held city of Madrid with four columns. He was asked in a broadcast whether this was sufficient to capture the city and he replied that he was relying on the support of the *quinta columna* [fifth column], which was already hiding inside the city and which sympathized with his side. *The Fifth Column* was the title of Ernest Hemingway's only play (1938).

Figaro.   A barber, also a roguish character – derived from the guileful, amusing character of Figaro in the plays by Beaumarchais, *Le Barbier de Séville* (1775) and *Le Mariage de Figaro* (1784). In addition, the title of the French newspaper *Le Figaro* (founded 1826) comes from the same source.

find the streets paved with gold, to.   Where did this near-cliché originate? In the story of Dick Whittington, he makes his way to London from Gloucestershire because he hears the streets are paved with gold and silver. The actual Dick Whittington was thrice Lord Mayor of London in the late fourteenth and early fifteenth centuries. The popular legend does not appear to have been told before 1605. *Benham's Book of Quotations* (1948) comments on the proverbial expression 'London streets are paved with gold' – 'A doubtful story or tradition alleges that this saying was due to the fact that *c.*1470, a number of members of the Goldsmiths' Company, London, joined the Paviors' Company.'

George Colman the Younger in *The Heir-at-Law* (1797) wrote:

Oh, London is a fine town,
A very famous city,
Where all the streets are paved with gold,
And all the maidens pretty.

The streets of heaven are also sometimes said to be paved with gold
– 'the street of the city was pure gold' (Revelation 21:21). Accordingly,
there is also a spiritual where the 'streets in heaven am paved with
gold'.

> He had played the traditional part of the country boy who comes up to
> London where the streets are paved with gold.
> G.K. Chesterton, *William Cobbett* (1925)

fine-tooth comb. *See* GO THROUGH (SOMETHING) WITH A . . .

fish. *See* NEITHER . . .

fit as a fiddle, to be. A fiddler, when playing quickly, has to be
so dextrous with his fingers and bow that he is assumed to be
especially lively and awake. Could, then, the phrase that we have be
a contraction of 'fit as a fiddler'? It was current by 1616.

fit to a T, to. To fit perfectly. A T-square is used by draughtsmen
to draw parallel lines and angles, though it seems 'to a T' was in
use by 1693 and before the T-square got its name. Perhaps the
original expression was 'fit to a tittle' – a tittle being the dot over
the letter *i* – so the phrase meant 'to a dot, fine point'. There are
other theories, none of them conclusive.

Flaming Nora! (sometimes **Ruddy Nora!**). A delightful expletive
which was certainly current by the 1970s. Beyond that, its source is
a mystery, as also is the identity of the particular Nora who must
have inspired it. Oddly, the name 'Nora' does not appear to be
euphemistic as GORDON BENNETT is.

flash Harry. (1) A self-confident, vulgar person. British slang.
Street Talk: The Language of Coronation Street (1986) nicely defines it
thus: 'A "greasy" character of extravagant habits, someone who is
common, vulgar, but self-assured, gangster-like. From "flash" meaning "loud" and in poor taste.' Known by 1960. (2) Nickname of Sir
Malcolm Sargent (1895–1967), the orchestral conductor. It is said

to have originated with a BBC announcer after Sargent had appeared on the *Brains Trust* radio programme and was also about to be heard in the following programme. Listeners were told that they were to be taken over to a concert conducted by Sargent in Manchester. It sounded as if he had gone there straight away, in a flash. This is the version given by Sargent himself in the *Sunday Times* (25 April 1965). However, the nickname also encapsulated his extremely debonair looks and manner – smoothed-back hair, buttonhole, gestures and all.

It has been suggested that 'Flash Harry' was originally the name given to the man who would 'flash' the furnaces every morning in Midlands factories – which might go some way to explain how the name 'Harry' came to be in the Malcolm Sargent nickname. Other similar coinages noted by Partridge/*Slang* are 'Flash Alf' and 'Flash Jack'.

flash in the pan. A short-lived success, failure after a showy attempt. From the irregular firing of a flintlock musket. A hammer was supposed to strike a flint and produce sparks which exploded the charge, but this did not always occur. The powder in the 'pan', a small depression, sometimes flashed but failed to ignite the charge. Figurative sense known by 1741.

flying colours. *See* WITH . . .

Flynn. *See* IN LIKE . . .

fogey. *See* YOUNG . . .

foodie/foodism/foodist. Words coined in the early 1980s for people – 'foodies' – who indulged in excessive fussing over the purchase and preparation of food. This fussing might take the form of going to great lengths to buy particular meats or cheeses or worrying unduly about obtaining the perfect recipe from some Spanish hillside to create a masterly dish. The term may also be applied to anyone whose main interest is food. If not actually coined by Ann Barr of *Harpers & Queen* Magazine, the term ought to have been. Celebrated in a book by her and Paul Levy, *The Official Foodie Handbook* (1984).

He told me about the foodie who sat next to him in a Chinese restaurant and went into transports of enthusiastic analysis about the way in which the chicken had been cooked.
Listener (27 September 1984)

Unpretentious, carefully seasoned and served dishes, made of cheap ingredients, are what avant garde foodies are taking to more and more.
Cosmopolitan (June 1986)

footprint.   An area covered. New applications for this word emerged in the 1980s. One was for the area covered by the signal from a communications satellite. Another was the area in which the warheads of a multiple-warhead missile land. In computers, it referred to the surface area on a desk taken up by equipment. A slightly earlier use than these had been for the area in which noise from a moving source, like an aeroplane, could be heard on the ground.

With features like a ... memory mapper and a footprint of only 12.6 inches by 15.7 inches, it's a difficult micro to fault.
Advertisement in *Mail on Sunday* (9 August 1987)

Trident's footprint is considerably large and each warhead can be targeted more accurately.
Independent (26 January 1988)

for a song.   *See* GO ...

for all mankind.   Portentous phrase for 'everybody' and used, for example, on the plaque left on the moon by the US crew of the Apollo XI space mission:

> HERE MEN FROM THE PLANET EARTH
> FIRST SET FOOT UPON THE MOON
> JULY 1969 AD
> WE CAME IN PEACE FOR ALL MANKIND.

Known by 1792.

The two clever ones embracing each other and dissolving into tears of tenderness for all mankind ...
Charles Dickens, *Little Dorrit*, Chap. 29 (1857)

The settlement agreed by Servo Computers with two former women employees was not merely a victory for the sensibilities of women; it was a victory for all mankind. Or at any rate, the substantial section of the

population who have, at some time in their working life, had to endure the office party from hell.
Daily Telegraph (15 February 1996)

for goodness' sake. Euphemistic exclamation (in place of 'for God's sake'), though originally the phrase simply meant something like 'in order to be kind'. The earliest citations in this earlier sense occur in Shakespeare's *King Henry VIII*, Prologue 23; III.i.159 (1612).

for the high jump, to be. To be obliged to face the reckoning for some action when called upon to do so by authority. Possibly from services slang, referring to a difficult test in athletics. Certainly known by the 1920s in military slang – the suggestion being that someone on a charge would need to jump very high to get out of the trouble.

fourth estate. The press (chiefly in Britain). In 1828, Thomas Macaulay wrote of the House of Commons: 'The gallery in which the reporters sit has become the fourth estate of the realm' – that is to say, after the Lords Spiritual, the Lords Temporal, and the Commons – and Macaulay has often been credited with coining this expression. But so have a number of others. The phrase was originally used to describe various forces outside Parliament – such as the Army (as by Falkland in 1638) or the Mob (as by Fielding in 1752). When William Hazlitt used it in 'Table Talk' in 1821, he meant not the press in general but just William Cobbett. Two years later, Lord Brougham is said to have used the phrase in the House of Commons to describe the press in general. So by the time Macaulay used it in the *Edinburgh Review* in 1828, it was obviously an established usage. Then Thomas Carlyle used it several times – in his article on Boswell's *Life of Johnson* in 1832, in his *The French Revolution* in 1837, and in his lectures 'On Heroes, Hero-Worship, & the Heroic in History' in 1841. But, just to keep the confusion alive, he attributed the phrase to Edmund Burke, who died in 1797 and is said to have pointed at the press gallery and remarked: 'And yonder sits the fourth estate, more important than them all.'

It has been suggested that the BBC (or the broadcast media in general) now constitute a *fifth* estate, as also, at one time, the trades unions.

fox. *See* CRAZY LIKE A . . .

foxed. *See* SLIGHTLY . . .

foxtrot. This dance was supposedly named after the US entertainer Harry Fox whose 1913 *Ziegfeld Follies* contained the steps for it. The word first appears in the 1915 Victor Record catalogue.

Before this, a 'foxtrot' was a term in horsemanship for a short-paced step in changing from trotting to walking. Not because a fox does anything similar but because of a development from *faux-droite* in Norman French where this was the name of a dance at the annual meeting of the Folk (*Volk*) People.

France. *See* LIVE LIKE GOD IN . . .

free. *See* SET THE PEOPLE . . .

freelance. Used to denote a self-employed person, especially a writer or journalist. The word (redolent of the Middle Ages, when an unattached soldier for hire – a mercenary – would have been appropriately called a 'free lance') is in fact a nineteenth-century coinage. Sir Walter Scott in *Ivanhoe* (1820) has: 'I offered Richard the services of my Free Lances'.

French leave. *See* TAKE . . .

Friends of the Earth. Name of an international lobbying organization of GREEN environmentalists. Originating in the US, the name was adopted in Britain in 1970.

frit. An abbreviation of 'fright/frightened' still widely used in the British north Midlands – including Grantham where Margaret Thatcher was born. When Prime Minister she challenged a prominent Labour minister, Denis Healey, in the House of Commons on 20 April 1983. He had suggested that she was preparing to 'cut and run' regarding a general election. 'Oh, the Right Honourable Gentleman is afraid of an election is he?' she taunted him. 'Afraid, afraid, afraid, frightened, frit, couldn't take it, couldn't stand it!'

The first recorded use of the word is by the Northamptonshire poet, John Clare. In 'The Village Minstrel' (1821), he wrote:

The coy hare squats nesting in the corn,
Frit at the bow'd ear tott'ring over her head.

from the cradle to the grave. The whole of a person's life. Something of a cliché phrase now. It appears to have been coined by Sir Richard Steele in an essay in the *Tatler* (No. 52, 1709): 'A modest Fellow never has a doubt from his Cradle to his Grave'.

> A sunbeam in a winter's day,
> Is all the proud and mighty have
> Between the cradle and the grave.
> John Dyer, *Grongar Hill* (1726)

> The move represents a tacit admission that the National Health Service has in parts of Britain lost sight of its commitment to offer care from the cradle to the grave.
> *Guardian* (28 February 1996)

from the grassroots. A political cliché of the early 1970s, used when supposedly reflecting the opinions of the 'rank and file' and the 'ordinary voter' rather than the leadership of the political parties 'at national level'. The full phrase is 'from the grassroots up' and has been used to describe anything of a fundamental nature since *c*.1900 and specifically in politics from *c*.1912 – originally in the US. A BBC Radio programme *From the Grassroots* started in 1970. Katherine Moore writing to Joyce Grenfell in *An Invisible Friendship* (letter of 13 October 1973): 'Talking of writing – why have roots now always got to be *grass* roots? And what a lot of them seem to be about.'

> In spite of official discouragement and some genuine disquiet at the grassroots in both parties, 21 such joint administrations have been operating in counties, districts and boroughs over the past year.
> *Guardian* (10 May 1995)

> The mood of the grassroots party, and much of Westminster too, is for an end of big government, substantial cuts in taxation, cuts in public spending, toughness on crime, immigration and social-security spending, and as little Europe as possible.
> *Ibid.*

from your mouth to God's ear (or ... **to the Gates of Heaven**). May God hear what I/you say and act upon it. Or, as defined in *The Taste of Yiddish* by Lillian Merwin Feinsilver (1970): 'Fun zayn moyl, in Gots oyer. Lit., From his mouth into God's ear.

May God hear what he has said (and fulfil it)!' The 'Gates of Heaven' may be an Arab version. Arabic also has a sarcastic if vulgar retort when the occasion arises: 'From your mouth to His arsehole', meaning 'like hell it will'. The first expression may stem from Psalm 130:2: 'Lord, hear my voice: let thine ears be attentive to the voice of my supplications.' The phrase also makes an appearance in the orthodox Jewish prayer book.

> *Goldeneye* is the best movie in the series since *Diamonds Are Forever* ... I told him I thought it would take $30 million in its opening weekend, to which he replied: 'From your lips to God's ears.'
> *Evening Standard* (London) (4 October 1995)

frying pan. *See* OUT OF THE ...

full monty. The full amount, everything included. A phrase suddenly popular in British English in the early 1990s but known since the early 1980s. Its appearance in *Street Talk, the Language of* Coronation Street (1986) shows that it was established in the north of England/Lancashire soap opera by that date. The dictionary explains: 'To avoid the awkwardness of stumbling through an unfamiliar menu, someone might tell the waiter: "We'll have the full monty"' (though the expression **full house** might just as easily be used in that context). The somewhat Cockney comedian Jim Davidson entitled his autobiography *The Full Monty* in 1993.

Could it be a corruption of the 'full amount'? Or could it have something to do with 'monty' (from the Spanish *monte*), a card game, or the Australian/New Zealand term for a horse considered certain to win a race? Or, again, could it have something to do with bales stuffed *full* of wool and imported from Montevideo? Or with Field Marshal Montgomery being kitted out with all his medals? Or, most convincingly of all, with being dressed in a full wedding suit (or similar) from the tailors Montague Burton (first established in Chesterfield in 1904)? It was possible to buy or hire a complete outfit – shirt, tie, suit and socks – so when you elected to have the whole lot you were wearing the 'full monty'.

> 'What we're after is a live skeleton – the full monty,' said the stage manager.
> *Guardian* (28 September 1989)

fumed oak. Oak which has been darkened by exposure to ammonia vapour. Furniture made of this wood was popular in the early 1900s especially. The phrase used allusively points to a certain suburban type of household where it would be found. Noël Coward gave the title *Fumed Oak* to one of his playlets in *To-night at 8.30* (1936).

> (Of a house called 'The Beeches' in Headington) This is a little half-timbered heaven furnished with 'fumed oak' and simple colours.
> John Betjeman, *Letters* (letter of 3 October 1927) (1994)

> One of the participants is Dillon himself, a *farouche* young actor-dramatist currently sponging on a suburban family straight out of Mr Coward's *Fumed Oak*.
> Kenneth Tynan in a 1958 theatre review, *Curtains* (1961)

funny bone. The part of the elbow over which the ulnar nerve passes – so called from the peculiar sensation experienced when it is hit. There is some suggestion that the term may be a pun on the Latin *humerus*, the medical name of the long bone in the upper arm. But how would this medical joke have gained common currency? Known by 1867.

funny old world. *See* IT'S A . . .

fuzz. A popular term for the police, out of the US in the 1960s, though current by the 1920s. Possibly because they are people who make a 'fuss', or a corruption of 'Feds' (federal agents).

G

gaff. *See* BLOW THE . . .

gaga. Meaning 'senile', this comes from a French word. Also in French, one can use the expression *c'est un vieux gâteux* to describe an old man who is completely gaga. Perhaps 'gaga' developed from '*gâteux*' which as a noun means 'dotard' and as an adjective, 'decrepit' (and has nothing to do with *gâteau*, cake), or it may just be imitative of the way such a person would sound if he tried to speak. Rosie Boycott's suggestion in *Batty, Bloomers and Boycott* (1982), that it has something to do with the Impressionist painter Paul Gauguin (1848–1903) seems unlikely. He may have been mentally disturbed in old age, but the word was known in French by 1875 when he was not. Known in English by 1920.

Gaiety Girl. Originally, one of the performers and beauties who appeared in shows at the Gaiety Theatre, London, in the 1890s. Then a somewhat dismissive phrase for a now faded chorus girl of any description.

game. *See* —'S MY NAME …

game isn't over. *See* IT'S NOT OVER …

gammy. Meaning 'lame, crippled' – a form of 'game' which is an eighteenth-century dialect word of unknown origin. *Brewer* gives it as 'a dialect form of the Celtic *cam* meaning crooked', though *OED2* disputes this. From 'Focus on Fact' in *Private Eye* (1981) we have: 'The Llewellyns are descended from medieval knight, Sir Dafydd Gam, who got an arrow in his eye at Agincourt … hence the expression "gammy" eye, leg etc.' 'Davy Gam, Esquire' is indeed mentioned in Shakespeare's *King Henry V*, IV.viii.106 (1599) as having fallen at Agincourt, and it appears that David ap Llewellyn of Brecon was so called because of a squint. So what one can say is, that though the origin of 'gammy' may be from the Celtic fringe, it was probably not derived from Dafydd Gam – merely applied to him.

gamp. A nickname for 'umbrella' which derives from the name of the character Sarah Gamp in *Martin Chuzzlewit* (1843–4) by Charles Dickens. She always carried a large one.

gang of four. Now meaning any group of four people working in concert, the original Gang of Four was led by Jiang Qing, the unscrupulous wife of Chairman Mao Tse-tung, and so labelled in the mid-1970s when the four were tried and given the death sentence for treason and other crimes (later commuted to life imprisonment). The other three members were Zhang Chunqiao, a political organizer in the Cultural Revolution; Wang Hogwen, a youthful activist; and

Yao Wenyuan, a journalist. Chairman Hua Kuo-feng attributed the phrase to his predecessor. Apparently on one occasion, Mao had warned his wife and her colleagues: 'Don't be a gang of four.' The nickname was later applied to the founders of the Social Democratic Party in Britain in 1981 – Roy Jenkins, David Owen, William Rodgers and Shirley Williams.

garbage in, garbage out.   A term from computing, known by 1964 (and sometimes abbreviated to **GIGO**, pronounced 'guy-go'). Basically, it means that if you put bad data into a computer, you can come up with anything you want but what comes out will be useless and meaningless. In the wider sense it conveys the simple idea that what you get out of something depends very much on what you put into it.

garden path.   *See* LEAD SOMEONE UP THE . . .

Gates of Heaven.   *See under* FROM YOUR MOUTH TO . . .

gauntlet.   *See* RUN THE . . .

gay.   Homosexual. It was at the end of the 1960s that homosexuals most noticeably hijacked the word 'gay'. This was at a time when the US Gay Liberation Front came 'out of the closet' and used such slogans as 'Say it loud, we're gay and we're proud' and '2–4–6–8, gay is just as good as straight'.

The word 'gay' had, however, been used in this sense since at least the 1930s and on both sides of the Atlantic. In the nineteenth century, 'gay' was used to describe female prostitutes and there is an even earlier use of the word applied to female licentiousness. It may (like CAMP) have gravitated towards its homosexual use from there. Although one regrets the loss of the word to mean 'joyful, lighthearted', perhaps this use goes some way towards making up for the pejorative use of 'bent', 'queer' and 'poof' to describe homosexuals. **Poof** (also 'pouf', 'poove', 'poofdah' and the Australian 'poofter') dates back at least to the 1850s, and 'puff' (pointing to the likely origin) was apparently tramps' slang for homosexual by 1870. *Private Eye* certainly popularized 'poof' in the 1960s but clearly did not invent it, as has been claimed.

gazumped, to be. Meaning 'to lose out on a house purchase agreement, when the vendor accepts a bid higher than that agreed with the first bidder', this specific meaning became popular in England and Wales during the early 1970s. The process can only occur in those countries where vendors are allowed to break a verbal agreement to sell if they receive a later, better offer. In Scotland where the 'sealed bid' system operates, gazumping is not possible.

But why the word 'gazump' – alternatively 'gazoomph', 'gasumph', 'gazumph', 'gezumph'? *OED2* has citations from English sources from 1928 onwards suggesting that the word has always had something to do with swindling. Might it come from 'goes up!' – meaning the price – along the lines of the term 'gazunder' for chamberpot (because it 'goes under' the bed)? Another suggestion is that it is a Yiddish word, *gezumph*.

gender bender. One who obscures the difference between the sexes – usually by wearing the clothes of the opposite sex but also through bisexual activity. A coinage of the 1980s.

> The cult hallows ambiguous sexuality: Mr David Bowie, the rock star 'gender bender', is a key hero.
> *Economist* (27 December 1980)

> Pale pinks and soft blues are this year's colours for casual shirts and fashion jeans ... It may not be Boy George's idea of gender-bending, but the visual reassembly of masculinity through popular fashion is becoming a real feature of the 1980s.
> *New Socialist* (February 1986)

gentleman caller. A man who calls on a woman and becomes a potential suitor. Also a euphemism for a male lover. The phrase occurs in the script of *Citizen Kane* (1941) – 'When I have a gentleman caller . . .' – but the concept is best known from Tennessee Williams's play *The Glass Menagerie* (1944).

gentleman's agreement. Meaning 'an agreement not enforceable at law and only binding as a matter of honour' – of US origin and not known before the 1920s. A.J.P. Taylor in *English History 1914–1945* (1965) says: 'This absurd phrase was taken by [von] Papen from business usage to describe the agreement between Austria and Germany in July 1936. It was much used hereafter for an agreement with anyone who was obviously not a gentleman and who would obviously not keep his agreement.'

gentrification. The embourgeoising of formerly working class dwellings (in Britain), a particular feature of 1960s property development. The *OED2* has the word in 1973.

> I propose to define it as that moment in the life of an old working man's cottage when the new owners paint the front door aubergine.
> Godfrey Smith, *Sunday Times* (30 January 1983)

George Spelvin. *See under* WALTER PLINGE.

gercha! (or **gertcha!**). Get out of it! This word had a burst of popularity in about 1980 when it was used in TV advertisements for Courage Best Bitter in the UK. Various grim-faced drinkers sat around in an East End pub and shouted it out during breaks in the music. Dave Trott, the copywriter responsible for using the word, suggested it derived from 'Get out of it, you!' This is supported by Partridge/*Slang* who was on to it – as 'gercher' – in 1937. The *OED2* has 'get away/along with you' as a 'derisive expression of disbelief'. The line got into the commercial from a song composed by the Cockney singers Chas and Dave. They originally pronounced it 'Wooertcha'.

Gesundheit! An exclamation made when someone sneezes, this is German for 'health', but it also has the rhythmic appeal of 'God bless you' and of a musical finish (as to a music-hall joke). Known in English by 1914. Sneezing was believed to be the expulsion of an evil spirit, hence the need for such an exclamation. The Romans cried ***absit omen!*** [flee, omen!].

get down to brass tacks, to. Probably of US origin, this phrase means 'to get down to essentials' and has been known since 1897, at least. There are various theories as to why we say it, including: (1) In old stores, brass tacks were positioned a yard apart for measuring. When a customer 'got down to brass tacks', it meant he or she was serious about making a purchase. (2) Brass tacks were a fundamental element in nineteenth-century upholstery, hence this expression meant to deal with a fault in the furniture by getting down to basics. (3) 'Brass tacks' is rhyming slang for 'facts', though the version 'to get down to brass nails' would contradict this.

get/be given the sack, to.   The suggestion is that this expression dates from the days when workers would carry the tools of their trade around with them, from job to job, in a bag which they would leave with their employer. When their services were no longer required, they would be given the bag back. Known in English since 1825, but in French since the seventeenth century: '*On luy a donné son sac*'.

get on one's wick, to.   To get on one's nerves. 'You really get on my wick, y'know that?' Probably a rhyming slang expression from 'Hampton Wick' [an area of London] = prick. Known by 1945.

get one's dander up, to.   Meaning 'to get ruffled or angry', the expression occurs in William Thackeray's *Pendennis*: 'Don't talk to me about daring to do this thing or t'other, or when my dander is up it's the very thing to urge me on' (Chap.44, 1848–50). Apparently of US origin (known by 1831), where 'dander' was either a 'calcined cinder' or 'dandruff'. It is hard to see how the expression develops from either of these meanings. The Dutch word *donder* meaning 'thunder', or 'dunder', a Scottish dialect word for 'ferment', may be more relevant.

get one's goat, to.   To be annoyed by something. 'The way she carries on, that really gets my goat!' Apparently another Americanism that has passed into general use (and current by 1910), this expression can also be found in French as *prendre la chèvre*, 'to take the milch-goat'. One is always suspicious of explanations that go on to explain that, of course, goats were very important to poor people and if anyone were to get a man's goat . . . etc. One is even more unimpressed by the explanation given by the *Morris Dictionary of Word and Phrase Origins* (1977): 'It used to be a fairly common practice to stable a goat with a thoroughbred [horse], the theory being that the goat's presence would help the high-strung nag to keep its composure. If the goat were stolen the night before a big race, the horse might be expected to lose its poise and blow the race.'

Robert L. Shook in *The Book of Why* (1983) wonders, interestingly, whether it has anything to do with a 'goatee' (a beard like a goat's). If you got someone by the 'goat', it would certainly annoy them.

All one can do is to point to the number of idioms referring to goats – 'act the goat', 'giddy goat', 'scapegoat', and, once more, emphasize the alliteration. Another version is 'to get one's nanny-goat'.

get one's just deserts, to. To suffer the fate or outcome of a situation which one deserves – especially if bad. The temptation to spell it 'desserts' should be resisted. Known by 1970 but surely of earlier provenance?

> Biggs [says], 'I've managed to avoid the grim grey cells for 30 years. I believe in the power of good. If I keep my nose clean it will be all right.' He pauses: 'Don't you agree that the villain always gets his just deserts?'
> *Sunday Telegraph* (5 February 1995)

> Sentences must reflect an assessment of the individual circumstances and of the offender's just deserts.
> *Guardian* (2 December 1995)

get/take one's kit off, to. To undress, take one's clothes off. Originally from removing one's football kit or other sports gear but, in the early 1990s in the UK, increasingly applied to actors and actresses or any other exhibitionists revealing their nakedness.

> In the late Sixties and early Seventies directors banged on endlessly about the artistic integrity of their nude scenes, though it was strange, as Bernard Levin perceptively observed, that only pretty women seemed to be required to get their kit off. Chaps still clung cravenly to their Y-fronts, and older, uglier women were generally spared strip-tease duties.
> *Daily Telegraph* (29 April 1994)

get one's oar in, to (also **put/stick**). To interfere in an unwelcome fashion with what someone else is doing or to interrupt what they are saying. From an older expression, 'to have an oar in another man's boat'. Known by 1543.

get out of the wrong side of the bed, to. To start the day in a bad mood. It was held to be unlucky to put the left foot on the ground first when getting out of bed. The superstition was commented on by 1540.

You rose o' the wrong side to-day.
Richard Brome, *The Court Beggar* (1632)

Why, brother Nixon, thou art angry this morning ... hast risen from thy wrong side, I think.
Walter Scott, *Redgauntlet* (1824)

get religion, to.   To become suddenly enthusiastic about religion and to attempt to involve others in your enthusiasm with all the fervour of a convert. Originally an American concept, this expression was known by 1772.

The Confirmation, when it took place, was a great affair ... The imposing appearance of the Bishop who confirmed us, and the general odour of sanctity that prevailed, combined to inspire me with the belief that I had at last 'got religion'.
Lord Berners, *A Distant Prospect* (1945)

get someone's number, to.   To work out what kind of character a person has. Origin obscure.

Whenever a person proclaims to you 'In worldly matters I'm a child'... you have got that person's number and it's Number One.
Charles Dickens, *Bleak House* Chap. 57 (1853)

get the bird, to.   Meaning, 'to be rejected by an audience'. Originally the expression was 'to get the big bird' and has been used as such since the nineteenth century. What do audiences do when they do not like something? They boo or they hiss, sounding something like a flock of geese, perhaps.

get under someone's skin, to.   (1) To annoy or upset them greatly. (2) To emphathize with them. Presumably the image is of some disease getting under the skin. Known since 1896 and 1927, respectively. In the famous song by Cole Porter, 'I've Got You Under My Skin' (1936), the malady of love is, of course, regarded as a benign contagion.

— get your gun.   The title of Irving Berlin's 1946 musical *Annie Get Your Gun* is utterly appropriate for the tale of Annie Oakley the gun-toting gal, but it is also allusive. A song 'Johnny Get Your Gun' with lyrics somewhat along the lines of, 'Johnny get your gun, get your gun, get your gun,/Keep them on the run, on the run, on the run' was written by 'F. Belasco' (Monroe H. Rosenfeld) and published in New York, 1886. It was a popular American song of the First World War. *Johnny Got His Gun* (US, 1971) was a film about a soldier mutilated in the 1914–18 war.

GI. An ordinary member of the US Armed Forces who enlisted to fight in the Second World War. From the initials applied to blankets, uniforms, haircuts, and so on and standing for 'Government Issue' (or perhaps 'General Issue'). **GI Joe** refers more specifically to the typical American foot soldier. It was the title of a comic strip created (1942) by David Breger for *Yank*, the US Army's enlisted man's magazine.

gibberish. Dr Johnson thought this word for nonsense derived from an Arabian alchemist called Geber in the eleventh century who had, in turn, translated into Latin the writings of an eighth-century alchemist called *Jabir* ibn Hayyan. He wrote in a mystical jargon because, if his writings had been discovered, he might have been put to death. The most obvious derivation is from 'gibber' which, like 'jabber', means to speak fast and inarticulately (compare 'gabber' and 'gab'). But the word appears to have an earlier source than this, which might just confirm Dr Johnson's theory. Partridge/*Slang*, meanwhile, thinks it developed from 'Egyptian', like 'gypsy'. Known by 1554.

gift horse. *See* LOOK A . . .

gifts. *See* BEWARE GREEKS BEARING . . .

GIGO. *See* GARBAGE IN . . .

gilded youth. *See under* GOLDEN YOUTH.

Ginger, you're barmy! Addressed to any male, this street cry merely means he is stupid or crazy. It may date from the early 1900s and most probably originated in the British music-hall song with the title 'Ginger, You're Balmy [the alternative spelling]!' written by Fred Murray and published in 1912. This was sung by Harry Champion (1866–1942). In the song the following phrase is 'Get your hair cut!' Also in the chorus occurs another line sometimes coupled with 'Ginger, you're barmy!' – 'Why don't you join the army'. Roy Dent of Harrow recalls a version fifty years ago that went: 'Ginger, you're BARMY/You ought to join the army/You'll get knocked out/By a bottle of stout/Ginger, you're BARMY!' Mrs B.J. Halliwell of Leominster thinks that it became a Navy taunt to the Army and remembers it from Hong Kong in the late 1950s: 'My children always looked out in case a certain red-nosed soldier was on duty at an army camp in the Clearwater Bay area. If he was, they all shouted out, "Ginger, you're BARMY, why did you join the Army?"' *Ginger, You're Barmy* was used as the title of a novel (1962) by David Lodge.

Separately, the word 'ginger' has been applied in the UK to male homosexuals (since the 1930s, at least) on account of the rhyming slang, 'ginger beer = queer'. 'Ginger' is also the name given to a red-headed man. But neither of these appears relevant to the song. Ian Gillies commented (1995): 'The plot of "Ginger" is very similar [to another Champion song] "Any Old Iron" – someone who fancies himself well-dressed, being shouted at in the one case because of his "old iron" watch-chain, and in the other because he isn't wearing a hat and not, apparently, because he is ginger. Indeed, there is no specific reference to his being ginger.' Here are the lines:

'Don't walk a-bout with our cady [= hat] on;
'Ginger, you're balmy!
Get your hair cut!', they all be-gin to cry.
'With nothing on your nap-per, oh, you are a pie!
'Pies must have a lit-tle bit of crust,
'Why don't you join the army?
'If you want to look a don you want a bit of something on –
'Ginger, you're balmy!'

give a dog a bad name. Meaning 'say bad things about a person and they'll stick', this possibly comes from the longer 'Give a dog an ill name and hang him' (known by 1818), suggesting that if a dog has a reputation for ferocity, it might as well be killed because no one will trust it.

give/grant no quarter, to. Not to concede any ground. Previously, 'give quarter' meant to spare the life of an enemy in one's power. Known by 1645. An old theory that 'quarter' referred to the share of a soldier's pay which would be claimed as ransom does not seem to stand up. Perhaps rather it refers to the *quarters* a prisoner would have to occupy.

give someone the cold shoulder, to.   Meaning 'to be studiedly indifferent towards someone'. Known by 1820, this expression is said to have originated with the medieval French custom of serving guests a hot roast. When they had outstayed their welcome, the host would pointedly produce a cold shoulder of mutton to get them on their way.

give the thumbs down, to.   To indicate disapproval or failure. From the traditional gesture supposedly made by members of the crowd at Roman gladiatoral combats. This meant that the gladiator was to die. Known by 1906.

glasnost.   Russian for 'openness' – a key word for the atmosphere that President Mikhail Gorbachev tried to instil in the USSR prior to its breakup in 1989. The word was being used in the West as early as 1972 but really became known in the period 1985–7.

glitzy.   Characterized by glitter and show, and thus probably mere-tricious and tawdry. 'Is the word "glitzy" now the flavour of the month?' wrote a pained reader to the *Guardian* in 1985. 'It seems to be appearing with boring frequency especially, I'm sorry to see, in your descriptions of television programmes.' Actually, the *OED2*'s first citation is from the US and in 1966. Elmore Leonard's novel with the title *Glitz* was published in 1985. The word **glitterati** used to describe the glittering stars of show business and society in a very general sense (and fashioned from 'literati'), similarly popular in the 1980s, goes back even further to the US and 1956.

Gnomes of Zurich.   A term used to disparage the tight-fisted speculators in the Swiss financial capital who questioned Britain's creditworthiness and who forced austerity measures on the Labour government of Prime Minister Harold Wilson when it came to power in 1964. George Brown, Secretary of State for Economic Affairs, popularized the term in November of that year. Wilson himself, however, had used it long before in a speech to the House of Commons (12 November 1956), referring to 'all the little gnomes in Zurich and other financial centres'. In 1958, Andrew Shonfield wrote in *British Economic Policy Since the War*: 'Hence the tragedy of the autumn of 1957, when the Chancellor of the Exchequer [Peter Thorneycroft] adopted as his guide to action the slogan: I must be hard-faced enough to match the mirror-image of an imaginary hard-faced little man in Zurich. It is tough on the Swiss that William Tell should be displaced in English folklore by this new image of a gnome in a bank at the end of a telephone line.' Gnomes, traditionally, were seen as guardians of the earth's treasures. ('Lord Gnome', the wealthy and unscrupulous supposed proprietor of *Private Eye* was presumably named after the 1964 use.)

go at something baldheaded, to. Meaning 'to act without regard for the consequences, to go at something full tilt' – e.g. from J.R. Lowell, *The Biglow Papers* (1848): 'I scent what pays the best, an' then/Go into it baldheaded.' This is an American expression, dating from the nineteenth century. The suggestion is that of a man who would tackle a problem as though he had just rushed out of the house without putting on his wig, or without wearing a hat.

Earlier sources have been suggested – notably that the Marquis of Granby, a colonel of the Blues, led a cavalry charge at the Battle of Warburg (1760) despite his hat and wig falling off. He was an enormously popular figure (hence the number of British pubs named after him), but it is unlikely that his fame was sufficient to have led to the expression being used in the US.

go (down) a bomb, to. To go over really well, 'with a bang' – though probably 'very fast' was the original image evoked. Known by 1962. This is very much a positive British expression which has to be compared with the negative American **to bomb**, meaning to fail, crash, come to grief.

> Heller was subsequently distracted by the writing and production of his first stage play – an army comedy called *We Bombed In New Haven*, which, indeed, bombed on Broadway.
>
> *Independent on Sunday* (25 September 1994)

go for a song, to. To be sold very cheaply, if not for free. *Going for a Song* was the title of a BBC TV antiques programme (from 1968). The expression 'for a song' was proverbial in Shakespeare's day and occurs in *All's Well That Ends Well*, III.ii.8 (1603): 'I know a man that had this trick of melancholy sold a goodly manor for a song.' 'I bought it for a song' occurs in *Regulus* (1694) by John Crowne. Possibly also from the 'trifling cost' (*Brewer*) of ballad sheets sold in olden days.

go for gold. A slogan meaning, literally, 'aim for a gold medal'. As far as one can tell, this slogan was first used by the US Olympic team at the Lake Placid Winter Olympics in 1980. (*Going for Gold* became the title of an Emma Lathen thriller set in Lake Placid, published in 1983, and there was a TV movie *Going for the Gold* in 1985). Other teams, including the British, had taken it up by the time of the 1984 Olympics. A BBC TV quiz called *Going for Gold* began in 1987.

Just to show, as always, that there is nothing new under the sun: in 1832, there was a political slogan 'To Stop the Duke, Go for Gold' – which was somehow intended, through its alliterative force, to prevent the Duke of Wellington from forming a government in the run up to the Reform Bill. The slogan was coined by a radical politician, Francis Place, for a poster, on 12 May 1832. (It was intended to cause a run on the Bank of England – and succeeded.)

go for it! A popular slogan from the early 1980s, mostly in America – though any number of sales managers have encouraged their teams to strive this way in the UK, too.

In June 1985, President Reagan's call on tax reform was, 'America, go for it!' Victor Kiam, an American razor entrepreneur, entitled his 1986 memoirs *Going For it!*; and 'Go for it, America' was the slogan used by British Airways in the same year to get more US tourists to ignore the terrorist threat and travel to Europe.

Lisa Bernbach in *The Official Preppie Handbook* (1980) pointed to a possible US campus origin, giving the phrase as a general exhortation meaning 'Let's get carried away and act stupid'. At about the same time, the phrase was used in aerobics. Jane Fonda in a work-out book (1981) and video (*c*.1983), cried, 'Go for it, **go for the burn!**' (where the burn was a sensation felt during exercise). There was also a US beer slogan (current 1981), 'Go for it! Schlitz makes it great'. Media mogul Ted Turner was later called a 'go-for-it guy', and so on.

Partridge/*Slang* has 'to go for it' as Australian for being 'extremely eager for sexual intercourse' (*c*.1925).

go haywire, to. To behave in an uncontrolled and crazy manner. This phrase is of American origin – *c.*1900, perhaps – and seemingly derives from the wire used to hold bales of hay together. If cut, the wire can whip round in a fearsome way.

According to *DOAS*, there is another use of the word 'haywire' in American slang. Something is described as 'haywire' if it is dilapidated and might be held together with such, just as in British English one might say something is 'held together with bits of string'.

go, man, go! A phrase of encouragement originally shouted at jazz musicians in the 1940s. Then it took on wider use. At the beginning of the number 'It's Too Darn Hot' in Cole Porter's *Kiss Me Kate* (film version, 1953) a dancer cried, 'Go, girl, go!'

TV newscaster Walter Cronkite reverted famously to 'Go, baby, go!' when describing the launch of Apollo XI in 1969 and this form became a fairly standard cry at rocket and missile departures thereafter. *Time* Magazine reported it being shouted at a test firing of a Pershing missile (29 November 1982). **Crazy, man, crazy!** originated at about the same time. One wonders whether T.S. Eliot's 'Go go go said the bird' ('Burnt Norton', *Four Quartets*, 1935) or Hamlet's 'Come, bird, come' (the cry of a falconer recalling his hawk) relate to these cries in any way . . .?

go on a Cook's tour, to. To travel in an organized manner, possibly on a tour of rather greater extent than originally intended. Thomas Cook was the founder of the world's original travel agency. His first tour was in 1841 when he took a party of fellow teetotallers on a railway trip in the British Midlands. Alas, there has always been a certain amount of prejudice against the organized tour. Amelia B. Edwards, the Victorian egyptologist, is suitably caustic in *A Thousand Miles Up the Nile* (1877): '[The newcomer in Cairo soon] distinguishes at first sight between a Cook's tourist and an independent traveller'.

go through (something) with a fine-tooth comb, to. 'To examine very closely' (known by 1891). Note, it is a 'fine-tooth comb' rather than 'fine tooth-comb' – the comb has fine teeth (enabling the smallest pieces of dirt to be removed) and isn't necessarily excellent.

go to pot, to. To go to ruin. This could refer to the custom of putting a dead person's ashes into an urn or pot. After that happens, there is no more to be done. Neil Ewart, *Everyday Phrases* (1983) on the other hand, prefers to think 'the phrase comes from the melting-pots into which broken items of metal, gold and silver, were thrown when they could no longer be used in their original form as they were either damaged, or stolen.'

The *Morris Dictionary of Word and Phrase Origins* (1977) thinks it means left-over meat and vegetables all chopped up and ready for their last appearance as stew or hash in the pot. This is supported by *OED2* which sees the phrases as shortened from 'go to the pot' (lit. 'to be cut in pieces like meat for the pot'). Known by 1530.

Whatever the case, the phrase has nothing whatever to do with the other type of **pot**, namely marijuana. This word is said to come from the Mexican Spanish word *potiguaya*, meaning marijuana leaves.

go up the aisle, to. To be married (in church) – an erroneous usage. Sir Thomas Bazley fired off a letter to *The Times* in July 1986: 'Sir, You report that Miss Sarah Fergusson will go up the aisle to the strains of Elgar's "Imperial March". Hitherto, brides have always gone up the nave. Yours faithfully ...' Indeed, the nave is the main route from the west door of a church to the chancel and altar; the aisles are the parallel routes at the side of the building, usually separated from the nave by pillars.

> Film star Julia Roberts got her manager to call actor Kiefer Sutherland to tell him the wedding was off – two weeks before she was due to walk up the aisle.
> *Daily Mirror* (28 February 1996)

go west, to. Meaning 'to die', this dates back to the sixteenth century and alludes to the setting of the sun and may have entered American Indian usage by 1801.

goat. *See* GET ONE'S ...

gobsmacked, to be. To be made speechless with surprise (where gob = mouth). The image evoked is of the hand being clapped over the mouth, a familiar gesture of surprise. This expression became popular in Britain during the 1980s. Claire Rayner, the advice columnist, said, 'I'm gobsmacked!' on being surprised for TV's *This*

Is Your Life (26 October 1988). Emma Thompson said it on winning an Oscar (April 1993).

> One of the actors, Barrie Rutter, surveying the intimidating amphitheatre of Epidaurus was 'a bit gobsmacked.'
> *Financial Times* (10 October 1983)

Also, 'to gobsmack' can be used in the sense of 'overwhelm, bowl over':

> She has been gobsmacking the punters in a recent cluster of Personal Appearances in gay clubs, straight clubs and 'kid clubs'.
> *Melody Maker* (24 October 1987)

God. *See* LIVE LIKE . . .

Godfrey Daniel! *See under* GORDON BENNETT!

Goetz. One who does not give in to mugging or any other form of criminal activity, after Bernhard Goetz who shot and seriously wounded a man who had approached him for money on the New York subway in 1984. A word that, despite predictions, has *not* entered the language. 'Katharine Whitehorn wrote recently that Goetz, the name of the New Yorker who shot four black youths he thought were muggers, "may pass into the language like BOYCOTT or BOWDLER or LYNCH" – *Observer* (17 March 1985).

However, there is something called, in German, the *Goetz Zitat* [the Goetz Quotation]. In Goethe's play *Goetz von Berlichingen*, set in the Peasant War (1524–5), when Goetz is told to surrender, he says: 'I have, as always, due respect for his Imperial Majesty. But as for your captain, tell him he can lick my arse.' Those who wish to use this expression more allusively may say, '*Goetz*, act III, scene 4'. Compare MOT DE CAMBRONNE.

gold. *See* GO FOR . . .; FIND THE STREETS PAVED WITH . . .

golden youth. A young man or woman with obvious talent who is expected to do well in life and career. Possibly recalling Shakespeare, *Cymbeline*, IV.ii.262 (1609): 'Golden lads and girls all must,/As chimney sweepers come to dust.' Also in the form **gilded youth**, a fashionable young man or men (usually), dedicated to the pursuit of pleasure (possibly based on the French *jeunesse dorée*).

What avail his golden youth, his high blood ... if they help not now?
Benjamin Disraeli, *Coningsby* (1844)

Annoyed because it was a corny Fleet Street idea of gilded youth?
Sunday Times Magazine (8 March 1981)

Look, I suppose if you must call us the *jeuness dorée* you must, but it's a pity there isn't another word for it.
Ibid.

gone for a Burton.   Missing, presumed dead. Early in the Second World War, an RAF expression arose to describe what had happened to such a person. He had gone for a drink (*in* the drink = the sea) or, as another phrase put it, 'he'd bought it'. Folk memory has it that during the 1930s 'Gone for a Burton' had been used in advertisements to promote a Bass beer known in the trade as 'a Burton' (though, in fact, several ales are produced at Burton-on-Trent). More positive proof is lacking. An advert for Carlsberg in the 1987 Egon Ronay *Good Food in Pubs and Bars* described Burton thus: 'A strong ale, dark in colour, made with a proportion of highly-dried or roasted malts. It is not necessarily brewed in Burton and a variety of strong or old ales were given the term.'

Other fanciful theories are that RAF casualty records were kept in an office above or near a branch of Burton Menswear in Blackpool, and that morse code instruction for wireless operators/air gunners took place in a converted billiards hall above Burtons in the same town (and failure in tests meant posting off the course – a fairly minor kind of 'death'). Probably no more than a coincidental use of the name Burton.

good and the great.   Those who are on a British Government list from which are selected members of Royal Commissions and committees of inquiry. In 1983 the list stood at some 4500 names. For the previous eight years custodians of the list had sought more women, more people under 40 and more from outside the golden triangle of London and the South-East in an attempt to break the stereotype enshrined in Lord Rothschild's parody of it as containing only 53-year-old men 'who live in the South-East, have the right accent and belong to the Reform Club'.

In the 1950s, the Treasury division which kept the list was actually known as the 'G and G'. On one occasion, it really did nominate two *dead* people for service on a public body (*The Times*, 22 January 1983). Term known by the mid-twentieth century.

good career move.   Ironic comment on an event in a person's life, most often their death. Gore Vidal said it on hearing of the death of Truman Capote (1984), confirmed by him in BBC TV *Gore Vidal's Gore Vidal* (1995). According to *Time* Magazine (8 April 1985), the graffito 'Good career move' had appeared following Elvis Presley's death in 1977.

goodness' sake.   *See* FOR . . .

goolies.   Testicles – as in 'he has been kicked in the goolies'. Simple, really: *Goli* is Hindustani for a bullet, ball or pill. Recorded by 1937.

goose step.   Name given to the type of march step, used especially by German troops on formal occasions before the Second World War. It takes its name from the exaggerated swinging up of each leg and foot without bending the knee.

The term dates from the nineteenth century when the Germans or Prussians and several other armies were already doing it (known by 1806). Beatrix Potter in *The Tale of Tom Kitten* (1907) reverts to a literal use of the term: 'The three Puddle-ducks came along the hard high road, marching one behind the other and doing the goose-step – pit pat paddle pat! Pit pat waddle pat!'

gooseberry.   The odd one out in a threesome – especially when the other two are lovers. From the earlier expression 'to play gooseberry': to act as an unwanted chaperon or third party so that two young lovers can be together with propriety. Current by 1837, this expression has no obvious derivation, though one is that the chaperon might find him/herself filling in time by picking goose-berries while the couple is more romantically engaged.

On the other hand, playing gooseberry is not a very enviable or enjoyable job and the chaperon may well feel a bit of a *fool* and 'gooseberry' is a slang word for 'fool', derived of course from the pudding known as gooseberry fool (or from the supposedly comic appearance of gooseberries) since the early eighteenth century.

Gordon Bennett!   A euphemistic exclamation suddenly popular – or popular again – in the Britain of the early 1980s. Understandably, people shrink from blaspheming. 'Oh Gawd!' is felt to be less offensive than 'Oh God!' At the turn of the century it was natural for people facetiously to water down the exclamation 'God!' by saying 'Gordon!' The name Gordon Bennett was to hand. The initial letters of the name also had the explosive quality found in 'Gor*b*limey! [God blind me!]'. But who was this man? James Gordon Bennett II (1841–1918) was the editor-in-chief of the *New York Herald*, the man who sent Henry Morton Stanley to find Dr Livingstone in Africa, and altogether quite a character. He was exiled to Paris after a scandal but somehow managed to run his New York newspaper from there. He disposed of some $40 million in his lifetime. He offered numerous trophies to stimulate French sport and, when the motor car was in its infancy, presented the Gordon Bennett cup to be competed for. He became, as the *Dictionary of American Biography* puts it, 'one of the most picturesque figures of two continents'.

This, if anything does, probably explains why it was *his* name that ended up on people's lips and why they did not go around exclaiming, 'Gordon of Khartoum!' or 'Gordon Selfridge!' or anything else. Gordon Bennett was a man with an amazing reputation. A decade or two later, in similar fashion – and with a view to circumventing the strict Hollywood Hay's Code – W.C. Fields would exclaim **'Godfrey Daniel!'**, a 'minced oath' in place of 'God, damn you!'

But who was Godfrey Daniel . . .?

> The plats de jour were ready, the sauces simmering; [but] not a stove, not a hotplate was free. 'Gordon Bennett,' said the chef. But the restaurant was in all the guides.
> *Guardian* (24 June 1995)

got your mojo working?   In 1960, Muddy Waters, the American blues singer (1915–83) was singing a song with the refrain, 'Got my mojo workin', but it just don't work on you.' He knew what he was singing about because he had written the song under his real name, McKinley Morganfield. *DOAS* defines 'mojo' simply as 'any narcotic' but a sleeve note to an album entitled *Got My Mojo Workin'* (1966) by the jazz organist Jimmy Smith is perhaps nearer to the meaning of the word in the song. It describes 'mojo' as 'magic – a spell or charm guaranteed to make the user irresistible to the opposite sex'. Known by 1926.

Indeed, it seems that 'mojo' could well be a form of the word 'magic' corrupted through Black pronunciation, though the *OED2* finds an African word meaning 'magic, witchcraft' that is similar. The *OED2* derives the narcotic meaning of the word from the Spanish *mojar*, 'to celebrate by drinking'.

grain of salt. *See* TAKE SOMETHING WITH A ...

grandmother. *See* DON'T TEACH YOUR ...

grass widow. A divorced woman or one apart from her husband because his job or some other preoccupation has taken him elsewhere. It originally meant an unmarried woman who had sexual relations with one or more men – perhaps on the grass rather than in the lawful marriage bed – and had had a child out of wedlock. This sense was known by the sixteenth century. Later it seems to have been applied to women in British India who were sent up to the cool hill country (where grass grows) during the hottest season of the year. An alternative derivation is from 'grace widow' or even 'Grace Widow', the name of an actual person.

grassroots. *See* FROM THE ...

grave. *See* FROM THE CRADLE TO THE ...

gravy train. *See* CLIMB ABOARD THE ...

great. *See* GOOD AND THE ...

great outdoors. *See under* ANSWER THE CALL OF NATURE.

great Scott! As with GORDON BENNETT!, one is dealing here with a watered-down expletive. 'Great Scott!' clearly sounds like 'Great God!' and yet is not blasphemous. The *Morris Dictionary of Word and Phrase Origins* (1977) says the expression became popular when US General Winfield Scott was the hero of the Mexican War (1847) and 'probably our most admired general between Washington and Lee'. No rival candidate seems to have been proposed and the origination is almost certainly American. *OED2*'s earliest British English example dates from 1885.

Greeks. *See* BEWARE ...

green. *See* SEE YOU ON THE ...

green. Concerned with the protection of the environment, particularly as a political issue. Derived from the German *grün* (green), which was used from the early 1970s by the West German environmental lobby – as, for example, in the name of the *Grüne Aktion Zukunft* [Green Campaign for the Future]. Traditionally, green has always been associated with nature and the countryside.

This association undoubtedly led to the choosing of the colour green to denote lead-free fuels on petrol pumps.

Green Goddess. An alliterative nickname which has been applied variously to Second World War fire engines (painted green), Liverpool trams, a crème de menthe cocktail, a lettuce salad and a lily. In 1983, Diana Moran, a keep-fit demonstrator on a BBC TV breakfast programme, was so billed. She wore distinctive green exercise clothing. Perhaps all these uses derive from William Archer's play entitled *The Green Goddess* (1923; film US, 1930).

greenfields site/start. In business and industry, where you choose to put a factory or development on a hitherto undeveloped site, perhaps literally in fields. Or, metaphorically, not a going concern. Known by the 1980s.

> [Rupert Murdoch] had always preferred acquiring existing publications, no matter how poor in shape they were in, to a so-called 'green-fields start', starting something from scratch.
> Michael Leapman, *Barefaced Cheek* (1983)

greenhouse effect. Trapping of the sun's heat in the lower atmosphere because of the build-up of pollutants. This may lead to global warming. By analogy with an actual greenhouse, where the glass allows the sun's warmth in but does not let the warmed air escape. Although much talked about in environmental discussions since the 1980s, the phrase was coined in the 1920s.

gremlin.   Name for a kind of sprite said to get into machinery and make it malfunction, it was popular in the RAF during the Second World War, although it may have originated during the First World War. The name first appeared in print in 1929, and seems to have been derived from 'goblin', possibly blended with 'Fremlin's' (the name of a Kent beer). Roald Dahl wrote a children's book *The Gremlins* as early as 1943 which undoubtedly popularized the term. *Gremlins* was the title of a Steven Spielberg film (US, 1984).

grey suit.   *See* MAN IN A . . .

grin like a Cheshire Cat.   Smile very broadly. The Cheshire Cat is most famous from its appearances in Lewis Carroll's *Alice's Adventures in Wonderland* (1865) – where it has the ability to disappear leaving only its grin behind – but the beast had been known since about 1770. Carroll, who was born in Cheshire, probably knew that Cheshire cheeses were at one time moulded in the shape of a grinning cat.

> British power was slowly disappearing during the Churchillian Era, leaving, like the Cheshire Cat, only a wide smile behind.
> Andrew Roberts, *Eminent Churchillians* (1994)

grind.   *See* HAVE AN AXE TO . . .

gringo.   Scornful Mexican word for a foreigner. Most likely derived from the Spanish word *griego* (Greek), as in 'It's all Greek to me' (i.e. 'it's nonsense'). Recorded by 1849. A more colourful derivation is from the Spanish pronunciation of the surname of Major Samuel *Ringgold*, a brave American soldier who fought in the Mexican War under General Zachary Taylor.

grockle.   A tourist, holidaymaker, summer visitor. This derogatory term originated in the South West of England and was known by 1964. A dialect expression of impenetrable origin.

grog.   Meaning 'rum diluted with water', it was introduced by the British Admiral Edward Vernon in an attempt to prevent scurvy among his crewmen in 1740. It did not work. Vernon's nickname was 'Old Grog' because of his fondness for a cloak made of grogram, a coarse material of silk and wool. The nickname was given by

113

sailors to public houses ashore – hence 'grog shops', places where spirits were sold.

groovy. Meaning 'very good' (particularly of music) this word was popular in the 1960s, although *DOAS* traces it back to the mid-1930s and its use among 'swing' musicians and devotees. It comes from 'in the groove', referring to the way a gramophone or phonograph stylus or needle fits neatly into the groove on a record. 'Groovy', meaning a 'tendency to run in grooves' is found by the *OED2* in *c*.1882.

> 'Mummy, don't you think Santa Claus is getting rather *groovy*?'
> Caption to *Punch* cartoon by Beauchamp in *Almanack for 1930*

grotty. Meaning, 'seedy; down-at-heel; crummy; unpleasant; nasty; unattractive,' this was a trendy word in the 1960s (compare the 1980s' NAFF). It is short for 'grotesque' and is very much associated with the Mersey culture that accompanied The Beatles out of Liverpool in 1962–3. Alun Owen put it in his script for the first Beatles film, *A Hard Day's Night* (1964) but the word was in general Scouse (Liverpudlian) use before that.

As for **grotesque** itself, it has been jokingly derived from the name of Mrs Grote, the wife of a nineteenth-century historian. The Rev. Sydney Smith said of her turban: 'Now I know the meaning of the word grotesque.' She was peculiar in other ways, too. She 'dressed in discordant colours, with her petticoats arranged to show her ankles and feet'; she wore a man's hat and a coachman's cloak when driving her dogcart; and, she had 'unwholesome attachments to other women' (Ronald Pearsall, *Collapse of Stout Party*, 1975). This, alas, is more a case of life imitating the dictionary than the other way round. 'Grotesque' is a word of Italian and Greek origin and is derived from the 'grotto' style of ornamentation.

ground. *See* HIT THE ...

Grundy. *See* MRS ...

guillotine. Decapitation equipment incorporating a vertically descending blade, much used during the French Revolution. The French physician Dr Joseph-Ignace Guillotin did not invent it – the device had already been used in Italy and elsewhere and was at first called a *louison* or *louisette* after Dr Antoine Louis who adapted this 'painless' and 'humane' form of execution. What Dr Guillotin did was to push a resolution through the French Constituent Assembly adopting it as the official means of executing criminals in 1792. His family did not take kindly to having their name attached to such a device and, after his death, changed their name rather than put up with it. He narrowly escaped being guillotined himself.

> ... Which product popular gratitude or levity christens by a feminine derivative name, as if it were his daughter: *La Guillotine!* ... Unfortunate Doctor! For two-and-twenty years he, unguillotined, shall hear nothing but guillotine, see nothing but guillotine ... his name like to outlive Caesar's.
> Thomas Carlyle, *The French Revolution*, IV.iv. (1838)

gum tree.   *See* UP A ...

gun.   *See* — GET YOUR ...; SON OF A ...

gung-ho.   Meaning 'enthusiastic, if carelessly so', the phrase derives from Chinese *kung* plus *ho* meaning 'work together'. In Geoff Chapple, *Rewi Alley of China* (1980), it is stated that the phrase was coined in 1938 and used as the motto of the Chinese Industrial Co-operatives Association. Lt. Gen. Evans F. Carlson of the US Marines borrowed these words to make a slogan during the Second World War. In 1943, a film about the Marines had the title *Gung Ho!*

guy.   An effigy of Guy Fawkes burned on a bonfire every 5 November to commemorate his part in the Gunpowder Plot, an attempt to blow up King James I and Parliament in 1605. Fawkes was executed and the name 'guy' was being applied to any such effigy by the early nineteenth century at least. From thence, the word was applied to any disreputable person, and thence – particularly in the US from the 1890s – to any man, good as well as bad.

H

hair of the dog (that bit me). Meaning 'another drink of the same to help cure a hangover', it comes from the old belief that a bite from a mad dog could be cured if you put hair from the same dog's tail on the wound. Known by 1760.

half. *See* HOW THE OTHER ...

ham. (1) A bad actor. (2) An amateur radio operator. Various suggestions have been made as to the origin of (1). Possibly it is short for 'hamfatter' – an actor who used fat from ham chops to take off his makeup (US origin, nineteenth century). The radio sense may derive from this in turn, conflated with '(h)amateur'.

hand over fist. As in 'to make money hand over fist'. A similar expression, 'pulling it in', provides the origin here. If you are pulling in a rope or hoisting a sail on board ship, you pass it between your two hands and, in so doing, unavoidably put one hand over the fist of the other hand. Current by 1825.

hands-on. Involving personal, practical experience. Of American origin, this adjective has been used principally in connection with computers where the use of an operator's hands is imperative to send commands through a keyboard or 'mouse'. To what extent the term was used in other fields – flying a plane, for example – is not clear. Now used about any kind of experience. Known by 1969.

> Peter Cadbury is very much a hands-on leader and that is how he sees his involvement with Working Woman.
> *Working Woman* (April 1986)

hang, draw and quarter, to. To execute for treason using a method last carried out in the UK in 1867 and known by the mid-seventeenth century. Term known by 1596. The order of procedure is actually 'drawn, hanged, and quartered' as is plain from the words of a British judge sentencing Irish rebels in 1775: 'You are to be *drawn* on hurdles to the place of execution, where you are to be *hanged* by the neck but not until you are dead; for, while you are still living, your bodies are to be taken down, your bowels torn out and burned before your faces; your heads then cut off, and your bodies *divided each into four quarters*, and your heads and quarters to be then at the King's disposal; and may the Almighty God have mercy on your souls.'

hang fire, to.   To be hesitant, hold back. This expression comes from gunnery – when the gun is slow to fire, or there is a delay between the fuse being ignited and the weapon firing. Current by 1781 and, figuratively, by 1801.

happening.   A 1960s word for an improvised theatrical event or deeply meaningful, possibly provocative act, supposedly of some significance but often disorganized and embarrassing to watch. An early example occurred at the Edinburgh Festival Drama Conference in 1963 when a nude woman was wheeled across a gallery above the speakers. A piper played, uproar ensued, and few delegates were any the wiser.

happy as Larry/a sandboy.   *See* AS . . .

happy clappy.   Name for a type of religious worship or worshipper identified in Britain in the early 1990s. From the clapping along with bouncy hymns used especially in 'evangelical' church services.

> The parish church has a knack of attracting those whose approach is more casual or nervous, and gently drawing them to faith. While it cannot be good if the end product of the system is semi-commitment, it certainly is good if this low-key style attracts many who would run a mile from a 'Happy Clappy' congregation.
> *Independent* (9 March 1991)

> [George Carey, Archbishop of Canterbury] attempted to distance himself from the 'evangelical' tag he has attracted, and emphasised that he wanted to affirm all traditions in the Church. 'I am not a "happy clappy" person, and I am not a fundamentalist,' he said.
> *Independent* (17 April 1991)

happy medium. A compromise, avoiding extremes. Known by 1778.

hard place. *See* BETWEEN A ROCK AND A . . .

Harry. *See* FLASH . . .

harvest moon. *See* 'SHINE ON . . .'

hat in the ring. *See* THROW ONE'S . . .

hatter. *See* MAD AS A . . .

have a cat in Hell's chance, not to. Meaning 'to have no chance whatsoever', the full expression makes the phrase clear: 'No more chance than a cat in hell *without claws*', which is recorded in Grose, *Dictionary of the Vulgar Tongue* (1796).

have a chip on one's shoulder, to. Meaning 'to bear a grudge in a defensive manner', the expression originated in the US where it was known by the early nineteenth century. A boy or man would, or would seem, to carry a chip (of wood) on his shoulder daring others to dislodge it, looking for a fight.

have a feather in one's cap, to. Meaning '[to have] an honour or achievement of which one can be proud'. The expression (known by 1700) probably dates from 1346, when the Black Prince was awarded the crest of John, King of Bohemia, which showed three ostrich feathers, after he had distinguished himself at the Battle of Crécy. This symbol has since been carried by every Prince of Wales. Later, any knight who had fought well might wear a feather in his helmet.

> It could be argued that when Logan struck the penalty that drew Stirling level, 6–6, after Stark had been caught offside, it was another feather in his cap.
> *Scotsman* (26 February 1995)

have an axe to grind, to. The expression, meaning 'to have an ulterior motive, a private end to serve', would appear to have originated in an anecdote related by the American statesman Benjamin Franklin (1706–90) in his essay 'Too Much for Your Whistle'. A man showed interest in young Franklin's grindstone and asked how it worked. In the process of explaining, Franklin – using much energy – sharpened up the visitor's axe for him. This was clearly what the visitor had had in mind all along. Subsequently, Franklin always had to ask himself whether other people he encountered had 'another axe to grind'.

have bats in the belfry, to (or **to be bats/batty**).   Meaning 'to be mentally deficient, harmlessly insane, or mad', these expressions convey the idea that a person behaves in a wildly disturbed manner, like bats disturbed by the ringing of bells. Stephen Graham wrote in *London Nights* (1925): 'There is a set of jokes which are the common property of all the comedians. You may hear them as easily in Leicester Square as in Mile End Road. It strikes the unwonted visitor to the Pavilion as very original when Stanley Lupino says of some one: "He has bats in the belfry." It is not always grasped that the expression belongs to the music hall at large.'

Attempts have been made to derive 'batty', in particular, from the name of William Battie (1704–76), author of *A Treatise on Madness*, though this seems a little harsh, given that he was the psychiatrist and not the patient. On the other hand, there was a Fitzherbert Batty, barrister of Spanish Town, Jamaica, who made news when he was certified insane in London in 1839. The names of these two gentlemen merely, and coincidentally, reinforced the 'bats in the belfry' idea – but there do not seem to be any examples of either expression in use before 1900.

have kittens, to.   To act nervously, behave in a hysterical manner. Originally American and known by 1900. The *Morris Dictionary of Word and Phrase Origins* (1977) explains that, in medieval times, if a pregnant woman was having pains, it was 'believed she was bewitched and had kittens clawing at her inside her womb'. Witches could provide lotions to destroy the imagined 'litter'. As late as the seventeenth century an 'excuse for obtaining an abortion was given in court as "removing cats in the belly".'

have one's feet (well) under the table, to.   (1) To be 'well in with' someone; to be familiar, cohabit, with. Probably Northern English use. Known by the 1960s? (2) To be at ease, not worried. Sometimes when actors or broadcasters are asked if they are nervous

119

they will reply, 'It'll be all right when I get my feet under the table' – i.e. get to work and put an end to anticipation. Known by the 1970s.

have seen better days, to.   To have been more successful, prosperous than at present. Originally from Shakespeare, *As You Like It*, II.vii. 113 & 120 (1598): 'If ever you have look'd on better days', 'True it is that we have seen better days.'

> The whole town bears evident marks of having seen better days.
> Robert Forsyth, *The Beauties of Scotland* (1806)

hawks/doves.   These terms are used to denote those for and against tough military action. The term 'war hawk' was coined by Thomas Jefferson in 1798. A dove traditionally has been a symbol of peace – perhaps since Noah sent one to see if the waters had abated and it returned with an olive leaf (Genesis 8:8–11). The modern division into hawks and doves, much used during the Vietnam War of the 1960s, dates from the Cuban missile crisis of 1962.

> The hawks favoured an air strike to eliminate the Cuban missile bases … The doves opposed the air strike and favoured a blockade.
> Charles Bartlett in *Saturday Evening Post* (1962)

haywire.   *See* GO . . .

heart.   *See* EAT YOUR . . .

heart of hearts.   *See* IN MY . . .

Heath Robinson.   Adjectival phrase applied to complicated, ingenious, and sometimes amateur and makeshift contraptions. It is derived from the name of W. Heath Robinson (1872–1944) whose drawings of such things appeared in *Punch* and elsewhere. The use was established by 1917.

Heaven.   *See* I'VE DIED AND GONE TO . . .

Hell.   *See* HAVE A CAT IN . . .; COME . . .

hello.   As a way of attracting attention or establishing you are 'there', particularly over the telephone (as opposed to a greeting or salutation). 'Hello' was in use this way by 1854 (hence before the invention of the telephone), as also 'halloa', 'halloo' etc. The word used on the first experimental switchboard at New Haven, Connecticut, in 1878 was **ahoy!** Following this 'Are you there?' was common for a while. Thomas Edison is said to have been the first person to answer the telephone with 'Hello?' in a way which has since become the popular form.

Henry. *See* HOORAY . . .

hidden agenda. The true meaning behind words and actions, often contradicting them. The expression is believed to have emerged following discussions in British educational circles in the late 1960s and early 1970s when the concept of a 'hidden curriculum' in schools (going against the actual curriculum that was taught) was much talked about. In 1990, a British film about the 'shoot-to-kill' policy of security forces in Northern Ireland was given the title *Hidden Agenda*.

The phenomenon is also sometimes referred to currently as the **subtext**.

> Those who vote Yes for the new constitution will vote ostensibly for reform in South Africa but will in effect be voting for the permanent rejection of the black majority – unless, as the Government repeatedly denies, there is a 'hidden agenda' for dramatic new reforms after the vote is won.
> *Financial Times* (5 October 1983)

> A Labour government, grabbing vast new powers and dispensing patronage on a scale never seen before, will give [political correctness] impetus, official backing and legislative authority. Here indeed is the hidden agenda, which does not figure in the manifesto because much of it will be enacted by private member's bills in a parliament with a 'progressive' majority.
> *Sunday Telegraph* (29 March 1992)

hi-de-hi! For several years from 1980 onwards, BBC TV had a long-running situation comedy series called *Hi-de-hi* set in a 1950s holiday camp. The title probably came to be used in this way from a campers' song special to Butlin's:

Tramp, tramp, tramp, tramp,
Here we come, to jolly old Butlin's every year.

All come down to Butlin's, all by the sea.
Never mind the weather, we're as happy as can be.
Hi-de-hi! Ho-de-ho!
(quoted in the *Observer* Magazine, 12 June 1983)

This possibly dates from the late 1930s. In May 1937, Stanley Holloway recorded a song called 'Hi-de-hi' (his own composition) on a promotional record for Butlin's Holiday Camps, though the lyrics differ from the above.

The origin of the phrase lies, however, in the dance band vocals of the 1920s/30s – the 'Hi-de-ho, vo-de-o-do' sort of thing. In particular, Cab Calloway's song 'Minnie the Moocher' (1931) contains the refrain, 'Ho-de-ho, hi-de-hi'. The line 'Hey, ho-de-ho, hi-de-hi!' also occurs in the Ira Gershwin lyrics for the song 'The Lorelei' (1933). In addition, according to Denis Gifford's *The Golden Age of Radio*, 'Hi-de-hi! Ho-de-ho!' was the catchphrase of Christopher Stone, the BBC's first 'disc jockey', when he went off and presented *Post Toasties Radio Corner*, a children's programme for Radio Normandy in 1937.

Shortly after this last, the phrase achieved notoriety when a commanding officer in the army faced a court of inquiry or court-martial for making his troops answer 'Ho-de-ho' when he (or his fellow officers) yelled 'Hi-de-hi'. This case was well in the past when *Notes and Queries* got around to it in 1943–4, and there was a revue with the title at the Palace Theatre, London, in 1943. Gerald Kersh referred to army use of the exchange (though not to the specific case) in *They Die with their Boots Clean* in 1941.

high jump. *See* FOR THE . . .

high water. *See* COME HELL AND/OR . . .

his nibs. *See under* NOB.

hit list. A list of opponents, originally of people to be killed off, by a gangster. Compare **enemies list** – a term which emerged when John Dean revealed to the Watergate hearings (1974) that President Richard Nixon had an actual such list of people who were consequently to be harassed. Compare such terms as **black list** (see BLACKLIST, TO) and **shit list** (of people who have somehow fallen into disfavour, perhaps by not paying money owed).

The bizarre phony-bomb incident got cops shuffling through their list of Gotti's enemies once again ... an enemies list the size of a small-town phone directory.
New York Post (27 March 1989)

hit the ground running, to. To get off to a good start, to go straight into successful mode. From the *Independent* (29 March 1989): '*The Late Show* has so far generated an overwhelmingly favourable response ... "To hit the ground running with four shows a week," said Alex Graham, editor of *The Media Show* on Channel 4, "that's really impressive."' This phrase probably comes from the military – leaping from assault craft and helicopters, even landing by parachute, immediately running off, and, without preamble, successfully getting straight on with the business in hand. Current by 1984.

> Pentagonese has given us infamous little expressions like: 'Hell, that guy's good. He hit the ground running.' Obviously, the guy got off to a splendid start.
> *The Times* (2 April 1984)

Compare **up and running**, meaning 'to be under way', current by 1987.

> Party chiefs will tell delegates that a Scottish Parliament will be up and running by 1999.
> *Daily Record* (28 February 1996)

Hobson's choice. No choice at all. Thomas or Tobias Hobson (*d* 1631) hired horses from a livery stable in Cambridge. His customers were always obliged to take the horse nearest the door. The man's fame was considerable, the expression was recorded by 1649, and Hobson was celebrated in two epitaphs by Milton. *Hobson's Choice* was the title of a play (1915; film UK, 1953) by Harold Brighouse.

hog-whimpering. Of drunkenness, in an extreme state. A delightful coinage which, nevertheless, defies plodding definition. Also, figuratively, anything you think is awful (or which is, so to speak, enough to make a hog whimper).

> Of course people get drunk, absolutely hog-whimpering drunk, and there's lots of straight sex about.
> *Sunday Times* Magazine (8 March 1981)

> I can hardly approve of this blatant pandering to the filthy, stinking, hog-whimpering rich, but I can forgive the magazine a lot for its slogan:

'Not since the last act of *La Traviata* has consumption been quite so conspicuous.'
Today (1 March 1987)

Blair ducked. 'I'll tell him what people will recall,' he said, then produced two soundbites of such hog-whimpering banality that they do not even deserve the name of weasel. They were gerbil soundbites.
The Times (1 December 1995)

hold a candle to someone/thing, unable to. In the pre-electric light era, an apprentice might have found himself holding a candle so that a more experienced workman could do his job. Or, in the days before street lighting, a linkboy would carry a torch for another person. Holding a candle, in either of these ways, was a necessary but menial task. If a person was so incompetent that he could not even do that properly, then he really was not fit for anything.

There seems to be nothing to do with examining eggs by holding them up to the light (as has been suggested) or with one person being *compared* with another. The meaning of the phrase is better expressed as 'not fit to hold a candle *for* another'. It has been known since the sixteenth century.

Though I be not worthy to hold the candle to Aristotle.
Sir Edward Dering, *The Four Cardinal Virtues of a Carmelite Friar* (1641)

hole in the head. *See* NEED SOMETHING LIKE A . . .

Holocaust. Term applied to the mass murder of Jews and the attempted elimination of European Jewry by the German Nazis during the Second World War. A holocaust is an all-consuming conflagration and is not perhaps the most obvious description of what happened to the estimated six million Jews under the Nazis, though many were burned after being gassed or killed in some other way.

The term seems to have arisen because 'genocide' hardly sounded emotive enough. The popular use of 'the Holocaust' for this purpose dates only from 1965 when Alexander Donat published a book on the subject entitled *The Holocaust Kingdom*. However, *OED2* has it in this sense in the *News Chronicle* by 1942, as well as various other 1940s citations. As early as 1951, the Israeli Knesset had 'The Holocaust and Ghetto Uprising Day' – translated from *Yom ha-Sho'ah*. The use was finally settled when a US TV mini-series called *Holocaust* (1978) was shown and caused controversy in many countries. Well before *that* happened, Eric Partridge was advising in his *Usage and Abusage* (1947): 'Holocaust is "destruction by fire": do not synonymize it with *disaster*. Moreover, it is properly an ecclesiastical technicality.'

In fact, the word derives from the Greek words *holos* and *kaustos* meaning 'wholly burnt' and was for many years used to describe a sacrifice or offering that was burnt. Some translations of the Bible use it to describe Abraham's preparations to slay his son Isaac. The term has latterly been used to describe what happened to the people of Cambodia at the hands of the Khmer Rouge in the 1970s, and also to the Vietnamese boat people.

homophobe. Person with a prejudice against homosexuals. First noticed in the UK in April/May 1988.

honeymoon. The name for the holiday taken by a bride and groom after their wedding comes from the old custom of newly married couples drinking mead (wine made with honey) for a month after the ceremony. Other languages follow the same pattern: French *lune de miel*, Italian *luna di miele*. Originally the word referred to 'the first month after marriage when there is nothing but tenderness and pleasure' (as Dr Johnson defined it) – but which like the moon would soon enough wane. Known by 1546.

honk one's chuff, to. To vomit. Known by 1985. To honk = to vomit has been known in British slang since the 1950s. However, 'chuff' has been known since the 1940s as 'anus, backside', so perhaps this really means evacuate, void one's bowels?

hook. *See* SLING ONE'S . . .

hooker. A prostitute, in American usage, it probably derives from Corlear's Hook (*or* 'the Hook'), a part of Manhattan where tarts used to ply their trade in the early nineteenth century. General Joseph Hooker may have helped popularize the name during the Civil War when an area of Washington DC became known as 'Hooker's Division' on account of the General's camp-followers. The term was well established by 1845, however, before the Civil War and the General came along.

hooligan. Meaning 'a destructive young ruffian; a vandal', this word derives from the English form of the common Irish name 'Houlihan', or maybe from 'Hooley's Gang', of which there appears to have been one in north London in the late nineteenth century. Which of the various 'Hooligans' is the original, is hard to say. Known by the 1890s.

Hooray (Henry). A loud-mouthed upper-class twit (in Britain). The phrase was coined by Jim Godbolt in 1951 to describe the upper-class contingent attracted to the jazz club at 100, Oxford Street, London by the Old Etonian trumpeter, Humphrey Lyttelton. It derives from a character in Damon Runyon's story 'Tight Shoes' (1936) who is described as 'strictly a Hoorah Henry'. In his *Second Chorus* (1958), Lyttelton discusses the habitués of jazz clubs: 'In jazz circles, aggressively "upper-class" characters are known as Hoorays – an adaptation, I believe, of Damon Runyon's "Hooray Henries".'

hoover, to. Meaning 'to use a vacuum cleaner' the verb is after William H. Hoover who marketed, but did not invent, the original Hoover model. James Murray Spengler invented the 'triple action' machine ('it beats as it sweeps as it cleans') in 1908. Alas for him, we don't say we are going to 'spengler' the carpet. Verb known by 1926.

horse of a different colour. That is, 'another matter altogether'. Known in the US since 1798. Robert L. Shook in *The Book of Why* (1983) demonstrates the bizarre lengths to which some etymologists will go to find an origin for a perfectly simple phrase. According to him, 'it may have grown out of an English archaeological phenomenon, the White Horse of Berkshire, which is an outline of a horse 374 feet long, formed by trenches in a chalk hillside. It is customary for neighbourhood citizens to clean the weeds from the trenches every so often, thus making it "a gorse of a different colour".'

horse's mouth. *See* STRAIGHT FROM THE . . .

hot and cold. *See* BLOW . . .

hot metal. Term for the traditional method of newspaper production (before the advent of computer type-setting). Known by

1969. Type would be set up by hand and then, when the page was complete, an impression would be made by pouring molten metal over it. From this would be made the plates for printing the finished newspaper. *Hot Metal* was the title of a TV satire about newspaper production, written by Andrew Marshall and David Renwick in 1986.

> The company also claims that an agreement to reduce National Graphical Association (NGA) composing-room staff from 372 to 186 has been badly held up as a consequence of delays in introducing new coldtype computer setting technology to replace the oldfashioned 'hot-metal' system, still used in most of Fleet Street.
> *Financial Times* (13 February 1982)

house and home. *See* EAT SOMEONE OUT OF . . .

how the other half lives. Meaning 'how people live who belong to different social groups, especially the rich', the expression was used as the title of a book (1890) by Jacob Riis, an American newspaper reporter. He described the conditions in which poor people lived in New York City. Indeed, the expression seems basically to have referred to the poor but has since been used about any 'other half'. Riis alluded to the core-saying in these words: 'Long ago it was said that "one half of the world does not know how the other half lives".' *OED2* finds this proverb in 1607 in English, and in French, in *Pantagruel* by Rabelais (1532). Alan Ayckbourn entitled a play (1970) *How the Other Half Loves*.

Hoyle. *See* ACCORDING TO . . .

humble abode. Self-deprecating term for where one lives. Appropriately, two of the most unctuous characters in all literature use it. Mr Collins in Jane Austen's *Pride and Prejudice* (1813) says: 'The garden in which stands my humble abode, is separated only by a lane from Rosings Park, her ladyship's residence.' Uriah Heap in Charles Dickens's *David Copperfield* (1849) says: 'My mother is likewise a very umble person. We live in a numble abode.'

> Venus the artist brings to Cancer the home-lover an ability to make a humble abode into a glorious palace.
> Horoscope, *Daily Mail* (16 February 1995)

In the village of Eastwood, 10 miles distant, stands the more humble abode of Nottinghamshire's other world-famous writer, D.H. Lawrence, at 8A Victoria Street, now, naturally, a museum, too, but one so lovingly and painstakingly restored that it is a cut above many a similarly sized establishment.

Herald (Glasgow) (3 April 1995)

humble pie. *See* EAT . . .

hundred days. This phrase is used to refer to a period of intense political activity (often immediately upon coming to power). During the 1964 general election, Harold Wilson said Britain would need a 'programme of a hundred days of dynamic action' such as President Kennedy had promised in 1961. In fact, Kennedy had specifically ruled out a hundred days, saying in his inaugural speech that even 'a thousand days' would be too short (hence the title of Arthur M. Schlesinger's memoir, *A Thousand Days*, 1965, referring also to the 1056 days of Kennedy's presidency). The allusion is to the period during which Napoleon ruled between his escape from Elba and his defeat at the Battle of Waterloo in 1815.

hush puppies. (1) Deep-fried corn meal batter, often served with fried fish in the Southern US. Known by 1918. (2) Soft shoes, popular in the 1960s in the US and UK. The food may have got its name from pieces being tossed to hounds with the admonition. 'Hush, puppy!' In 1961, the Wolverine Shoe and Tanning Corp. registered 'Hush Puppies' as a trade name in the US. Adrian Room in his *Dictionary of Trade Name Origins* (1982) suggests the name was adopted because it conjures up softness and suppleness. Pictures of beagle-like dogs were shown on the display material. The only connection between the food and the shoe seems to have been a would-be homeliness.

hype. Referring to publicity, often particularly in the publishing world, where the promotion is more substantial than the product, the word probably derives from US slang expressions referring to deception, short-changing and confidence tricks, dating from around the 1920s. Some give the origin of the word as a short form of 'hyperbole' or 'high-pressure'; others say it is short for 'hypodermic' (something used to give an unnatural boost).

I

I am Marie of Romania. Expression of disbelief, found for example in a detective novel – Val MacDermid's *Clean Break* (1995): 'If what you had nicked off your wall is a Monet, I am Marie of Romania'. The source of this expression is Dorothy Parker's jaunty little 'Comment' (1937):

Oh, life is a glorious cycle of song,
    A medley of extemporanea;
And love is a thing that can never go wrong;
    And I am Marie of Roumania.

The question is, what was so funny about Marie of Romania (1875–1938)? She was one of Queen Victoria's grandchildren and became the queen of King Ferdinand I. She paid a famous visit to the US in the 1920s. No doubt this was what captured Parker's amused attention.

I do/I will. When taking marriage vows, which reply is correct? In the Anglican Prayer Book, the response to 'Wilt thou have this man/woman to thy wedded husband/wife ...?' is obviously, 'I will.' In the Order of Confirmation, to the question: 'Do ye renew the solemn promise and vow that was made ... at your baptism?' the response is obviously, 'I do.' But in some US marriage services, the question is posed: 'Do you take so-and-so ...?' to which the response has to be, 'I do.' 'Will you ...' is said to be more popular with American clergy, 'Do you ...' at civil ceremonies. Jan de Hartog's play *The Four Poster* was turned into a musical with the title *I Do! I Do!* (1966).

—, I love ya! Clark Gable's stock phrase from several films in the 1930s. Celebrated in a sequence in the compilation *That's Entertainment Part Two* (1976).

I should cocoa! A slightly dated British English exclamation meaning 'certainly not!' Longman's *Dictionary of English Idioms* (1979) adds a word of caution: 'This phrase is not recommended for use by the foreign student.'

But why 'cocoa'? As always when in difficulty with a phrase origin, turn to rhyming slang. 'Cocoa' is from 'coffee and cocoa', almost rhyming slang for 'I should hope so!' Often used ironically. Current by 1936.

I sing . . . A poet's phrase which is used most notably in the first line of Virgil's *Aeneid*: '*Arma virumque cano*' [I sing of arms and the man]. Robert Herrick in *Hesperides* (1648) begins: 'I sing of brooks, of blossoms, birds, and bowers'. William Cowper begins 'The Sofa' in *The Task* (1785):

> I sing the Sofa. I who lately sang
> Truth, Hope and Charity, and touch'd with awe
> The solemn chords . . .
> Now seek repose upon a humbler theme.

'One's Self I Sing', 'For Him I Sing' and 'I Sing the Body Electric' are the titles of poems by Walt Whitman.

I'm not well. Sometimes recalled as 'I've not been well.' Catchphrase of the British comedian George Williams (1910–95). Denis Gifford in an obituary for the *Independent* (8 May 1995) wrote: 'It was in 1934 that he coined the catchphrase "I'm not well". He played the patient in a hospital sketch. His face chalked white, he was pushed on in a bathchair and got such uproarious laughter that the chap playing the doctor, fed up with the long wait, shouted his feed line at the top of his voice, "What's the matter with you?" The laughter died away and at last Williams spoke, "I'm not well," he said. Again there was audience uproar. It told Williams he had chanced on the gag of a lifetime.'

I've died and gone to Heaven. I'm in ecstasy, in a state of bliss (but also used ironically in situations where the opposite is the case). American, possibly Black origin, and in vogue by the 1980s. An early appearance occurs in the film *Barefoot in the Park* (1967): 'I feel like we've died and gone to heaven . . . only we had to climb up.' Compare:

We ... to persuade ourselves that we had not really died and gone to heaven, took a most unangelic tiffin.
Sara J. Duncan, *A Social Depart* (1890)

ice. *See* CUT NO ...

idiot. *See* BLINKING ...

idiot's lantern. *See under* BOX.

if anything can go wrong it will. *See* MURPHY'S LAW.

iffy. Dubious, odd, of questionable merit. As in, 'I think that TV show's a bit iffy, don't you?' Known by 1937, but had something of a revival in about 1982.

illegitimi non carborundum. This cod-Latin phrase – supposed to mean 'Don't let the bastards grind you down' – was used by US General 'Vinegar Joe' Stilwell as his motto during the Second World War, though it is not suggested he devised it. Partridge/*Catch Phrases* gives it as '*illegitimis*' and its origins in British army intelligence very early on in the same war. Something like the phrase has also been reported from 1929. 'Carborundum' is, in fact, the trade name of a very hard substance composed of silicon carbide, used in grinding.

The same meaning is also conveyed by the phrase ***nil carborundum*** ... (as in the title of a play by Henry Livings, 1962) – a pun upon the genuine Latin *nil desperandum* [never say die – lit.: there is nought to be despaired of] which comes from '*nil desperandum est Teucro duce et auspice Teucro*' [nothing is to be despaired of with Teucer as leader and protector] (Horace, *Odes*, I.vii.27).

Perhaps because it is a made-up one, the phrase takes many forms, e.g.: '*nil illegitimis ...*', '*nil bastardo illegitimi ...*', '*nil bastardo carborundum ...*' etc. When the Rt Rev. David Jenkins, as Bishop of Durham, was unwise enough to make use of the phrase at a private meeting in March 1985, a cloth-eared journalist reported him as having said, '*Nil desperandum illegitimi ...*'

in apple-pie order. Meaning 'with everything in place, smart', the expression possibly derives from the French *cap-à-pied*, wearing armour 'from head to foot'. Known in English since 1780. Another suggested French origin is from *nappe pliée*, a folded table cloth or sheet (though

131

this seems a more likely source for the term **apple-pie bed**, for one made so that you can't get into it). On the other hand, a folded cloth or napkin does convey the idea of crispness and smartness.

in cold blood.   With cool deliberateness, especially as in 'murdered in cold blood'. Known by 1711. *In Cold Blood* was the title of Truman Capote's 'non-fiction novel' (1965).

> When regarded backwards from our benefits of new knowledge the deaths of those regretted twenty men in the Wejh streets seemed not so terrible. Vickery's impatience was justified, perhaps, in cold blood.
> T.E. Lawrence, *Seven Pillars of Wisdom* (1926)

> 'The obvious motive was payment of money and the act was carried out in cold blood,' the Recorder of London, Sir Lawrence Verney, told Te Rangimaria Ngarimu.
> *Guardian* (23 December 1994)

> It wasn't akin to the actions of a street brawler at pub throwing-out time, it was a case of a highly trained athlete attacking someone in cold blood.
> *Today* (26 January 1995)

in like Flynn.   Someone who is 'in like Flynn' is a quick seducer – at least, according to the Australian use of the phrase. Appropriately, it is derived from the name of Errol Flynn (1909–59), the Australian-born film actor. It alludes to his legendary bedroom prowess, though the phrase can also mean that a person simply seizes an offered opportunity (of any kind).

According to *The Intimate Sex Lives of Famous People* (Irving Wallace *et al*, 1981), Flynn frowned on the expression when it became popular, especially among servicemen, in the Second World War. It 'implied he was a fun-loving rapist', though 'in fact, Flynn's reputation stemmed partly from his having been charged with statutory rape'. After a celebrated trial, he was acquitted. Nevertheless, he 'boasted that he had spent between 12,000 and 14,000 nights making love'.

Rather weakly, a US film of 1967 was entitled *In Like Flint*.

Partridge/*Catch Phrases* turns up an American version which refers to Ed Flynn, a Democratic machine politician in the Bronx, New York City, in the 1940s. Here the meaning is simply 'to be in automatically' – as his candidates would have been.

in my heart of hearts.   In my deepest and most hidden thoughts and feelings. Apparently a coinage of Shakespeare's. In *Hamlet*,

III.ii.73 (1600–1) there is: 'In my heart's core, in my heart of heart.'

> 'In my heart of hearts, I always know that God comes first,' [Dolly Parton] says. 'But in my body of bodies, some other urges can be absolutely irresistible.'
> *Northern Echo* (7 February 1995)

in the buff.   *See under* BUFF.

in the cart, to be.   Meaning 'to be in trouble', this expression may come from the fact that prisoners used to be taken in a cart to punishment or execution, or from when a horse was put in a cart (because it was ill or dead), the owner being left in a spot. Probably known in this sense by the late nineteenth century.

in the club.   Pregnant. The full expression is probably 'in the pudding club' where pudding = semen. Known since the 1930s.

in the kitty.   Money is put in the kitty or 'the pool' in card games and the expression has been known since 1887. Robert L. Shook in *The Book of Why* (1983) suggests that it comes from 'kit', short for 'kitbag', which was used among soldiers as a receptacle in which to pool their money.

in the limelight.   The centre of attention – from the type of lighting used in nineteenth-century theatre following the discovery of the brilliant luminosity of incandescent lime by Thomas Drummond, a British army surveyor, in 1825. Figurative use by 1877.

> The most limelighted person in Europe this morning is Queen Wilhelmina of Holland.
> *Daily Chronicle* (10 April 1903)

in the mind's eye.   In the imagination. After Shakespeare, *Hamlet*, I.ii.184 (1600–1): 'Methinks I see my father … in my mind's eye, Horatio'. However, this is a traditional metaphor dating back to Plato.

in the same boat, to be.   In the same position – often a difficult one. Known by 1845. This has been traced back to *in eadem es navi*, a Latin tag used in a letter by Cicero in 53 BC.

> They [the Japanese] have attacked us at Pearl Harbor. We are all in the
> same boat now [December 1941].
> President Roosevelt quoted by Winston Churchill in *The Second World War*, Vol. 3
> (1950)

in two shakes of a lamb's tail.   Very quickly, in no time at all –
as in the script of the film *Pulp Fiction* (US, 1994): 'I'll be with you
in two shakes of a lamb's tail.' Known since 1840. Possibly an
elaboration of the simpler 'in two shakes' (of a dice or a cloth or
whatever) and often simply abbreviated to that even now.

indeedy-doody!   American affirmative, noted in TV's *The Muppet
Show* (1980 series). *DOAS* finds 'indeedy' on its own by 1856, as in
'yes, indeedy' or 'no, indeedy'.

Industrial Light and Magic.   Name of the production company
founded in 1975 by the noted Hollywood director and producer,
George Lucas, creating the special effects for the films *Star Wars*,
ET, *Indiana Jones* and *Terminator 2*, and others. Based in northern
California, the company with the fascinating name is the leader in
film technical effects.

> Industrial light and magic on show at the Vatican [exhibition about social
> problems born of the Industrial Revolution].
> Headline, *Independent on Sunday* (17 November 1991)

infiltrate as a mole, to.   The name 'mole' is applied to one who
'tunnels' into a large organization, but particularly a spy who is
placed in another country's intelligence network, often years before
being needed. The CIA term for this process is 'penetration' and
former CIA chief Richard Helms told William Safire (*Safire's Political
Dictionary*, 1978) that he had never encountered use of the word
'mole' in this regard. Although flirted with by other writers (as early
as Francis Bacon), the term was introduced by John Le Carré in his
novel *Tinker, Tailor, Soldier, Spy* (1974). In a BBC TV interview in
1976, he said he *thought* it was a genuine KGB term which he had
picked up.

it is a sorry sight.   It is a miserable, sad, pitiable sight. Apparently
a coinage of Shakespeare's. *Macbeth*, II.ii.20 (1606) has: 'This is a
sorry sight'.

it's a funny old world.   Expression of reluctant acceptance of some blow that fate has delivered. In the 1934 film *You're Telling Me*, W.C. Fields delivers the line, 'It's a funny old world – a man's lucky if he gets out of it alive.' In the *Independent* (22 November 1990), Margaret Thatcher was reported as having exclaimed 'It's a funny old world' (with tears in her eyes) at the previous day's Cabinet meeting at which she announced she had been ousted from the Prime Ministership.

> Well it's a funny old world. Think of Philby, Profumo, Stonehouse. Strange things do happen. Let's run the story: LOST PREMIER WAS RED SPY.
> *Guardian* (20 May 1985)

> It's a funny old world. Here you have, in his final months of office, that aged American butcher, Mr Ian MacGregor, quietly going about his lawful occasion at Hobart House.
> *Guardian* (7 May 1986)

it's a wrap.   'That's it, we've finished for the day'. From film/TV slang, after the expression 'to wrap it up', for to put an end to something, presumably because wrapping up the goods is the last thing you do when a purchase has been completed. Noted by 1974. From 'The Writer in Disguise', Alan Bennett's published diary of filming for TV plays (entry for 15 March 1978): 'We finish at 11.30 with the customary call, "Right, that's a wrap." The judge could have said the same. "Manslaughter. Seven years. And that's a wrap."'

it's an old — custom.   Joking excuse for some aspect of behaviour that has been questioned. Since the 1920s/30s. 'Belgian' might be inserted after a belch ('belchin', geddit?) 'Spanish' is one of the more common interpolations. Compare OLD SPANISH CUSTOMS. 'Southern' followed its use in a US song *c.*1935.

it's not over till it's over (sometimes **the game isn't over . . .**).   A warning comparable to 'the opera ain't over till the fat lady sings' and of American origin also.

> Brigadier General Richard Neal, the US spokesman in Riyadh, warned 'let there be no mistake the [Gulf] war is over. Parts of the Iraqi army are still in Kuwait City'. . . He added: 'It's not over until it's over.'
> *Independent* (27 February 1991)

ivory tower. *See* LIVE IN AN . . .

Ivy League. Name given to the old north-eastern university colleges in the US – Harvard, Yale, Princeton and Columbia. Nothing to do with ivy-covered walls, but rather with the interscholastic 'Four League' which was always written with Roman numerals as the 'IV League' and pronounced 'I-V League'. 'Ivy' came to be the accepted version in the 1930s and the official 'Ivy League' was formed after the Second World War.

J

Jack Russell. Name of a breed of terrier dog (which the Kennel Club refuses to recognize as a breed). So named after a Rev. John Russell (1795–1883), a West Country parson in the days when clergymen rode to hounds and bred ferrets in preference to preaching sermons. Russell encountered Trump, the progenitress of the breed, in the company of a milkman at Oxford. Recorded in use by 1907.

Jack the Ripper. Nickname of the unknown murderer of five or more prostitutes who mutilated his victims in the East End of London (1887–9). He may have been a sailor, a butcher, or even a member of the Royal Family, according to various theories. The first time the name was used was in a letter signed by a man claiming to be the killer, which was sent to a London news agency in September 1888.

The murders were such a long-lasting sensation that the nickname 'Ripper' has been bestowed on subsequent perpetrators of similar crimes – for example, the **Yorkshire Ripper**. This tag was applied to the murderer of some thirteen women in the north of England during the period 1975—80, by a Yorkshire newspaper during the course of a prolonged police pursuit. As eventually revealed, he was Peter Sutcliffe (*b* 1946).

Jackanory. The title of the BBC TV story-telling series for children (from the 1960s onwards) comes from a nursery rhyme first recorded in 1760:

I'll tell you a story
About Jack a Nory,
And now the story's begun;
I'll tell you another
Of Jack and his brother,
And now my story is done.

jacuzzi. The name for a type of hot tub or swirling bath used for relaxation, originally in California. In 1968, Roy Jacuzzi saw the commercial possibilities of using a portable pump invented by his relative, Candido Jacuzzi, for the treatment of rheumatoid arthritis, to make a whirlpool bath. The word 'Jacuzzi' for a type of hydro-massage was known, however, by 1966.

jakes. Old term for a lavatory. This is an archaism but an interesting one. Just as there is a current (mostly American) use of the name **john** for a lavatory, so, in Elizabethan times (and later) there was a use of 'jakes' (a form of John/Jack) for the same thing.

It is said that this derives from the name of Sir John Harrington (1561–1612) who invented a flush lavatory, hence 'Jake's place', once a respectacle euphemism (according to Vernon Noble, *Speak Softly – Euphemisms and Such*, 1982). Sir John, Queen Elizabeth's 'saucy godson', installed a WC at Hampton Court and even published instructions as to how such devices could be manufactured, but either because of the difficulty of installation or frequent breakdowns – or perhaps because people simply could not be bothered – more than a century and a half elapsed before the household version was generally adopted.

It would be good to believe all this, but one cannot be sure. *OED2* has '*c.*1530' for the use of 'jakes' to mean a privy, which would effectively eliminate Sir John.

And, as for the American use of 'john', the *Morris Dictionary of Word and Phrase Origins* (1977) records the first appearance of the word in print in this sense. It is contained in an official regulation of Harvard College published in 1735. 'The expression in full was

"Cousin John"… the regulation read: "No Freshman shall go into the Fellows' Cousin John".'

jalopy. An old motor car. Possibly from the name of an early brand of car in the US? Known there (as 'jaloppi') since 1929.

jam tomorrow. A promise unlikely to be fulfilled, by allusion to Lewis Carroll's *Through the Looking Glass* (1871). The White Queen wants Alice to be her maid and offers her twopence a week and jam every other day, except that she can never actually have any – it's never jam today. An early version of Catch-22. The Queen explains: 'The rule is, jam to-morrow and jam yesterday – but never jam *to-day* …' Quite often the phrase is used in connection with the unfulfilled promises of politicians. Did Carroll adopt an older phrase?

Others recall being taught that this was an academic joke. In Latin there are two words meaning 'now': *nunc* and *iam*. The former is used in the present tense, whereas the latter is the correct word for past and future tenses, i.e. yesterday and tomorrow.

jaywalking. Describing what a pedestrian does who ignores the rules in a motorized zone, the word is a US coinage from the early twentieth century. 'Jay' was a slang term for a rustic or countrified person, so jaywalking was inappropriate in a city where newfangled automobiles were likely to interrupt the reveries of visitors from quieter parts. 'Jaywalker' has been known since 1917.

jeans. These hard-wearing trousers get their name from the French 'Gênes' for Genoa, in Italy, where a similar cloth to DENIM, *jene fustian*, was once made. Use recorded by 1843. *See also* LEVIS.

jerkwater. Small or insignificant, when applied to a place. From the towns where American railroad engines would stop solely to take water on board. The water was 'jerked' on board using leather buckets. Known in the US by 1878.

Not to be confused with **dirtwater**, as in *The Duchess and the Dirtwater Fox*, a film title (US, 1976) where 'the dirtwater fox' is the name of a card sharp.

Jerry. *See* STICK IT, …

jerry-built. Meaning 'built badly of poor materials'. The word was in use by 1869 (which rules out any connection with buildings put up by German or 'Jerry' prisoners-of-war). There are various suggestions as to its origin: that it has to do with the walls of Jericho which came tumbling down; or that there were two brothers called Jerry who were notoriously bad builders in Liverpool; or that it has something to do with the French *jour* [day] – workers paid on a daily basis were unlikely to make a good job of things. Or that, as with the nautical term 'jury' ('jury-rigging', 'jury mast') it is something temporary.

Jerusalem artichoke. An English misnomer, it derived possibly from a mishearing of the Italian *girasole articiocco* [sunflower artichoke]. Known in English by 1620.

jib. *See* LIKE THE CUT OF SOMEONE'S ...

Job's comforter. An expression used to describe one who seeks to give comfort but who, by blaming you for what has happened, makes things worse. It comes from the rebukes Job received from his friends, to whom he says: 'miserable comforters are ye all' (Job 16:2).

joey. A handicapped person (British use only) – an unfortunate coinage. The BBC TV children's programme *Blue Peter* featured a quadraplegic spastic called Joey Deacon who was unable to communicate in normal language. His 'autobiography' had already been dramatized for adult viewers in 1974. The idea was to create a caring attitude in young viewers. Alas, cruelly, the word 'Joey' came to be used by children in quite the wrong way, as in 'You are a joey', or 'That was a real joey thing to do.'

(The word is also applied, incidentally, to owls, to clowns – backstage, in honour of Grimaldi's Joey the Clown – to a hunchback's hunch and, in Australia, to a baby kangaroo.)

John. Mode of address in England, referring to any man (compare 'Jimmy' in Scotland and 'Boyo' in Wales). Became particularly noticeable in the 1970s, not least when Alexei Sayle had a hit record with "'Ullo, John, Got a New Motor?" in 1984.

Earlier use of 'John' to refer to the average fellow is said to go back to the fourteenth century. It is also a slang term for a prostitute's customer (though this might have something to do with 'John Thomas' as a nickname for the penis).

See also under JAKES.

John Birch Society.   The name of an extreme right-wing, anti-Communist politicial group in the US (founded 1958). Capt. John Birch was a USAF officer who had been killed by Chinese Communists in 1945 and is sometimes referred to as 'the first casualty of the Cold War' (William Safire, *Safire's Political Dictionary*, 1978).

John Bull.   *See under* BULLDOG BREED.

John Doe.   In American legal actions, an unknown person is referred to as 'John Doe' – a usage which began in England in the fourteenth century. Curiously for a name which is supposed to signify 'A.N. Other', it is a most uncommon one. Known in the US by the 1840s.

John Hancock.   This US nickname for a signature or autograph, derives from John Hancock, a Boston merchant, who was one of the first signatories of the Declaration of Independence in 1776. His signature is quite the largest on the document and he is variously reported to have made it that way 'so the King of England could read it without spectacles' and said: 'There! I guess King George [or John Bull] will be able to read that!' Known as such by 1903.

jolly as a sandboy.   *See* AS HAPPY AS . . .

Joneses.   *See* KEEP UP WITH THE . . .

jot and tittle.   Meaning 'the least item or detail', the words come from St Matthew 5:18: 'Till heaven and earth pass, one jot or one tittle shall in no wise pass from the law, till all be fulfilled.' 'Jot' is *iota*, the smallest Greek letter (compare 'not one iota') and 'tittle' is the dot over the letter *i* (Latin *titulus*).

joyriding.   Name given to the practice of young people stealing motor cars and then driving them at high speed. Possibly of American origin, known by the 1910s. Believing that the word was clearly inappropriate for such an anti-social acitivity, the *Daily Telegraph* (13

January 1993) attempted to engineer the language and impose 'mad-riding', 'bad-tripping', 'auto-abuse', but inevitably failed.

jumbo.   Meaning 'big, elephantine', it comes from the name of a notably large African elephant and the first to be seen in England. Jumbo was exhibited at the London Zoo from 1865 to 1882. It was then sold to Barnum and Bailey's circus in the US where it was killed by a railway engine in 1885.

jump.   *See* FOR THE HIGH . . .

just deserts.   *See* GET ONE'S . . .

just like mother makes/used to make.   Like home cooking and very acceptable. This expression seems to have acquired figurative quotation marks around it by the early years of the twentieth century. As such, it is of American origin and was soon used by advertisers as a form of slogan (compare the US pop song of the Second World War, 'Ma, I Miss Your Apple Pie'). 'The kind mother used to make' was used as a slogan by New England Mincemeat around 1900.

K

kangaroo court.   The name applied to a self-appointed court which has no proper legal authority – as in the disciplinary proceedings sometimes to be found among prisoners in gaol. Recorded by 1853. Ironically, *Macquarie* (1981), the Australian dictionary, calls this an American and British colloquialism, but surely it must have something to do with the land of the kangaroo? Perhaps it alludes to the vicious streak that such animals sometimes display? Possibly it was coined in the lawless Californian goldfields where there were many Australians – probably of a criminal bent.

karzy.   A lavatory. This word has limited British use and one had always assumed that it was spelt *khazi* and had some connection with India. However, Partridge – while drawing attention to other spellings viz. *kharsie* and *carzey* – derives it from the more English *carsey*, a low Cockney word for a privy and dating from the late nineteenth century. A carsey was also a den or brothel and presumably derives from the Italian *casa*, meaning 'house'.

keen as mustard. Very sharp, clever, 'doesn't miss a trick', extremely keen. According to the *Independent* (3 November 1993), the Thomas *Keen* who is buried in West Norwood cemetery, near London is the one 'whose family firm made mustard and whose activities led to the phrase "keen as mustard".' A nice thought, but 'the keenest mustard' was a phrase by 1658.

keep the ball rolling, to. To keep something going, especially a conversation. Possibly from an elementary game where this had to be done or from bandy (a type of hockey). If the ball was not kept rolling it was a slow game and uninteresting for the spectators. Known by 1840.

To Keep the Ball Rolling was the overall title given to Anthony Powell's autobiographical sequence (1976–82). He said it came from Joseph Conrad's *Chance* (1913): 'To keep the ball rolling I asked Marlow if this Powell was remarkable in any way. "He was not exactly remarkable," Marlow answered with his usual nonchalance. "In a general way it's very difficult to become remarkable. People won't take sufficient notice of one, don't you know."'

keep up with the Joneses, to. Meaning 'to strive not to be outdone by one's neighbours', the expression comes from a comic strip by Arthur R. 'Pop' Momand entitled *Keeping up with the Joneses*, which appeared in the New York *Globe* from 1913 to 1931. It is said that Momand had at first intended to call his strip 'Keeping up with the Smiths' but refrained because his own neighbours were actually of that name and some of the exploits he wished to report had been acted out by them in real life.

kermit. A Frenchman – after Kermit the Frog, an endearing character in the TV show *The Muppets*. It became British student and other slang by 1981 and alludes, of course, to 'frog' as the traditional name for French people (who are curiously noted for eating frogs' legs as a delicacy).

The name 'Kermit', while not common, was bestowed, for example, as a forename on a son of President Theodore Roosevelt. It was derived from his mother's surname.

keyhole.   *See* THROUGH THE ...

kibosh.   *See* PUT THE ...

kick the bucket/dust, to.   This euphemism for 'to die', derives from either the suicide's kicking away the bucket on which he/she is standing, in order to hang him/herself, or from the 'bucket beam' on which pigs were hung *after* being slaughtered. The odd post mortem spasm would lead to the 'bucket' being kicked.

'Kick the dust' for 'to die' is nicely illustrated by a passage from Thoreau's *Walden* (1854): 'I was present at the auction of a deacon's effects ... after lying half a century in his garret and other dust holes ... When a man dies he kicks the dust.' The *OED2* mentions neither this expression, nor 'kiss the dust', though it does find **bite the dust** in 1856.

Psalm 72:9 has **lick the dust**: 'They that dwell in the wilderness shall bow before him; and his enemies shall lick the dust' – though this is suggesting humiliation rather than death.

kick-start, to.   Figuratively, to start something or force it into action by the administration of a mighty jolt or effort. After the action required to move the pedal which starts the engine on a motorbike. Known by 1914.

> The Netherlands, too, seems to be trying to 'kick-start manufacturers into the wind energy industry,' according to one British turbine designer. It is said to be offering a 40 per cent subsidy on investment to Dutch developers of new wind farms.
> *New Scientist* (17 March 1988)

kike.   A Jew – an offensive, mostly US term, and thought to be a variant of *kiki*, a duplication of the common *-ki* ending of the names of many Jews from Slav countries. Leo Rosten, however, in *The Joys of Yiddish* (1968) suggests that the word comes from Ellis Island immigration officers who, faced with Jewish immigrants unable to write their names in the Roman alphabet, instructed them to sign their names with a cross. For understandable reasons, they chose to put instead a circle as a means of identification. For the Jews, a circle (Yiddish, *kikel*) is a symbol of unending life. To the immigration officers, a person who asked to be allowed to make a *kikel* or a *kikeleh* (a little circle) soon became a 'kikee' or simply a 'kike'. Known by 1904.

kill. *See* DRESSED TO . . .

kilter. *See* OUT OF . . .

King. *See* CHICKEN À LA . . .

kipper's knickers. *See under* BEE'S KNEES.

kir. A drink made from dry white wine and a drop of *crème de cassis*, known originally as *blanc cassis*, it derives from the name of a notable imbiber rather than its inventor. Canon Félix Kir was a hero of the French Resistance and Mayor of Dijon who died in 1968 aged 92. The term was known by 1966. The drink had been known for long before Canon Kir came along, praising it as a cure all and giving it his name.

kit. *See* GET/TAKE ONE'S . . .

kittens. *See* HAVE . . .

kitty. *See* IN THE . . .

knee trembler. Name for a type of sexual intercourse, traditionally done in a bus shelter or against a wall, where both the participants are standing up. Known by 1971, though Partridge/*Slang* thinks it may have been around in 1850.

> There is usually a bit of amateur comfort available – a few port-and-lemons (or whatever the modern equivalent is), a portion of fish and chips, and a knee-trembler behind the scout hut.
> *Daily Telegraph* (29 April 1995)

knickers. Female underwear, short for knickerbockers. Many of the original Dutch settlers in New York (originally New Amsterdam) were called Knickerbocker. Dutchmen wore loose knee-pants or breeches and they, via a common process, came to be called 'knickerbockers' especially after the garments had been shown in illustrations for Washington Irving's book *Knickerbocker's History of New York* (1809). The term has also been applied to the wide trousers, gathered just below the knee, favoured by golfers.

In Britain, shortened to 'knickers', the word has been more usually applied to female underwear formerly called 'drawers' and which, initially at least, looked like the old Dutch breeches.

The excellent expression **don't get your knickers in a twist** (meaning 'don't get worked up or confused about something') is, for this reason, probably denied to the Americans. Known by 1971.

knobs. *See* WITH ...

knock off work, to. To finish work for the day. The *Morris Dictionary of Word and Phrase Origins* (1977) explains that this dates from the days of slave galleys. The man who beat time to keep the oarsmen pulling in unison would give a special knock to indicate when there was to be a change of shift. Not recorded before 1902 (in the UK).

knock seven bells out of —, to. To beat severely, if not actually knock someone out. It is nautical in origin (and known by 1929), but why seven out of the eight bells available aboard ship? Also figurative use.

> If they [louts] misbehave, the players leave the pitch and kick seven bells out of them.
> *People* (19 February 1995)

> There is something reassuringly solid about sculptors, especially those who work on the grand scale. Perhaps belting seven bells out of a ton of granite all day long dispels any high-flown airs and graces.
> *Scotland on Sunday* (2 July 1995)

knock spots off (the competition), to. To do something better than somebody else. American origin, known by 1861. But what spots are alluded to?

know. *See* ANYONE WE ...

know the ropes, to. To understand the procedures to be followed in any situation. From nautical use where, literally, to know the ropes was vital for survival. Recorded in 1874.

know what I mean?   Verbal filler which in the 1970s took over from the shorter **you know?** at the end of sentences. It was used almost as a catchphrase in the TV film *The Knowledge* by Jack Rosenthal (1979). A possible popularizer was Michael Caine who in the film *Alfie* (1966) had delivered such lines as: 'So what's the answer? That's what I keep asking meself. What's it all about? Know what I mean?'

So irritating and omnipresent was this phrase that in *c.*1981 it was sometimes written and pronounced **narmean?** by its critics.

know where the bodies are buried, to.   To know the secrets of an organization and thus to be in a position where you are not likely to be 'let go'. In the film *Citizen Kane* (US, 1941), Susan Alexander, Kane's estranged wife, says of the butler at Xanadu that he 'knows where all the bodies are buried'. Particularly popular from the 1980s onwards in the US and UK.

> A senior member of the PLP [in the Bahamas] said: 'If he is sent to America, he will sing like a canary – and this guy knows where the bodies are buried.'
> *Sunday Times* (29 September 1985)

> Like Martha Mitchell, the political wife who spilled the beans, she knows where the bodies are buried in the Rose Garden.
> *Financial Times* (9 June 1986)

> Politicians trust John [Cole]. They talk to him because he would never say where the bodies are buried.
> *Independent* Metro (2 June 1995)

know which way the wind blows, to.   To be aware of a tendency or change in affairs or conditions. A proverbial expression of 1546 was 'I knew which way the wind blew.' The title of the memoirs of Lord Home, the former British Prime Minister, was *The Way the Wind Blows* (1976). He explains that it was what a gamekeeper said of his family's abilities, 'The Home boys always seem to know which way the wind blows', and adds, '[He] was not thinking of me as a political trimmer, but simply stating a fact of our family life ... on the right interpretation of wind or weather depended the action of the day.'

Compare **when the wind blows**. This phrase was used as the title of a children's story (1982) by Raymond Briggs about the aftermath of a nuclear holocaust. 'When the wind blows the cradle will rock' is a line from the nursery rhyme 'Hush-a-bye, baby, on the tree top' (known since 1765). 'Grass never grows when the wind blows' is a proverb cited in G.L. Apperson's *English Proverbs and Proverbial Phrases* (1929) as dating from 1846.

knowledge. The process of acquiring and learning the traffic routes around London which is part of the training of licensed taxi-cab drivers. Celebrated in a TV comedy drama called *The Knowledge* (1979).

knuckle down, to. To get down to doing, to apply one's self seriously to a difficult task. Known by 1740 – from placing the knuckles on the ground in shooting or playing at marbles.

> 'I play well in some matches but not in others so in my next match I need to knuckle down and produce a good performance,' said Henman. *Herald* (Glasgow) (17 January 1996)

knuckle under, to. To give in to someone else, to give way to a superior force. Known by 1740.

> Protesters denounced the ban on travel to jobs in Israel and the expansion of Jewish settlements in the West Bank. 'No to starvation, no to settlements. We are a people who won't knuckle under,' they chanted. *Independent* (14 February 1995)

L

lager lout. Term for a young person in the UK, noted for lager consumption and a tendency to violence, particularly when attending football matches. The species was identified in 1988, the name clearly owing much to alliteration. According to Simon Walters, political correspondent of the *Sun*, in a letter to the *Independent* (13 April 1989): 'It dates back to last August when the Home Office referred to the "lager culture" among young troublemakers ... from that I coined the term "lager lout" to give it more meaning.'

lamb's tail. *See* IN TWO SHAKES OF A . . .

lame duck. Someone or something handicapped by misfortune or by incapacity. It was the name originally given to a defaulter on the London Stock Exchange and known by 1761. In William Thackeray's *Vanity Fair*, Chap. 13 (1847–8), the money-conscious Mr Osborne is suspicious of the financial position of Amelia's father: 'I'll have no lame duck's daughter in my family.' It is said that people who could not pay their debts would 'waddle' out of Exchange Alley in the City of London – hence perhaps, the 'duck'.

In the US, since the 1860s, the term has come to be applied to a President or other office-holder whose power is diminished because he is about to leave office or because he is handicapped by some scandal. In *c.*1970, the term was also applied by British politicians to industries unable to survive without government financial support.

landlubber. A person more happy on land than on sea. Known by 1752. It is not that he is a 'land-lover' (though he might well have this preference) but that he is a 'lubber' – a big, clumsy, stupid fellow. By 1579, 'lubber' was a seaman's name for a clumsy novice. The addition of 'land-' only served to emphasize the insult. Presumably such a person would be equally clumsy on land as on sea.

landscape. *See* BLOT ON THE . . .

large. *See* BY AND . . .

Larry. *See* AS HAPPY AS . . .

late unpleasantness. A euphemism for the previous war or recent hostilities, it was introduced by the US humorist David Ross Locke in *Ekkoes from Kentucky* (1868). Writing as 'Petroleum V. Nasby', he referred to the recently ended Civil War as 'the late onpleasantniss' and the coinage spread.

> Here, for instance, is Dan Rather, America's father-figure, on the hot-line to Panama during the late unpleasantness [an invasion] . . .
> *Independent* (20 January 1990)

laugh? I thought I should have died. I thought something was extremely funny. Now often said ironically to mean the reverse, that you were so taken aback by someone else's cheek, for example, that you did not find their behaviour at all funny but all you could do was laugh it off. It occurs in Albert Chevalier's song 'Knocked 'Em in the Old Kent Road' (*c*.1892), but also, in nascent form, in Jane Austen's *Pride and Prejudice*, Chap. 39 (1813) – Lydia says: 'Lord! how I laughed! ... I thought I should have died.'

laugh like drains, to.   To laugh very hard and loud. Probably of British origin in the mid-twentieth century. Possibly reflecting that, just as drains sometimes gurgle so that is the way extreme laughter can sound. Recorded by 1948.

> Some people at the screening I went to laughed like drains. Maybe they were Alan Parker's family, or his backers. Most of us sat in pained silence.
> *Independent on Sunday* (5 February 1995)

lawk(s)-a-mussy!   Euphemistic exclamation since the late nineteenth century. A softening of 'Lord have mercy!'

lay an egg, to.   To fail, flop. Although *OED2* says the source is American, more than one transatlantic source gives the English game of cricket as the origin of this expression. A zero score was called a 'duck's egg' because of the obvious resemblance between the number and the object. Early twentieth century. In the US in baseball there developed a similar expression, 'goose egg'.

> Wall Street lays an egg ... The most dramatic event in the financial history of America is the collapse of the New York Stock Market.
> Headline and text, *Variety* (30 October 1929)

lay it on with a trowel, to.   To be generous in supplying something – usually when engaged in flattery. Benjamin Disraeli is said to have told Matthew Arnold: 'Everyone likes flattery; and when you come to Royalty you should lay it on with a trowel.' But the figure of speech was an old one even in the nineteenth century. 'That was laid on with a trowel' appears in Shakespeare's *As You Like It*, I.ii.98 (1598) which the Arden edition glosses as 'slapped on thick and without nicety, like mortar'.

The trowel in question is not a garden one, but of the kind used by painters for spreading paint thickly.

lead someone up the garden path, to.   To mislead. Known since 1925. Possibly from the place where promises of matrimony were made and not always carried out. Compare the title of a book by Beverly Nichols, *Down the Garden Path* (1932).

leap in the dark.   A venture, an action, a decision, where the outcome is unknown or unknowable. Known by the seventeenth century.

> I am about to take my last voyage, a great leap in the dark.
> Last words of Thomas Hobbes (*d* 1679), quoted in John Watkins *Anecdotes of Men of Learning* (1808)
>
> A little before you made a leap into the dark.
> Thomas Brown, *Letters from the Dead to the Living* (1702)

left footer.   A Roman Catholic. Twentieth-century origin, possibly a coinage of Northern Ireland protestants. In the Irish Republic it is assumed that a spade is pushed into the ground using the left foot by agricultural labourers. Hence, as anyone from southern Ireland is likely to be a Roman Catholic, then he is likely to be a left-footer. Recorded by 1944.

leg.   *See* BREAK A ...; MAKE A ...; SHAKE/SHOW A ...

legion.   *See* MY NAME IS ...

leotard.   Tight, one-piece garment worn by ballet dancers, acrobats and other performers. From the name of Jules Léotard (1830–70), the French trapeze artist, who popularized it. He was the original 'daring young man on the flying trapeze' and celebrated in the song 'The Man on the Flying Trapeze' by George Leybourne and Alfred Lee (1868).

let bygones be bygones.   Let us not dwell on things that have happened in the past. 'Bygones' here means 'things that are past'. A proverbial expression known in English by 1546, but the thought is expressed by the Greek philosopher Epictetus.

let the cat out of the bag, to.   Meaning 'to reveal a secret', this saying derives from the trick played on unsuspecting purchasers of sucking-pigs at old English country fairs. The pig would be shown to the buyer, then put in a sack while the deal was finalized. A quick substitution of a less valuable *cat* would then be made, and this is what the buyer would take away. When he opened the sack, he would 'let the cat out of the bag' and the subterfuge would be revealed. Known by 1760.

> We are commanded to be silent lest we should let the cat out of the bag. The cat out of the bag! There are in this novel about a hundred cats contained in a hundred bags, all screaming and mewing to be let out. Every new chapter contains a new cat. When we come to the end of it out goes the animal, and there is a new bag put into our hands which it is the object of the subsequent chapter to open. We are very willing to stroke some of these numerous cats, but it is not possible to do it without letting them out.
> *The Times* (30 October 1860), reviewing *The Woman in White* by Wilkie Collins

let's get down to the (real) nitty-gritty.   Meaning, 'let's get down to the real basics of a problem or situation' (like GET DOWN TO BRASS TACKS). Sheilah Graham, the Hollywood columnist, in her book *Scratch an Actor* (1969) says of Steve McQueen: 'Without a formal education – Steve left school when he was fifteen – he has invented his own vocabulary to express what he means . . . His "Let's get down to the nitty-gritty" has gone into the American language.'

All she meant, one feels, is that McQueen popularized the term, for it is generally held to be an African-American phrase and was talked about before the film star came on the scene. It seems to have had a particular vogue among Black Power campaigners *c.*1963, and the first *OED2* citation is from that year. In 1963, Shirley Ellis recorded a song 'The Nitty Gritty' to launch a new dance (like 'The Locomotion' before it). The opening line of the record is, 'Now let's get down to the real nitty-gritty'.

Stuart Berg Flexner in *Listening to America* (1982) comments: 'It may have originally referred to the grit-like nits or small lice that are hard to get out of one's hair or scalp, or to a Black English term for the anus.'

Levis (or **Levi's**).   The name of a specific type of blue denim JEANS originated by Levi Strauss of San Francisco. He turned up during the California Gold Rush in 1850 with a roll of tent canvas under his arm. When he ran out of canvas for making tough trousers, his brothers in New York imported the material from its French source. The form Levi's is now a proprietary name. *See also* DENIM.

licensed to kill. The James Bond label appears frequently in the works of Ian Fleming. In *Dr No* (1958): 'The licence to kill for the Secret Service, the double-o prefix, was a great honour.' There was a Bond film with the title *Licence to Kill* (UK, 1989). Compare this by William Godwin Jnr (son of the philosopher-novelist) in *Blackwood's Edinburgh Magazine* (October 1833): 'My Lord of the thirty thousand acres expired on a couch of down . . . each moment of his fluctuating existence watched by an obsequious practitioner, "licensed to kill", whose trade it is to assuage the pangs of death . . .' The quotation marks make it look like an established joke at the expense of doctors.

lick into shape, to. To put the final touches to something, make it more presentable or efficient. Known by 1413. From the belief that bear cubs are born shapeless and have to be licked into shape by their mothers. Told in the encyclopedia compiled by the Arab physician Avicenna (979–1037).

> Enforced, as a Bear doth her Whelps, to bring forth this confused lump, I had not time to lick it into form.
> Robert Burton, *The Anatomy of Melancholy* (1621)

> A cast of 35, aged from 11 to 25 will be taking part in the Lionel Bart musical *Blitz*. They have had just seven days of intensive rehearsals to lick it into shape.
> *Northern Echo* (8 August 1995)

lick the dust. *See under* KICK THE BUCKET.

life is just a bowl of cherries. Everything is wonderful. A modern proverbial expression that apparently originated in the song by Lew Brown (music by Ray Henderson), first heard in the American musical *Scandals of 1931*.

life is (just) one damn(ed) thing after another (also rendered as **ODTAA**). Expression of dismay at a series of misfortunes. Originally a famous quotation of the remark by either Elbert Hubbard (1856–1915) or Frank Ward O'Malley (1875–1932). John Masefield published his novel *Odtaa* in 1926.

lifestyle. One's complete life, physical and spiritual, and what one does with it. The word was coined by the philosopher Alfred Adler

(1870–1937) in *Problems of Neurosis* (1929). He originally meant a person's character as formed in early childhood, but the word has come to mean a way of living. Latterly taken by those who always prefer a longer word to a shorter. Where 'life' would be the short direct way of saying what is meant, 'lifestyle' is wheeled out instead.

> Testimony from a group of bright articulate lesbians covering: lesbian sexuality, problems of lesbian mothers ... and the lesbian lifestyle.
> *Ms* Magazine (July 1974)

> *Lifestyles of the Rich and Famous.*
> Title of US TV series (current 1987)

lifetime. *See* ALL IN A ...

light. *See under* ROAD TO DAMASCUS.

lightning never strikes twice in the same place. Taken literally this is an untrue statement. Lightning is often drawn repeatedly to the same spot. However, when used as a figurative, superstitious expression, it means that you are going to tempt providence because the chances are that you will not suffer a misfortune of the kind (large or small) undergone by a previous doer of what you are about to do. Mostly twentieth century use?

> They also say that lightning never strikes twice, which makes York Minster a rare sanctuary if you're unlucky enough to be an astrapophobe.
> *Independent* (5 February 1996)

> 'They say that lightning never strikes twice in the same place but that's exactly what we're all hoping for,' said Rush.
> Press Association (24 January 1996)

like a bat out of hell. With extreme (and desperate) speed. The image is clear. Known by 1921.

> Once I went through Spain, like a bat out of hell, with a party that included ... a distinguished American of letters.
> Dorothy Parker, in the *New Yorker* (25 July 1931)

> She'll shoot out of Greenwich like a bat out of hell, if she thinks there's a chance of seeing you.
> Dorothy Parker, 'Dusk Before Fireworks' (before 1944)

like the cut of someone's jib, not to. Meaning 'not to like the look of someone', the expression has a nautical origin – the 'cut' or condition of the 'jib' or foresail signifying the quality of the sailing vessel as a whole. Current by 1823.

limelight.   *See* IN THE . . .

limey.   An old American and then Australian term for 'a Britisher', deriving from the free issue of lime juice to British sailors to protect them from scurvy, in the eighteenth century. It is short for 'lime-juicer' and was in use by 1888.

lindy hop.   A vigorous dance popular in the 1930s which evolved into the jitterbug of the 1940s and perhaps even led to the jive and rock'n'roll of the 1950s.

Its name comes from an age perhaps more inclined to celebrate progress than our own. In 1927, Colonel Charles Lindberg, the American pilot, flew the Atlantic – the first non-stop solo crossing – and set off a tremendous, euphoric response. Most reference books connect the dance which began to flourish shortly after the flight with Lindberg's nickname 'Lindy'. The word known by 1931.

lion's share.   The largest portion of anything. This probably derives from Aesop's fable of the lion, the fox and the ass. They went hunting and killed a stag. The ass divided it into equal proportions but the lion looked upon this as an insult to his dignity and killed the ass. The fox, more craftily, nibbled a bit and left the 'lion's share' to the bigger beast.

In fact, a lion does get the largest share of the food obtained for him by the lionesses in his pride. The expression recorded by 1790.

The art of finding a rich friend to make a tour with you in autumn, and of leaving him to bear the lion's share of the expenses.
Punch (22 June 1872)

The lion's share – £215m – would be used to develop distribution networks, said Mr Marcelino Oreja, commissioner for culture.
Daily Telegraph (9 February 1995)

little black dress.   Referring to a simple frock suitable for most social occasions and sometimes abbreviated to 'lbd', it was popular from the 1920s and 30s onwards. The supposed original, a creation of Coco Chanel, was sold at auction for £1500 in 1978. In Britain, the designer Molyneux perfected the dress as the ideal cocktail party wear of the between-the-wars years.

live in an ivory tower, to.   Meaning 'to live in intellectual seclusion and protected from the harsh realities of life', the expression comes from Sainte-Beuve writing in 1837 about the turret room in which the Comte de Vigny, the French poet, dramatist and novelist, worked. He described it as his *tour d'ivoire*, possibly after the Song of Solomon 7:4: 'Thy neck is as a tower of ivory; thine eyes like fishpools ...'

live like God in France, to.   To live in ease and comfort. This is a common expression in Dutch (*Hij leeft als God in Frankrijk*) and German, and occurs also in Frisian. Several far-fetched explanations have been proposed, none supported by convincing evidence. An example in Dutch dates from 1771 (with *Gods*, plural). Perhaps the expression simply combines an allusion to the well-known splendour of the French court under Louis XIV with the older idea that gods lead privileged lives. Lutz Röhrich has this in German by 1693 and offers a number of origins. One is that it is a reference to the comfortable life of the French clergy in the Middle Ages. Another is that it is a mixture of the older 'To live like a God' and 'To live like a lord in France.'

Llanfair P.G.   A small Welsh village on Anglesey in Wales has the longest place name in the British Isles (or had until someone invented an even longer one elsewhere in Wales). The longest place name in the world is the official name for Bangkok, Thailand. The longest in use is in New Zealand. In full Llanfair is: 'LLANFAIRPWLL-GWYNGYLLGOGERYCHWRYNDROBWLLLLANTYSILIO-GOGOGOCH', meaning 'St Mary's Church in the hollow of the white hazels near to the rapid whirlpool of Llantysilio by the red cave.' It said to have been deliberately concocted by a Victorian innkeeper in order to attract tourists or by a local bard, John Evans (1827–95) as a hoax. The railway station displaying the name on a sign reopened in 1973.

load of old cobblers.   *See under* CODSWALLOP.

lobster Newburg.   Lobster cooked in a rich, thick, creamy sauce flavoured with brandy, sherry or wine, with paprika or cayenne pepper and egg yolks. This was a speciality of Delmonico's, the fashionable New York restaurant of the late nineteenth century. (In 1895 it was being called 'Lobster à la Newburg'.)

Originally, so the story has it, it was named 'Lobster Wenberg', after a particular customer, Ben Wenberg, a sea-captain who supplied the cayenne pepper and also related how a similar South American dish had been prepared. When he fell out of favour with the management – for fighting in the restaurant – his name was ana-grammatised, more or less, into 'Newburg'.

Loch Ness Monster. Name for a mythical creature, sometimes known as 'Nessie'. For many hundreds of years has been thought to exist in the waters of Loch Ness in Scotland. The first *OED2* citation of this descriptive name is 1933 (during the 1930s revival of interest in the supposed phenomenon) but the phrase is apparently alluded to in a *Punch* cartoon (26 May 1909).

lock stock and barrel. Meaning, 'the whole lot', this term comes to us from the armoury where the lock (or firing mechanism), stock and barrel are the three principal parts of a gun. Known by 1842.

> The whole thing, lock, stock, and barrel, isn't worth one big yellow sea-poppy.
> Rudyard Kipling, *The Light That Failed* (1891)

> He went into any game lock, stock and barrel ... He would get whatever he needed – the best horses, coaches, equipment ...
> Christopher Ogden, *Life of the Party* (1994)

long chalk. *See* NOT BY A ...

long hot summer. A journalistic cliché from the 1960s. This is usually blamed on the title of the 1958 film *The Long Hot Summer* based on the stories of William Faulkner and also of a spin-off TV series (1965–6). The film was based on 'The Hamlet', a story published by Faulkner in 1928, which contains the chapter heading 'The Long Summer' (*sic*). On the second page of Wilkie Collins, *The Woman in White* (1860) is: 'It was the last day of July. The long, hot summer was drawing to a close.'

long in the tooth. Older people suffer from receding of the gums and their teeth appear to be longer. The same probably applies to horses, so compare LOOK A GIFT HORSE IN THE MOUTH. Known by 1852 (W.M. Thackeray, *Esmond*).

loo. A euphemism for the lavatory, established in well-to-do British society by the early twentieth century and in general middle-class use after the Second World War. Of the several theories for its origin, perhaps the most well known is that the word comes from the French *gardez l'eau* [mind the water], dating from the days when chamber pots or dirty water were emptied out of the window into the street and recorded by Laurence Sterne as *garde d'eau* in *A Sentimental Journey* (1768). This cry was also rendered 'gardyloo' in old Edinburgh and recorded by Tobias Smollett in *Humphrey Clinker* (1771).

However, Professor A.S.C. Ross who examined the various options in a 1974 issue of *Blackwood's Magazine* favoured a derivation, 'in some way which could not be determined', from 'Waterloo'. At one time people probably said: 'I must go to the water-closet' and, wishing not to be explicit, substituted 'Water-loo' as a weak little joke. The name 'Waterloo' was there, waiting to be used, from 1815 onwards.

look a gift horse in the mouth, to. Meaning 'to find fault with a gift, to spoil an offer by inquiring too closely into it', the proverb alludes to the fact that the age of horses is commonly assessed by the length of their teeth. If you are offered the gift of a horse, you would be ill-advised to look in its mouth. You might discover information not to your advantage. Known by 1546 (as 'given horse').

looking/dressed up like a dog's breakfast/dinner. When the first saying (known by 1937) suggests something *scrappy* and the second (known by 1934) something *showy*, what are we led to conclude about the differing nature of a dog's breakfast and dinner? A dog's breakfast might well have consisted (before the invention of tinned dog food) of the left-over scraps of the household from the night before. So that takes care of that, except that there is also the phrase **cat's breakfast**, meaning a mess. Could both these derive from a belief that dogs and cats on occasions appear to eat their own sick?

A dog's dinner might well not have differed very much (and, on occasions, can mean the same as a dog's breakfast) except for the case described in 2 Kings 9 where it says of Jezebel that, after many years leading Ahab astray, she 'painted her face, and tired her head', but failed to impress Jehu, whose messy disposal of her fulfilled Elijah's prophecy that the 'dogs shall eat Jezebel by the wall of Jezreel'. Hence 'done up like a dog's dinner' has been interpreted as 'dressed to kill, dressed stylishly'.

Quite how one should distinguish between the two remains a problem, as is shown by this use of both phrases in a letter from Sir Huw Wheldon (23 July 1977), published in the book *Sir Huge* (1990) and concerning his TV series *Royal Heritage*: 'It was very difficult, and I feared it would be a Dog's Dinner. There was so much ... to draw upon ... I think it matriculated, in the event, into a Dog's Breakfast, more or less, & I was content.'

loose cannon. A person who is not attached to a particular faction and acts independently and, possibly, unreliably. Of American origin. The reference is either to a cannon that is not properly secured to the deck of a ship or to an artillery man who is working independently during a land battle.

> A subcategory of journalese involves the language used to indicate a powerful or celebrated person who is about to self-destruct or walk the plank ... Soon Mr Brilliant will be labeled a 'loose cannon' and transmute himself into an adviser, the Washington version of self-imposed exile.
> *Time* Magazine (1 September 1986)

> Gung-ho, loose cannon, cowboy, Jesus freak – there is already a cottage industry manufacturing Ollie epithets. Lynching [Oliver] North is quickly becoming a national sport.
> *Observer* (26 July 1987)

lounge lizard. Alliterative coinage for a man who lounges about fashionable society (in hotel lounges, too) seeking support from a wealthy female patroness. The *OED2* says the phrase is of American origin and finds its earliest citation in 1937. However, a cartoon in *Punch* (9 March 1927) has the caption 'Where are the lounge lizards?'

love. *See* —, I LOVE YA!; SUMMER OF ...

love. Scoring call for 'no points' in the game of tennis. As modern tennis grew out of the older game of real or Royal tennis, the scoring terms would seem to be derived from the courtly language of French.

Supposedly 'love' is '*l'oeuf*' 'the egg', hence 'zero'. However, it would be more likely in French to say *un oeuf* and the French nowadays denote no score by saying 'zéro'. Another explanation is that if in the expression 'neither love nor money', love signifies nothing, the antithesis of wealth, then 'love' in tennis equals nothing either. Recorded (in the game of whist) by 1742.

Deuce for both sides having three points each seems somehow rather more likely to come from the French *deux*, 'two'. (In cards, 'deuce' also means a score of two.)

love me, love my dog. Meaning 'if you are inclined to take my side in matters generally, you must put up with one or two things you don't like at the same time', it comes from one of St Bernard's sermons: '*Qui me amat, amat et canem meum*' [Who loves me, also loves my dog]. Alas, this was a different St Bernard from the one after whom the breed of Alpine dog is named. It was said (or quoted) by St Bernard of Clairvaux (*d* 1153) rather than St Bernard of Menthon (*d* 1008).

A good illustration comes from an article by Valerie Bornstein in *Proverbium* (1991): 'I told my mother that she must love my father a lot because she tolerated his snoring!... She became aggravated with me and stated the proverb "*Aime moi, aime mon chien*". She told me that when you love someone, you accept all the things that go along with them, their virtues and faults.'

lucky Jim. Title of a US song by Frederick Bowers (*d* 1961) and his vaudeville partner Charles Horwitz (though it is usually ascribed to Anon). It tells of a man who has to wait for his childhood friend to die before he can marry the girl they were once both after. Then, married to the woman and not enjoying it, he would rather he was dead like his friend: 'Oh, lucky Jim, how I envy him.'

Lucky Jim became the title of a comic novel (1953) by Kingsley Amis, about a hapless university lecturer, Jim Dixon.

lumbered. Put in an impossible position (sometimes 'dead lumbered'), burdened. Not too clear, this one. In one sense, of course, lumber is simply timber, wood. The verb 'to lumber' used to mean 'to arrest, put in prison' and the phrase 'in lumber' meant in prison', so that might have contributed to the present meaning.

Another derivation is from 'lumber-room', i.e. the room in a house in which disused or useless articles of furniture are dumped. People who cannot bear to part with objects like this often prefer to give them to other people rather than throw them away. Recipients of such questionable gifts from the lumber-room might be said to have been lumbered with them.

Brewer notes that lumber (from Lombard) was also the name given to a pawnbroker's shop. Perhaps the owners of these shops, if they were not careful, sometimes lent money in return for items they would never be able to get rid of if they were not reclaimed – and were thus 'lumbered'? Known since 1671 (pawn sense), 1745 (encumbered), 1812 (prison).

lump-love. *See under* CUPBOARD LOVE.

lush. Meaning 'a drunk', this term seems to have originated in the US by the beginning of the nineteenth century, building on the English origins of a slang word for 'beer'. In the eighteenth century, there was a London actors' drinking club called 'The City of Lushington'. There may also have been a London brewer called Lushington, and Dr Thomas Lushington (*d* 1661), chaplain to Bishop Corbet, was a noted tippler.

> The first long step in crime taken by the half-grown boy ... is usually to rob a 'lush', i.e. a drunken man who has strayed his way.
> J.A. Riis, *How the Other Half Lives* (1890)

luvvies. Actors, particularly British ones, from their tendency to call each other 'love'. The term was coined in the late 1980s to describe the sizeable branch of the theatrical profession who kiss at every opportunity and perhaps are a little uncritical in their attitude to each other. The comic actor John Sessions is sometimes credited with the coinage. *Private Eye* magazine has run a column devoted to 'gems from the acting profession' since 1991.

> The Trotskyist lobbyists outside the TUC conference, of whom it was complained that they preferred to chant slogans through megaphones rather than reason with the delegates – wonderful, luvvies, terrific vintage feeling, somewhere between Eisenstein and Façade.
> *Guardian* (9 September 1989)

Kenneth Branagh's *Peter's Friends*: The witty script by Rita Rudner and Martin Bergman had me rolling in the aisles, while the luvvies in the cast played together perfectly.
Herald (Glasgow) (26 December 1992)

Compared to mincing luvvies and temperamental musos, there is something reassuringly solid about sculptors.
Scotland on Sunday (2 July 1995)

lynch mob.   A group of people administering summary justice by execution. There are several candidates for the origin of this name. Most likely is Colonel William Lynch (*d* 1820) of Pittsylvania County, Virginia, who certainly took the law into his own hands, formed a vigilante band and devised what became known as the Lynch Laws. However, as Tom Burnam, *More Misinformation* (1980) points out, even the Colonel did not really behave in the way 'to lynch' came to mean. There was also an old English word *linch*, meaning punishment by whipping or flogging, and this was sometimes imposed by the 'Lynch' courts of Virginia. The verb was in use by 1836.

M

McCoy.   *See* REAL ...

MacGuffin (or **McGuffin**).   This was the name given by the film director Alfred Hitchcock to the distracting device, the red herring, in a thriller upon which the whole plot appears to turn but which, in the end, has no real relevance to the plot or its solution. For example, the uranium in *Notorious* (1946) turns out to be less important than the notorious woman falling for the US agent.

mac(k)intosh.   The original waterproof coat is named after Charles Macintosh (1766–1843) who patented it in 1823. He invented a method of binding together two layers of fabric with india rubber dissolved in naphtha. Later waterproof garments tended to be treated with silicone which allows air to permeate the fabric, making it more comfortable to wear. The word is now used loosely – with or without the 'k', or as 'mac' – to describe any raincoat.

mad as a hatter.   Utterly crazy. The Hatter in Lewis Carroll's *Alice's Adventures in Wonderland* (1865) is not described as the *Mad* Hatter, though he is undoubtedly potty. His behaviour encapsulates a once-popular belief that people working as hat-makers could suffer brain damage by inhaling the nitrate of mercury used to treat felt. In fact, Carroll may not have been thinking of a hatter at all but rather of a certain Theophilus Carter, a furniture dealer of Oxford, who was notable for the top hat he wore, was also a bit potty and known as the Mad Hatter. And it is the March Hare who is marginally more mad (after the much older expression **mad as a march hare** – known by 1529).

Another suggested derivation is from the Anglo-Saxon word *atter*, meaning poison (and closely related to the adder, the British snake whose bite can cause fever). The phrase 'mad as a hatter' is not recorded before 1837. On the other hand, by 1609, there was a phrase 'mad as a weaver' which takes us back to the peculiarity of specific tradespeople.

madeleine.   A small fancy sponge cake, which in the first volume of *A La Recherche du Temps Perdu* by Marcel Proust triggers off memories of youth. In *Du Côté de Chez Swann* (1913), the author/narrator is reminded of the taste of a little crumb of madeleine which 'on Sunday mornings at Combray' his Aunt Leonie used to give him: 'Dipping it first in her own cup of real or of lime-flower tea'. The name may come from Madeleine Paulmier, a nineteenth-century French pastry cook.

Mae West.   The nickname for an inflatable life-jacket issued to the services in the Second World War, it gets its name from the curvaceous American film star, Mae West. It was in use by May 1940.

make a beeline for, to.   Meaning 'to go directly', from the supposition that bees fly in a straight line back to the hive. Possibly American in origin; known by 1849.

make a leg.   A 'leg' is defined by the *OED2* as 'an obeisance made by drawing back one leg and bending the other; a bow, scrape'.

It has it by 1589. Hence, 'to make a leg' means to make such a gesture, literally or figuratively. Making a leg to the reader (*see* citation below) is an indication of respect or request for the indulgence of that person.

Brewer (14th edition) quotes: 'The pursuivant smiled at their simplicitye. And making many leggs, tooke their rewards' from Percy's *Reliques* (The King and the Miller of Mansfield, Pt II, 1765).

> Not the least hint of the Round Table is detectable in the stories – no sassy showing off, no making a leg at the reader.
> Brendan Gill, Introduction to *The Collected Dorothy Parker* (1973)

make a u-turn, to.   The word 'u-turn' was probably first used in the US (by 1937) to describe the turn a motor car makes when the driver wishes to proceed in the opposite direction to the one he has been travelling in. The political use of the term to denote a reversal of policy was established in the US by 1961. In British politics, it was in use by the time of the Heath government (1970–4).

make no bones about, to.   Meaning 'to get straight to the point; not to conceal anything', the expression refers either to drinking a bowl of soup in which there are no bones, which is easy to swallow and there is nothing to complain about; or, from 'bones' meaning 'dice'. Here 'making no bones' means not making much of, and not attempting to coax the dice in order to show favour. Known by 1459.

make-do and mend.   Popularized during the Second World War, when there were Make-do-and-Mend departments in some stores, this phrase was designed to encourage thrift and the repairing of old garments, furniture, etc., rather than expenditure of scarce resources on making new. It was possibly derived from 'make and mend' which was a Royal Navy term for an afternoon free from work and devoted to mending clothes.

——-making.   Adjectival suffix, as in 'shy-making' and 'sick-making'. Partridge/*Slang* states that Evelyn Waugh 'fathered' this device and that it 'raged in 1930–3'. Certainly, Waugh's *Vile Bodies* (1930) has it. Note also in a cartoon about the Bright Young Things:

'Dear child, too totally toshmaking.'
Caption, *Punch* (23 April 1930)

male chauvinist (pig) (or **MCP**). This phrase for a man who is
sunk in masculine preoccupations and attitudes erupted in 1970 at
the time of the launch of the women's movement in the US and
elsewhere. The optional use of 'pig' was a reversion to the traditional,
fat, porky use of the word after the recent slang borrowing to
describe the police (mostly in the US).

Male chauvinism was a phrase in the 1950s. **Chauvinism** itself
is a venerable coinage and originally referred to excessive patriotism.
Nicolas Chauvin was a French general during Napoleon's campaigns
who became famous for his excessive devotion to his leader.

This has been a good lesson to all concerned that male chauvinism is
un-American to the core.
S.J. Perelman, 'Hell Hath No Fury . . . And Saks No Brake' (1951)

Hello, you male-chauvinist racist pig.
New Yorker (5 September 1970)

man in a grey/dark suit. A colourless administrator or technocrat
who is probably as grey in his personality as in the colour of his
suit. When The Beatles set up the Apple organization in the 1960s,
John Lennon said this was an attempt 'to wrest control from the
men in suits'. Sometimes such people are simply called 'suits'.

The **men in grey suits** are, however, something a little different.
In the November 1990 politicking which saw the British Prime
Minister Margaret Thatcher eased out of office by her own party,
there was much talk of the 'men in (grey) suits', those senior members
of the Tory party who would advise Mrs Thatcher when it was time
for her to go. Here, although still referring to faceless administrative
types, the term is not quite so pejorative. In the *Observer* (1 December
1990), Alan Watkins adjusted the phrase slightly: 'I claim the paternity
of "the men in suits" from an *Observer* column of the mid-1980s.
Not you may notice, the men in dark suits, still less those in grey
ones, which give quite the wrong idea.'

With this latest career move can we expect to see the wunderkind [John
Birt] transformed into the proverbial Man In A Grey Suit?
Broadcast Magazine (1987)

[John] Major's spectacular ordinariness – the Treasury is now led by a 'man in a suit' whose most distinguishing feature is his spectacles.
Observer (29 October 1989)

man on the Clapham omnibus.   The ordinary or average person, the man in the street, particularly when his/her point of view is instanced by the courts, newspaper editorials, etc. This person was first evoked in 1903 by Lord Bowen when hearing a case of negligence: 'We must ask ourselves what the man on the Clapham omnibus would think.'

Quite why he singled out that particular route we shall never know. It sounds suitably prosaic, of course, and the present 77A to Clapham Junction (1995) does pass though Whitehall and Westminster, thus providing a link between governors and governed.

There is evidence to suggest that the 'Clapham omnibus' in itself had already become a figure of speech by the mid-nineteenth century. In 1857, there was talk of the 'occupant of the knife-board of a Clapham omnibus'.

mankind.   *See* FOR ALL ...

Mappa Mundi.   This is the name given specifically to the primitive world map, dating from *c*.1300, which is to be found in Hereford Cathedral, but a 'mappamonde' was a normal medieval term for one of these (it occurs in Chaucer *c*.1380). The Latin means 'map of the world', although '*mappa*' also means 'napkin, cloth' (upon which the map was drawn). Compare the modern *mappamondo*, the modern Italian word for 'globe'.

march.   *See* STEAL A ...

march hare.   *See under* MAD AS A HATTER.

Marie of Romania.   *See* I AM ...

Marines.   *See* TELL IT TO THE ...

marmalade.   In Europe, this is still a word used for jams in general, though in Britain it has for a long time been applied to a preserve made of orange, lemon or grapefruit. *Marmelo* is the Portuguese word for quince: quince jam is '*marmelada*', '*marmelade*' is the French form. As the word has been known since at least 1480, the theory that it derives from the favourite food of Mary Queen of Scots (*b* 1542) when she was ill – '*Marie Malade*' – is clearly mistaken.

martinet. A strict person. Jean Martinet (*d* 1672) was a French colonel, general or even marquis, who served under Louis XIV and helped remodel the king's army. He was known as an especially severe, almost fanatical disciplinarian, relying heavily upon drill and punishment using a whip (which also became known as a martinet). Acquired the more general meaning in the early nineteenth century.

> Martinet dowagers and venerable beaux acted as masters and mistresses of ceremonies.
>
> Lord Cockburn, *Memoirs* (1821–30)

martini. There has been a firm, Martini and Rossi, makers of Italian vermouth since 1894, but the origin of the term 'dry martini' may have nothing to do with the firm (even though it can, of course, be made with Martini). The 'dry martini' is said to have been invented by Martini di Armi di Taggia, head bartender at the Knickerbocker Hotel, New York City, *c.*1910. He stipulated one third vermouth, two thirds dry gin. However, Stuart Berg Flexner in *Listening to America* (1982) finds that people were drinking something called a *martinez* in the US in the 1860s (half gin, half dry vermouth).

martyr to be smarter. *See under* FASHION VICTIM.

masochism. Sexual activity in which gratification is derived from humiliation and pain inflicted by oneself or by other people. The term takes its name from Leopold von Sacher-Masoch (1835–95), an Austrian novelist, who submitted to various women who gratified his wishes in this way, and ended up in an asylum. The German psychiatrist Krafft-Ebing coined the word to describe the condition. More recently, the meaning of the word has been broadened beyond the primarily sexual to include more general forms of enjoying humiliation.

masterpiece. A work of acknowledged greatness in any of the arts. Originally, however, it had a specific meaning, not necessarily in relation to the visual arts. At the end of his apprenticeship or training, a craftsman would produce a work to mark his transition to being a 'master' of his guild. Dutch originally and known by 1579; the more general sense by the following century.

maven (or **mavin**).   An expert, connoisseur or enthusiast. A Hebrew word (from *mevin* = understanding) which has entered US slang but which resolutely contrives not to catch on in British English. Someone who is sufficiently mad enough about word and phrase origins to write a book about them might well be termed a 'word maven'. Known by the 1960s in general American English.

> Whitney was dubbed 'Aga John' by All-American football player and society maven Shipwreck Kelly.
> Christopher Ogden, *Life of the Party* (1994)

maverick.   Meaning 'an individualist, an unorthodox independent-minded person', the word derives from Samuel A. Maverick (1803–70), a Texas cattle-owner who left the calves of his herd unbranded because he said the practice was cruel. It also enabled him to claim any unbranded calves he found on the range. In the 1880s, the word came to be used in politics and more generally, describing someone who would not affiliate with a particular party or cause.

mea culpa.   An expression of self-acceptance of fault or blame, and thus repentance. From the Latin phrase meaning 'through my own fault' which occurs in the confession from the Latin church liturgy. Then more widely used to admit 'I'm to blame'. Known by 1374 (Chaucer).

> *Mea culpa* ... We all do stupid things sometimes.
> D. Shannon, *Crime File* (1975)

> His sermon was peppered with mea culpas and apologies about how much he was to blame for their breakup.
> Christopher Ogden, *Life of the Party* (1994)

medallion man.   A man who, conscious that he is getting older and entering middle age, dresses in a consciously vulgar manner. This may include the wearing of gold medallions with open-neck shirts, hairy chests and tight pants. A species first identified in the 1970s when the pattern for such behaviour was given by the then young John Travolta in the film *Saturday Night Fever* (US, 1978).

Singer Tom Jones ... remains a macho sex symbol after 25 years, but now feels his Medallion Man image can be an embarrassment.
The Times (13 March 1991)

Melba toast.   *See under* PEACH MELBA.

melting pot.   Where something is scrapped and a new beginning made or where ideas are going to be put into an imaginary 'pool' and mixed together. From the image of the process of making things from metals that have been melted down. 'The jackboot is thrown into the melting-pot' is cited by George Orwell in 'Politics and the English Language' (*Horizon*, April 1946) as a metaphor where the images clash. Known by 1887 in the non-literal sense.

In a figurative sense, the image of a melting pot has been used to describe the United States where members of different races and many nationalities have been blended together to form a new society.

America is God's Crucible, the great Melting-Pot where all the races of Europe are melting and re-forming!
Israel Zangwill, *The Melting Pot*, Act I (1908)

He said the whole question would be thrown into the melting pot in an 'audit' of EU legislation which he secured as part of the Maastricht Treaty package.
Daily Mail (9 June 1994)

Many of today's artists ... have used the millennium as a metaphor for the post-nuclear, post-Aids culture in which politics, economics, sexual identity, and religion have been thrown up into a melting pot of uncertainties.
Guardian (8 April 1995)

mend.   *See* MAKE-DO AND ...

Menshevik.   *See under* BOLSHOI.

merde!   *See* MOT DE CAMBRONNE; *under* BREAK A LEG!

mesmerize, to.   Meaning 'to fascinate; act in a spellbinding way', the verb derives from Dr Franz or Friedrich Anton Mesmer (1734–1815), a German physician who practised a form of hypnotism in Vienna as a way of treating ailments. His theory of 'animal magnetism' was discredited in his lifetime but his reputation was rescued by a pupil who identified what Mesmer had done and gave it the name 'mesmerism'. Known in the original sense by 1829 and in the figurative by 1862.

Mexican wave. Stadium crowds have long entertained themselves (and observers) by rising up and down from their seats in an orderly sequence, thus giving the impression (when viewed from a distance) of a rippling wave or flag. The name 'Mexican wave' was given to the practice following much use of it during the football World Cup in Mexico in 1986. Until then it had been known as a 'human wave'.

Micawber. Meaning 'an incurable optimist', the word comes from the character Wilkins Micawber, in Charles Dickens's *David Copperfield* (1849), who lives a hand-to-mouth existence with his family but is always hoping that something will 'turn up'.

mickey. *See* TAKE THE . . .

Mickey Finn. Anything slipped into people's drinks in order to knock them out. *DOAS* claims that, to begin with, the term meant a laxative for horses. The original Mickey Finn may have been a notorious bartender in Chicago (*d* 1906) who proceeded to rob his unconscious victims. The word recorded by 1928.

Middle America. Originally a geographical expression (by 1898), this phrase was applied to the US conservative middle class in 1968 during Richard Nixon's campaign for the presidency. It corresponded to what he was later to call the Silent Majority and was what was alluded to in the expression 'It'll play in Peoria'. The expression is said to have been coined by the journalist Joseph Kraft.

middle of the road. The safe option, middle-brow taste (especially in music), the political centre, the middle way, moderate and unadventurous. Known since 1777 in the US, though not until the nineteenth century in a political sense. Known since 1958 in connection with music (where latterly it has been sometimes abbreviated to MOR).

> We know what happens to people who stay in the middle of the road. They get run over.
> Aneurin Bevan, quoted in the *Observer* (9 December 1953)

169

mid-life crisis. A crisis of confidence occurring especially in the middle-aged male. It may derive from his perception of the value of the work he does – or his waning sexuality – and may prompt him to try and change his behaviour and the course of his life. Apparently coined by E. Jaques in 'Death and the Mid-life Crisis' (1965), though Erik Erikson is also associated with the phrase.

> Jon Cousins is enjoying a spectacular mid-life crisis, shutting down his £12m-a-year advertising agency and taking a year off to travel the globe. *Daily Telegraph* (28 February 1996)

Compare **mid-career crisis**, a specifically work-related malaise. The phrase was used as the title of a book by John Hunt (1983).

> This feeling is contributing to what is being called 'mid-career crisis'. This used to take place when executives hit their fifties and realised there would be no more promotions. In the past decade it has been spotted in those nearing 40. Now it is starting to affect executives of 30. *Independent on Sunday* (28 May 1995)

milk of human kindness. Compassion. It appears to have originated in Shakespeare, *Macbeth*, I.v.16 (1606): 'Yet do I fear thy nature:/It is too full o'th' milk of human kindness/To catch the nearest way.'

mind one's ps and qs, to. Meaning 'to be careful, polite, on one's best behaviour', the phrase has several suggested origins: the letters 'p' and 'q' look so alike, a child might well be admonished to be careful writing them or a printer to take care in setting them; because a well-mannered person has to be careful to remember 'pleases and thankyous'; because in a public house 'pints' and 'quarts' would be chalked up on a blackboard for future payment; and, in the days of wigs, Frenchmen had to be warned not to get their *pieds* [feet] mixed up with their *queues* [wig-tails] when bowing and scraping. Recorded by 1779.

mind's eye. *See* IN THE . . .

minder. A bodyguard. There have been machine minders and baby minders for a long time but the special meaning with reference to the person who protects a criminal is not recorded before 1924. The sense became popular in British English when *Minder* was the title of an ITV series (from 1979) about just such a person in south London. In time the term came to be extended to include a person who was more of a 'personal assistant', smoothing the way for a politician, say, or on hand to rescue him from gaffes and difficult situations.

> Train drivers' leader Ray Buckton has joined the ranks of arrogant leaders who feel the need for a "minder" now that they are rich and famous.
> *Private Eye* (17 December 1982)

minutes. The written record of a meeting. This has nothing to do with the minutes of time that might pass during a meeting, though the term comes from the same Latin word *minutus*. No, in this context, the meaning is as in 'minute' (pronounced 'my newt'). The original minutes were taken down in minute or small writing so that they could be 'engrossed' or put into larger writing later.

moaning Minnie. Someone who complains. On 11 September 1985, the British Prime Minister Margaret Thatcher paid a visit to Tyneside and was reported as accusing those who complained about the effects of unemployment of being 'Moaning Minnies'. In the ensuing uproar, a Downing Street spokesman had to point out that it was the reporters attempting to question her, rather than the unemployed, on whom Mrs Thatcher had bestowed the title.

As a nickname, it was not an original alliterative coinage. A 'minnie' can mean a lost lamb which finds itself an adoptive mother. From the *Observer* (20 May 1989): 'Broadcasters are right to complain about the restrictions placed on them for the broadcasting of the House of Commons … But the Moaning Minnies have only themselves to blame.'

The original 'Moaning Minnie' was something quite different. In the First World War, a 'Minnie' was the slang name for a German *minenwerfer*, a trench mortar or the shell that came from it, making a distinctive moaning noise. In the Second World War, the name was also applied to air-raid sirens which were also that way inclined.

mod. The word 'mod' or 'Mod' had emerged by 1960 in Britain to denote tidy, clean-cut, slightly effete and clothes-conscious teenagers who rode around on motor-scooters. This was in contrast with the rougher, hairier Rockers with their leather jackets and motorbikes who had developed out of the 1950s Teddy Boys and rock'n'roll enthusiasts. The name 'mod' derives not so much from 'modern' as from 'modernist'.

mojo. *See* GOT YOUR . . .

mole. *See* INFILTRATE AS A . . .

Molotov cocktail. The incendiary device, similar to a petrol bomb, acquired its name in Finland during the early days of the Second World War and was known as such by 1940. V.M. Molotov had become Soviet Minister for Foreign Affairs in 1939. The Russians invaded Finland and these home-made grenades proved an effective way for the Finns to oppose their tanks.

moment of truth. Meaning, 'a decisive turning point; a significant moment', the phrase comes from '*el momento de la verdad*' in Spanish bullfighting – the final sword-thrust that kills the animal. *Il Momento della Verità* was the title of an Italian/Spanish film (1964) on a bullfighting theme. In *I, Claud* (1967), Claud Cockburn said of European intellectuals who had fought in the Spanish Civil War: 'They proclaimed, however briefly, that a moment comes when your actions have to bear some kind of relation to your words. This is what is called the Moment of Truth.' Not really known in English before Ernest Hemingway's *Death in the Afternoon* (1932).

> 'We have 50,000 moments of truth out there every day,' said Carlzon, defining a moment of truth as each time a customer came into contact with the company.
> *Financial Times* (15 September 1986)

monkey wrench. A spanner or wrench with an adjustable jaw – a notable tool that any engineer might possess. But why a *monkey* wrench? It is said that it was invented by Charles Moncke, a London blacksmith, or by a Mr Monk, who was an American (*c.*1856). Known as such by 1858.

monty. *See* FULL . . .

moola. Money, in US slang. Sometimes 'moolah' or 'moo'. For once, nobody has the slightest idea where this word comes from. An early use:

I never saw the day wherein no matter how much moola I had I could
not use some more.
John O'Hara, *Pal Joey* (1939)

moon.   *See* OVER THE . . .

moonshine.   Meaning 'illicit liquor', the word is of US origin where
it was used to describe whisky illegally *made* at night. Even before
this, however, the word had been used in England to denote brandy
illegally *smuggled* in by moonlight (known by 1785).

Morton's fork.   *See* APPLY . . .

mot de Cambronne.   Euphemism for the French expletive '*Merde!*'
[= shit!]. At the Battle of Waterloo in 1815 the commander of
Napoleon's Old or Imperial Guard is *supposed* to have declined a
British request for him to surrender with the words, '*La garde meurt
mais ne se rend jamais/pas* [The Guards die but never/do not surrender].'
However, it is quite likely that what he said, in fact, was, '*Merde! La
garde muert* . . . [Shit! The Guards die . . .]'
   The commander in question was Pierre Jacques Etienne, Count
Cambronne (1770–1842). At a banquet in 1835 Cambronne specifically denied saying the more polite version. That may have been
invented for him by Rougemont in a newspaper, *L'Indépendent.*
   In consequence of all this, *merde* is sometimes known in France
as *le mot de Cambronne*, a useful euphemism when needed. Un-
fortunately for Cambronne, the words he denied saying were put
on his statue in Nantes, his home town.

mother.   *See* JUST LIKE . . .

mould.   *See* BREAK THE . . .

mount a boycott, to.   'The lively Irish have invented a new word;
they are saying now to "boycott" someone, meaning to ostracize
him' – translated from *Le Figaro* (24 November 1880). Captain
Charles Boycott was an ex-British soldier who acted as an agent for
absentee landlords in Co. Mayo, Ireland, during the late nineteenth
century. He was extremely hard on the poor tenants and dispossessed
them if they fell behind with their rents. By way of retaliation, the
tenants isolated him and refused to have any dealings with him or

his family. They were encouraged in this by Charles Parnell of the Irish Land League who said that those who grabbed land from people evicted for non-payment of rent should be treated like 'the leper of old'. Eventually, the tenants brought about Boycott's own downfall by leaving his harvest to rot and he fled back to England where he died in 1897. Note that the verb 'to boycott' describes what was done *to* him rather than what was done *by* him.

mouth to God's ear. *See* FROM YOUR ...

Mr Clean. Originally the name of an American household cleanser, this is a fairly generally applied nickname. Among those to whom it has been applied are: Pat Boone (*b* 1934), the US pop singer and actor noted for his clean image and habits (he would never agree to kiss in films); John Lindsay (*b* 1921), Mayor of New York (1965–73); Elliot Richardson (*b* 1920), US Attorney-General who resigned in 1973 rather than agree to the restrictions President Nixon was then placing on investigations into the Watergate affair.

> The Secretary of State, James Baker, always regarded as Mr Clean among several highly-placed roguish officials in Ronald Reagan's administration ...
>
> *Independent* (15 February 1989)

Mrs Grundy. Meaning 'a censorious person; an upholder of conventional morality', the name comes from Thomas Morton's play *Speed the Plough* (1798) in which a character frequently asks: 'What will Mrs Grundy say?' Compare the later names of Mrs Ormiston Chaunt, an actual woman who campaigned in the late nineteenth century against immorality in the music-hall, and Mrs (Mary) Whitehouse who attempted to 'clean up' British TV from 1965 onwards.

ms. A woman of indeterminate marital status. 'Ms' (pronounced 'miz') is 'a title substituted for "Mrs" or "Miss" before a woman's name to avoid making a distinction between married and unmarried women,' according to the *Collins Dictionary of the English Language* (1979). Thus, it is a compromise (between 'Mrs' and 'Miss'), designed to solve a problem, and sounding every bit like the compromise it is.

'Ms' became popular with feminists in about 1970 at the start of the modern thrust by the women's movement. The New York

Commission on Human Rights adopted it for use in correspondence at about that time. By 1972, a feminist magazine called *Ms* was being launched.

The idea had been around for some time before it became – in the words of the *OED2* – 'an increasingly common, but not universally accepted, use.' This, from the early 1950s:

> Use the abbreviation Ms for *all women* addressees. This modern style solves an age-old problem.
>
> *The Simplified Letter* (National Office Management Association, Philadelphia) (4 January 1952)

mud. *See* NAME IS . . .

mugwump. A fool, but also with a precise political connotation. Originally, a *mugquomp* in the language of the Algonquin Indians described a great chief or person of high rank (and was so recorded by 1663). In 1884, however, the word was popularized and used to describe 'the little men attempting to be big chiefs' who felt unable to support James Blaine as the Republican candidate for the US Presidency and transferred their allegiance to the Democrat, Grover Cleveland. Hence, in American political parlance, a mugwump came to describe a 'bolter' or someone who held himself self-importantly aloof.

> A mugwump is a sort of bird that sits on a fence with his mug on one side and his wump on the other.
>
> *Blue Earth* (Minnesota) *Post* (early 1930s)

mum's the word. Meaning 'we are keeping silent on this matter'. No mother is invoked here: 'mum' is just a representation of 'Mmmm', the noise made when lips are sealed. The word 'mumble' obviously derives from the same source. Shakespeare has the idea in *Henry VI, Part 2*, I.ii.89 (1590): 'Seal up your lips and give no words but mum.' *See also* CRY MUM.

Murphy's Law. This saying (indistinguishable from **Sod's Law** and the less commonly heard **Spode's Law**), dates back to the 1940s. In other words, **if anything can go wrong, it will**. The *Macquarie Dictionary* (1981) suggests that it was named after a character who always made mistakes, in a series of educational cartoons published by the US Navy.

The *Concise Oxford Dictionary of Proverbs* (1982) suggests that it was invented by George Nichols, a project manager for Northrop, the Californian aviation firm, in 1949. He developed the idea from a remark made by a colleague, Captain Edward A. Murphy Jnr of the Wright Field-Aircraft Laboratory, 'If there is a wrong way to do something, then someone will do it.'

Some have argued that the point of Captain Murphy's original observation was constructive rather than defeatist – it was a prescription for avoiding mistakes in the design of a valve for an aircraft's hydraulic system. If the valve could be fitted in more than one way, then sooner or later someone would fit it the wrong way. The idea was to design it so that the valve could only be fitted the right way.

Allusions have included the film titles *Murphy's Law* (US, 1986) and *Murphy's War* (UK, 1971).

mustard. *See* CUT THE . . .; KEEN AS . . .

my name is legion. 'We/they are many, innumerable.' What the untamed 'man with an unclean spirit' speaking to Jesus in Mark 5: 9 actually says is, 'My name is Legion: for we are many'. Jesus has said, 'Come out of the man, thou unclean spirit' and asked, 'What is thy name?' And this is the answer given. After Jesus expels the devils from the man, he puts them into a herd of swine which jump into the sea. The man is then referred to as 'him that was possessed with the devil, and had the legion'.

—'s my name/—'s my game. Rhyming phrase of assertion and identification. Probably since the Second World War – US services' slang.

Aardvark's my name, and navigation is my game.
Joseph Heller, *Catch-22* (1961)

N

naff. 'In poor taste; unfashionable; bad' – and largely restricted to British use. This word had a sudden vogue in 1982. Attempts have been made to derive it from 'fanny' in back-slang, from the acronym NAAFI, and from the French '*rien à faire*', none very convincingly. In the BBC radio series *Round The Horne*, the word 'naph' (as it was spelt in the scripts) enjoyed another revival as part of camp slang. From the edition of 30 April 1967: 'Don't talk to us about Malaga!' – 'Naph, is it?' – 'He's got the palare off, hasn't he?' – 'I should say it is naph, treashette. Jule had a nasty experience in Malaga ...'

Also used as a euphemistic expletive. Keith Waterhouse used the participle 'naffing' in his novel *Billy Liar* (1959), remembering it from his service in the RAF (*c.*1950). That novel also includes the 'naff off!' expletive (echoic of 'eff off!') which was once used notably by Princess Anne to press photographers at the Badminton horse trials (April 1982).

naked truth. This was the title of a film (UK, 1957) and as a phrase for 'the absolute truth', it comes from an old fable which tells how Truth and Falsehood went swimming and Falsehood stole the clothes that Truth had left upon the river bank. Truth declined to wear Falsehood's clothes and went naked. Known in English by 1600; in Latin, as in the works of Horace, the phrase is '*nudas veritas*'.

namby-pamby. Meaning 'insipid; wishy-washy; soft', the phrase derives from Ambrose Philips (*d* 1749), a writer and politician whom the dramatist Henry Carey ridiculed with this nickname (in 1726) after Philips had written some insipid verses for children.

name. *See* CRAZY ...; —'S MY ...

name is mud, one's. This exclamation might be uttered as an acknowledgement that one has made a mistake and is held in low esteem. When John Wilkes Booth was escaping from the Washington DC theatre in which he had just assassinated President Lincoln in 1865, he fell and broke his leg. A country doctor called Dr Samuel Mudd tended Booth's wound without realizing the circumstances in which it had been received. When he did realize, he informed the authorities, was charged with being a co-conspirator, and sentenced to life imprisonment.

As the *Morris Dictionary of Word and Phrase Origins* (1977) points out, however, 'mud' in the sense of scandalous and defamatory charges, goes back to a time well before the American Civil War. There had been an expression 'the mud press' to describe mud-slinging newspapers in the US before 1846, so it seems most likely that the expression was well established before Dr Mudd met his unhappy fate. Indeed, *OED2* has an 1823 citation from 'Jon Bee' in *Slang* for 'And his name is mud!' as an ejaculation at the end of a silly oration, and also by then from *A Dictionary of the Turf* as a name for a stupid fellow.

> The younger Mosley, a very honourable man, found it hard to cope with the fact that his father's name was mud in polite society.
> *Daily Mail* (3 February 1996)

names.   *See* NO . . ., NO PACKDRILL.

Naples.   *See* SEE . . .

narmean?   *See under* KNOW WHAT I MEAN?

need something like a hole in the head, to.   Meaning 'not to need something at all'. Leo Rosten in *Hooray for Yiddish* (1982) describes this phrase as 'accepted from Alaska to the Hebrides' and states that it comes directly from the Yiddish *lock in kop*: 'It was propelled into our vernacular by the play *A Hole in the Head* (1957) by Arnold Schulman and more forcibly impressed upon mass consciousness by the Frank Sinatra movie (1959).' *OED2* finds it by 1951.

neither fish, flesh/fowl, nor good red herring.   Meaning 'neither one thing nor another; suitable to no class of people', the phrase sometimes occurs in the form: 'neither fish, flesh, nor fowl', where the origin of the expression (which dates from the Middle Ages) is that whatever is under discussion is unsuitable food for a monk (fish), for people generally (flesh), or for the poor (red, smoked, herring). Known by 1682.

Compare RED HERRING.

Nelson touch. Denoting any action bearing the hall mark of Horatio Nelson, his quality of leadership and seamanship, this term was coined by Nelson himself before the Battle of Trafalgar (1805): 'I am anxious to join the fleet, for it would add to my grief if any other man was to give them the Nelson touch.' The *Oxford Companion to Ships and the Sea* (1976) describes various manoeuvres to which the term could be applied, but adds, also: 'It could have meant the magic of his name among officers and seamen of his fleet, which was always enough to inspire them to great deeds of heroism and endurance.' The British title of the film *Corvette K-225* (US, 1943) was *The Nelson Touch*.

nerd. A boring stupid person (sometimes **nurd**, perhaps alluding to 'turd'). This US slang expression became popular in the 1970s, became part of Valspeak (see VALLEY GIRL) in the early 1980s, but had been around since the 1950s (for example in a Dr Seuss children's book). *The Nerd* was the title of a play (1986) by Larry Shue and similarly, a US 'college hi-jinks' film, *The Revenge of the Nerds* (1984).

netty. Lavatory, privy. This term to be heard in certain parts of northern Britain and recorded in the *English Dialect Dictionary* (1898) – is short for *gabinetti*, the Italian word for closets, small rooms, lavatories. Presumably, it must have been picked up from Italian immigrants at some stage.

Compare the equally cosy Australian term **dunny**, for an outside lavatory. This, however, comes from the same root as 'dung', via 'dunnakin', eighteenth-century English slang.

news. The word meaning 'tidings' is the plural of 'new', and not an acronym of the four main points of the compass, as has sometimes been proposed. Nowadays, the word is singular, but Shakespeare's *King Henry VI, Part 2*, III.ii.378 (1590–1) has: 'Ay me! What is this world! What news are these!' Queen Victoria, in an 1865 letter reacting to the assassination of President Lincoln, wrote: 'These

American news are most dreadful and awful! One never heard of such a thing! I only hope it will not be catching elsewhere.'

newt. *See* PISSED AS A . . .

nibs. *See under* NOB.

nil carborundum. *See* ILLEGITIMI NON . . .

nimby. Word from the acronym NIMBY, meaning 'not in my back yard' and used to describe people who object to having unpleasant developments near their homes but, by implication, don't mind them being sited elsewhere. In 1988, the British Environment Secretary, Nicholas Ridley, was so named when he objected to housing developments near his own home when he had previously criticized people who took this attitude. In fact, 'NIMBY' was an American coinage *c.*1980, for people who objected to the siting of something like a nuclear waste dumping site or a sewage treatment plant.

Trendy diners turn NIMBY over New York drugs clinic.
Headline, *Guardian* (12 November 1991)

nine days' wonder. Referring to something of short-lived appeal and soon forgotten, the expression comes from an old proverb: 'A wonder lasts nine days, and then the puppy's eyes are open' – alluding to the fact that dogs (like cats) are born blind. After nine days, in other words, their eyes are open to see clearly. The saying was known in this form by 1594.

Another etymologist finds a link with the old religious practice of selling indulgences, one of which – guaranteeing the purchaser nine days' worth of prayers – was called a *novem*. The indulgence was held to be a bit suspect – rather like this explanation.

Chaucer expressed the old proverb thus: 'For wonder last but nine night never in town.' Surely, we need look no further for the origin of an expression of which the truth is self-evident: wonder dies in time.

Incidentally, there is an Italian proverb: 'No wonder can last more than *three* days.'

nine lives. *See* CAT HAS . . .

nine points of the law. *See* POSSESSION IS . . .

nine yards. *See* WHOLE . . .

nines. *See* DRESSED UP TO THE . . .

nineteen to the dozen. *See* TALK . . .

nipple count. This phrase came into use in the 1970s when the *Sun* and other British newspapers began a 'war' in which the number of pin-ups' nipples shown per issue was of importance (compare 'body count' in the Vietnam War). The American drive-in movie critic, Joe Bob Briggs, who wrote for the *Dallas Times Herald* in the 1980s, literally counted the *breasts* he saw and rated the films accordingly. He did not actually use this phrase, however.

nitty-gritty. *See* LET'S GET DOWN TO THE . . .

no comment. This useful phrase, when people in the news are being hounded by journalists, has not quite been condemned as a cliché. After all, why should people in such a position be required to find something original to say? Nevertheless, it has come to be used as a consciously inadequate form of evasion, often in an obviously jokey way (compare 'We are just good friends'). Perhaps it arose initially by way of reaction to the ferretings of Hollywood gossip columnists in the 1920s and 30s, though perhaps it was simply a general reaction to the rise of the popular press in the first half of the century.

Winston Churchill appears not to have known it until 1946, so perhaps it was not generally known until then, at least not outside the US. After a meeting with President Truman, Churchill said, 'I think "No Comment" is a splendid expression. I got it from Sumner Welles.' Also in 1946, critic C.A. Lejeune's entire review of the US film *No Leave, No Love* was 'No comment.'

> Mr [Norman] Willis [TUC General Secretary at book award ceremony] is not going to rock the boat by descending to literary chat. 'No comment,' he says vigorously when asked if he has read any of the short-listed books.
> *Guardian* (25 January 1989)

no names, no packdrill.   Meaning that the speaker is not going to betray any confidences by mentioning names. Somehow this alludes to a one-time British army punishment when soldiers were made to march up and down carrying a heavy pack – a very physical punishment for use in the field where fines or confinement to barracks would be meaningless or impossible. It is probably a short form of saying, 'As long as I don't give away any names, I won't get punished for it – that's why I am not telling you.' Recorded by 1923.

Paul Beale gave this even lengthier paraphrase (1988): 'I will tell you this discreditable story, because it is a good story and shows the criminal ingenuity, or at least low cunning, of some people I know. But I won't tell you their names (even though you might guess who they are) because I don't want *them* to get into trouble – after all they are my mates, my muckers, and I'm only telling you so that you can admire their cleverness: it's all "off the record".' Beale added: 'Only secondarily was there any implication of "*I* don't want to get punished", except in as far as "the mates" might round on an informant. It's really an expression of the old army muckers-stick-together, and to hell with anyone of any rank higher than private/trooper/gunner/sapper or effing fusilier.'

no room to swing a cat.   Description of a confined space. As is well known, the 'cat' was the name given on old sailing vessels to a whip used in discipline. It left scars on the back reminiscent of a cat's scratches. A sailor condemned to be so punished had to be taken up on deck because below deck there literally was no room to swing the whip. Some still believe, however, that the expression merely refers to the amount of space in which you could swing an actual cat around by its tail. This may in fact be the true original. Known by 1665.

nob.   A grand person. Thought once to be a contraction of 'nobleman', but a number of other formations cast doubt on this. One theory is that it is simply short for *nabob* (from the Hindustani *navah* or *nawab*) which described a governor or ruler of a district under the old Mogul regime in India. Subsequently, the word was applied to Britons (and others) who had been to India and acquired great wealth.

Consequently, in San Francisco, many of the merchants who had made their fortunes by trading with the Far East lived in splendour in an area called Nabob Hill. This is now known as Nob Hill.

References to **his nibs** (someone grander than yourself) probably derive from the same source.

Nobby. The inevitable nickname for someone with the surname 'Clark'. A version of NOB and perhaps here more of a contraction of 'noble'. A clerk was originally a learned person and to be respected as though he were a member of the nobility. Also, in the City of London, clerks wore top hats – the sign more usually of nobility.

Nora. *See* FLAMING ...

nose. *See* PAY THROUGH THE ...; POWDER ONE'S ...

nosy parker. Meaning 'an interfering, inquisitive person', from the fact that the nose has long been associated with an inquisitive nature. Traditionally, a link has been suggested with Matthew Parker, Elizabeth I's Archbishop of Canterbury. But Partridge/*Slang* wonders whether the word 'parker', meaning 'park-keeper', might also have described someone who enjoyed spying on love-making couples in London's Hyde Park. Not found before 1907, however.

not by a long chalk. Meaning 'not by any means', this probably refers to the method of making chalk marks on the floor to show the score of a player or team. A 'long chalk' would mean a lot of points, a great deal. Other explanations refer specifically to keeping the score at darts and to the tally of beers drunk in a public house. Originally, the expression may have been 'by long chalks'. Known by 1835.

nth degree. *See* TO THE ...

number. *See* GET SOMEONE'S ...

Number 1, London. The legendary address of the 1st Duke of Wellington when he resided in Apsley House near Hyde Park Corner. From E.V. Lucas, *A Wanderer in London* (1906; 1926 ed.): 'No. 1 London enjoys its priority only I think in verbal tradition. To the postman such an address might mean nothing . . . The official address of Apsley House is, I fancy, 149 Piccadilly.'

O

oar. *See* GET ONE'S . . .

oats. *See* FEEL ONE'S . . .; SOW ONE'S WILD . . .

ODTAA. *See* LIFE IS ONE DAMN(ED) THING AFTER ANOTHER.

OK! The origin of this expression has occasioned more debate than any other in this dictionary. Here are some of the suggested origins, though one probably need go no further than explanations (1) and (2).

(1) President Andrew Jackson (*d* 1837), when a court clerk in Tennessee, would mark 'OK' on legal documents as an abbreviation for the illiterate 'Oll Korrect'. The first recorded use in the US of this jocular form is in the Boston *Morning Post* (23 March 1839).

(2) It was used by President Martin van Buren as an election slogan in 1840. The initials stood for 'Old Kinderhook', his nickname, which derived from his birthplace in New York State.

(3) Inspectors who weighed and graded bales of cotton as they were delivered to Mississippi river ports for shipment would write *aux quais* on any found faulty (i.e. this meant they were not OK and had to be sent back to the jetty).

(4) It comes from Aux Cayes, a port in Haiti famous for its rum.

(5) It is an anglicization of the word for 'good' in Ewe or Wolof, the West African language spoken by many of the slaves taken to the Southern US.

(6) It derives from the Greek words *ola kala* meaning 'all is fine; everything is good'.

(7) In the First World War, soldiers would report each night the number of deaths in their group. 'OK' stood for '0 killed'.

(8) A railroad freight agent, Obadiah Kelly, used his initials on bills of lading.

(9) An Indian chief, Old Keokuk, used his initials on treaties.

(10) It stood for 'outer keel' when shipbuilders chalked it on timbers.

(11) Teachers used it instead of *omnes korrectes* on perfect exam papers.

(12) From boxes of Orrins-Kendall crackers, popular with Union troops in the Civil War.

(13) From an English word 'hoacky', meaning 'the last load of a harvest'.

(14) From a Finnish word *oikea* meaning 'correct'.

(15) From a Choctaw word *okeh* [it is] or *hoke*.

Old Bill.   A nickname for the police (and, in particular, the Metropolitan Police of London), known by 1939. So many policemen wore walrus moustaches after the First World War that they reminded people of Bruce Bairnsfather's cartoon character 'Old Bill'. He was the one who said: 'If you know a better 'ole – go to it'. Partridge/ *Slang*, which provides this explanation, also wonders whether there might be some connection with the US song 'Won't You Come Home, Bill Bailey' (*c*.1902) or with the Old Bailey courts. **The Bill** is an abbreviation of the name and was used as the title of an ITV cops series (from *c*.1990).

old boy net(work).   British term for the informal system of support given to one another by men who once attended the same school. Not recorded before the 1950s but said to have been known in the Second World War, where the 'old boy *net*' referred to use of the wireless 'net' to organize military support from old friends and colleagues. Here the meaning of 'old boy' seems to move away from that of 'former schoolboy' to anyone you might address using the words, 'I say, old boy . . .'

From Claud Cockburn, *In Time of Trouble* (1956): 'My father . . . knew quite enough about the working of what is nowadays called "The Old Boy Net" to realize that as things now stood he had considerably less chance of entering the Indian Civil Service than he did of entering the Church of England and becoming a Bishop.'

Old Contemptibles. This nickname was gladly taken unto themselves by First World War veterans of the British Expeditionary Force who crossed the English Channel in 1914 to join the French and Belgians against the German advance. It was alleged that Kaiser Wilhelm II had described the army as 'a contemptibly little army' (referring to its size rather than its quality). The British press was then said to have mistranslated this so that it made him appear to have called them a 'contemptible little army'. The truth is that the whole episode was a propaganda ploy masterminded by the British. Recorded use by 1916.

Old Man of the Sea. The name of a troublesome character in *Tales of the Arabian Nights* who climbed on the back of Sinbad the Sailor and was hard to dislodge, hence, the phrase for 'a burden'. The title of Ernest Hemingway's novel *The Old Man and the Sea* (1952; film US, 1958) presumably alludes lightly to him.

old Spanish customs. The phrase refers to practices which are of long standing but are unauthorized. Although the journal *Notes and Queries* was vainly seeking the origin of the phrase in 1932, the term came to prominence in the 1980s to describe the irregular behaviour of British newspaper production workers in Fleet Street (cheating over pay-packets, especially). The use seems mainly British, though this does not explain how Groucho Marx came to make the pun 'old Spinach customs' in *Animal Crackers* (1930).

Why the Spanish are blamed is not clear, except that Spaniards tend to attract pejoratives – not least with regard to working practices (the *mañana* attitude). In Elizabethan times, William Cecil is quoted as saying of Sir Thomas Tresham, architect of Rushton Triangular Lodge, that he was not given to **Spanish practices** (i.e. Roman Catholic ones). In 1584, also, Lord Walsingham referred to 'Spanish practices' in a way that meant they were 'deceitful, perfidious and treacherous'. This could provide us with an origin for the modern phrase. Indeed, latterly (late 1980s), the two have been used interchangeably in the newspaper context.

> Receiving visits ... when you are from Home, is not consisting with our Spanish Customs.
> William R. Chetwood, *The Voyages and Adventures of Captain Robert Boyle* (1724)

The biggest internal cost is production wages ... embroidered round with 'old Spanish customs', which was regarded as virtually outside management control.
Simon Jenkins, *Newspapers: The Power and the Money* (1979)

omelette Arnold Bennett. Not created *by* but *for* the novelist (1867–1931). It is an omelette of haddock, grated cheese and cream, put under the grill. Bennett was a great frequenter of the Savoy Hotel in London where the recipe was concocted. The hotel also features in a number of his novels.

OMOV. *See* ONE MAN, ONE VOTE.

on board. *See* TAKE SOMEONE'S IDEA(S) ...

on cloud nine (or **cloud seven**). Meaning 'in a euphoric state'. Both forms have existed since the 1950s. The derivation appears to be from terminology used by the US Weather Bureau. Cloud nine is the cumulonimbus which may reach 30–40,000 feet. The *Morris Dictionary of Word and Phrase Origins* (1977) notes, 'If one is upon cloud nine, one is high indeed,' and also records the reason for cloud nine being more memorable than cloud seven: 'The popularity ... may be credited to the *Johnny Dollar* radio show of the 1950s. There was one recurring episode ... Every time the hero was knocked unconscious – which was often – he was transported to cloud nine. There Johnny could start talking again.'

Nurse John McGuinness Shares Double Rollover Lottery Jackpot ... 'It still hasn't sunk in and I've been on cloud nine since the draw.'
Daily Mirror (29 January 1996)

Scotland's rugby centre Scott Hastings is on cloud nine after becoming a father for the second time. The newest arrival to the Hastings clan, Kerry Anne, was not expected until later in the week but she was born on Sunday night, weighing in at 7lb 2oz.
Herald (Glasgow) (7 February 1996)

on one's tod, to be. Meaning 'to be on one's own', this expression derives from rhyming slang: Tod Sloan was a noted US jockey (*d* 1933). The expression was recorded by 1934. In Australia, there is the equivalent **to be on one's Pat**, meaning to be on one's own, after a certain Pat Malone. Known by 1908.

once and future —. Format phrase, based on '*Hic jacet Arthurus, rex quondam rexque futurus* [Here lies Arthur, the once and future king]', which is what, according to Sir Thomas Malory in *Le Morte d'Arthur* (1469–70), was written on the tombstone of the legendary King Arthur (hence the title of T.H. White's Arthurian romance, *The Once and Future King*, 1958.) Now either used in a literal sense (see first citation) or to call up a vaguely mythical atmosphere. The phrase 'once and future king' also occasionally appears in description of Prince Charles, with the 'once and' used meaninglessly.

> Jack Russell who is (at least I hope he is) the once and future England wicketkeeper.
> *The Times* (8 May 1993)

> The image of PC Dixon endures. He is the once and future constable, mystical paradigm of community policing.
> *Guardian* (8 May 1993)

> While our once and future king witters about the perpetuation of Shakespeare as cultural heritage.
> *Guardian* (24 June 1993)

one damned thing after another. *See* LIFE IS ...

one man, one vote. A slogan first coined in the nineteenth century for a campaign led by Major John Cartwright (1740–1824), a radical MP ('the Father of Reform'), in the fight against plural voting. It was possible in those days for a man to cast two votes, one on the basis of residence and the other by virtue of business or university qualifications. This right was not abolished until 1948. The phrase arose again during the period of the (illegal) Unilateral Declaration of Independence in Rhodesia (1965–80) to indicate a basic condition required by the British government before the breakaway could be legitimized. The phrase has also been used in the US, in civil rights contexts.

In 1993, when the British Labour Party was trying to overthrow the 'block votes' that gave its trade union membership a disproportionate say in the formulation of policy, the phrase was rendered by the acronym **OMOV**.

one of *them*. Derogatory phrase for (usually) a homosexual. Known by the 1950s/60s.

one over the eight. This expression for 'drunk' is services' slang, but not before the twentieth century. For some reason, eight beers was considered to be a reasonable and safe amount for an average man to drink. One more and you were incapable.

open Pandora's box, to. To let loose a whole stream of difficult problems. In Greek mythology, Pandora – the first mortal woman – kept a box in which were sealed all the evils of the world. They escaped when she opened the box, with only hope remaining. Now, possibly the most used of surviving classical references.

> The favours of Government are like the box of Pandora, with this important difference, that they rarely leave hope at the bottom.
> J.E.T. Rogers, *Economic Interpretations of History* (1888)

> Every idea has tended to fall victim to political wrangling between idealists concerned exclusively for the architectural fabric of Venice, environmentalists worried that solving one problem can open up a Pandora's box of others, and trade unionists keen to protect jobs on the mainland.
> *Independent* (1 February 1996)

open sesame! Meaning, 'open up (the door)!' or as a mock password, the phrase comes from the tale of 'The Forty Thieves' in the ancient Oriental *Tales of the Arabian Nights*. When it was spoken, the robbers' door flew open.

Sesame seed is also famous for its other opening qualities, as a laxative.

> Genius was understood and poetry a sort of 'open Sesame' to every noble door.
> Mrs Oliphant, *Literary History of England* (1882)

order. *See* IN APPLE-PIE ...

Oscar. An Academy Award, one of a number of statuettes presented each year since 1928 by the American Academy of Motion Picture Arts and Sciences. The nickname originated in a comment made by Margaret Herrick, a secretary at the Academy (*c.*1931): 'Why, it looks just like my Uncle Oscar' (who was Oscar Pierce, a wheat and fruit grower).

out of kilter.   Awry, in a mess, out of condition. Known since 1628 in the US. Of unknown origin, although the word 'kilter' = 'order, condition' is an old one.

> Mr John Cox, director-general of the Chemical Industries Association, said that this perceived imbalance between the industry's value and its social costs is not only out of kilter but is also a threat to the industry's 'licence to operate'.
> *Financial Times* (4 February 1995)

> The popular mood and the political mood are out of kilter. None of Sweden's main political parties has publicly campaigned for an end to the monopoly.
> *Financial Times* (8 February 1995)

out of the frying pan into the fire.   Out of one bad situation and into another. Most languages have similar expressions for this predicament: the Italians have 'from the frying pan into the coals' and the ancient Greeks 'out of the smoke and into the flame'. Known in English by 1532 (Thomas More).

over.   *See* IT'S NOT . . .

over the moon.   In about 1978, two cliché expressions became notorious in Britain if one wished to express either pleasure or dismay at the outcome of anything, but especially of a football match. The speaker was either 'over the moon' or **sick as a parrot**.

It probably all began because of the remorseless post-game analysis by TV football commentators and the consequent need for players and managers to provide pithy comments. Liverpool footballer Phil Thompson said he felt 'sick as a parrot' after his team's defeat in the 1978 Football League Cup Final.

Ironically, *Private Eye* fuelled the cliché by constant mockery, to such an extent that by 1980 an 'instant' BBC Radio play about the European Cup Final (written on the spot by Neville Smith according to the outcome) was given the alternative titles *Over the Moon/Sick as a Parrot*.

Some failed to note the cliché. *The Times* (21 January 1982) reported the reaction of M. Albert Roux, the London restaurateur, on gaining three stars in the *Michelin Guide*: '"I am over the moon," M. Roux said yesterday . . . he quickly denied, however, that his brother [another celebrated restaurateur] would be "sick as a parrot".'

'Over the moon' is probably the older of the two phrases. Indeed, in the diaries of May, Lady Cavendish (published 1927) there is an entry for 7 February 1857 saying how she broke the news of her youngest brother's birth to the rest of her siblings: 'I had told the little ones who were first utterly incredulous and then over the moon.' The family of Catherine Gladstone (*née* Gwynne), wife of the Prime Minister, is said to have had its own idiomatic language and originated the phrase. However, the nursery rhyme 'Hey diddle diddle/The cat and the fiddle,/The cow jumped over the moon' dates back to 1765 at least and surely conveys the same meaning. Besides, the Rev. Sydney Smith was reported in 1833 as having said 'I could have jumped over the moon.'

The specific application to football was already in evidence in 1962, when Alf Ramsey (a team manager) was quoted as saying, on one occasion, 'I feel like jumping over the moon.'

over the top (or **OTT**).   Exaggerated in manner of performance; 'too much'. The expression 'to go over the top' originated in the trenches of the First World War. It was used to describe the method of charging over the parapet and out of the trenches on the attack.

In a curious transition, the phrase was later adopted for use by show business people when describing a performance that has gone beyond the bounds of restraint, possibly to the point of embarrassment. Also by other people, and known in a variety of contexts by 1968.

In 1982, a near-the-bone TV series reflected this by calling itself *OTT*. After which, you heard people saying that something was 'a bit OTT' instead of the full expression. On 15 February 1989, the *Independent* quoted from a play called *State of Play* at the Soho Poly theatre: 'Look at sport – I'm sure you'll agree:/It's much more fun when it's OTT.'

Oxbridge.   Pertaining to the two ancient (though not necessarily eldest) universities in Britain, Oxford and Cambridge. Since the 1950s this has been the main way of distinguishing from the newer so-called 'red brick' universities. In fact, the term had been coined before – along with the now redundant 'Camford' – in William Thackeray's novel *Pendennis* (1849): '"Rough and ready, your chum seems," the Major said. "Somewhat different from your dandy friends at Oxbridge"'; 'He was a Camford man and very nearly got the English Prize poem'. Here the intention seems merely to be imprecise over which particular old university is being described.

oysters. *See* DON'T EAT . . .

P

P. *See* CAN I HAVE A . . .

packdrill. *See* NO NAMES, NO . . .

paddle one's own canoe, to. To control one's own affairs. American origin – early nineteenth century. There was a poem with the phrase in *Harper's Magazine* (by Sarah Bolton) in May 1854 and an American 'proverb song' called 'Paddle Your Own Canoe' (*c.*1871) written by Harry Clifton:

Then love your neighbor as yourself,
As the world you travel through.
And never sit down with a tear or frown,
But paddle your own canoe.

Page Three girl. Meaning 'a topless photographic model', the allusion is specifically to the kind regularly featured on page three of the *Sun* newspaper, but can be broadly applied to any nude model. Larry Lamb, the editor, introduced the feature on 17 November 1970, exactly a year after the paper's acquisition by Rupert Murdoch, the Australian-born newspaper proprietor. Initially, the nudes were not known by this phrase, though they were indeed on page three.

pale. *See* BEYOND THE . . .

pan. *See* FLASH IN THE . . .

Pandora's box. *See* OPEN . . .

paparazzo. A photographer who snatches photographs of celebrities by hanging about – though not necessarily in trees like a parrot, for which this is the Italian. The surname was bestowed by Federico Fellini, the Italian film director (1920–93), on the character of such a sensation-seeking photographer in *La Dolce Vita* (1960). Normally found in the plural – *paparazzi* – as they tend to hunt in packs. An earlier use of the term is said to occur in a novel by George Gissing.

paper tiger. A person who appears outwardly strong but is, in fact, weak. The phrase was popularized by the Chinese leader, Mao Tse-tung, who told a US interviewer in 1946: 'All reactionaries are paper tigers. In appearance, the reactionaries are terrifying, but in reality they are not so powerful.' Taken from Mao's *Selected Works*, this is how the saying appears in his famous *Quotations* – the little red book brandished during the Cultural Revolution (1966–9). *Paper Tiger* was also the title of a film (UK, 1975) about a coward (David Niven) who pretended to be otherwise until he was finally put to the test.

Evidence that the saying pre-dates Mao is provided by Ernest Bramah's *Kai Lung Unrolls His Lat* (1928) in which he writes: 'Even a paper leopard can put a hornless sheep to flight', and as early as 1900 Bramah uses the precise expression in *The Wallet of Kai Lung*: 'If it is the wish of this illustriously-endowed gathering that this exceedingly illiterate paper tiger should occupy their august moments with a description of ... Chee Chou ...' Bramah was a lover of chinoiserie rather than an expert Sinologist, and must undoubtedly have come across the phrase in English or some other western language rather than in Chinese.'

park home. A mobile home, possibly given this euphemistic term because it spends most of its time 'parked' permanently and the speaker for some reason wishes to avoid the term 'caravan'. Known by the 1980s.

A decent park home with two or three bedrooms ... can be bought on site, already connected to mains water and sewers.
Observer (24 July 1988)

parkin. Cake made from oatmeal and molasses which is traditionally eaten on Bonfire Night (5 November). North of England origin? Known by 1800.

parky. Nippingly cold, as in 'It's a bit parky, isn't it?' Known by 1895. Some wonder whether it has something to do with 'park', i.e. the weather you might expect out of doors in a park. Partridge wonders about PARKIN cake which you would eat in such weather. No one knows for sure.

parrot. *See under* OVER THE MOON.

parrots and monkeys. Personal possessions, goods and chattels. Army use since the 1930s but probably originating with the pets that a seaman might bring back with him from abroad.

parting shot. An action or remark usually made dismissively as a last gesture (giving one's opponent no chance to respond). Originally, this was **Parthian shot**, so called from the ancient Parthian horsemen who would turn in flight and fire arrows at their pursuers.

> Bremond had to retire from the battle in good order, getting in a Parthian shot at me ... by begging Feisal to insist that the British armoured cars in Suez be sent down to Wejh. But even this was a boomerang since they had started!
> T.E. Lawrence, *Seven Pillars of Wisdom*, Chap. 18 (1926/35)

party pooper/poop. Someone who manages to spoil or put a damper on fun by their actions or behaviour. American slang originally and known since the mid-1940s.

> No one can call Mr Bulganin and Mr Khrushchev party poopers ... The Russian leaders demonstrated their suavity and cleverness at the party.
> Earl Wilson column (5 July 1956), cited in *DOAS*

pass the buck, to. Meaning 'to shift responsibility on to someone else', the phrase derives from some card games, where a marker called a 'buck' is put in front of the dealer to remind players who the dealer is. When it is someone else's turn, the 'buck' is 'passed'. The original marker may have been a buckthorn knife or, in the Old West, a silver dollar – hence the modern use of the word 'buck' for a dollar. Known by 1865.

passing show. Contemporary life seen as a procession, pageant or slowly moving public spectacle. A theatrical 'revue' of such events. Possibly American in origin.

A whole passing show ... Your friends grotesquely photographed.
Sear's Roebuck Catalogue (1908)

The Passing Show
Title of revue by Arthur Wimperis (1915)

past master. A person of acknowledged skill in some activity. From the term applied to a former master of a guild, company or freemasons' lodge. Known by 1868, though in the original sense by 1762.

Pat. *See under* ON ONE'S TOD.

pathetic fallacy. The attribution of human feelings to nature or, to put it another way, the belief that nature reflects human feelings when this belief is expressed, usually in literature. So, a thunderstorm may be represented as echoing some human drama played out beneath it. The phrase was coined by John Ruskin in his *Modern Painters*, Vol. 3 (1856): 'All violent feelings ... produce ... a falseness in ... impressions of external things, which I would generally characterize as the "Pathetic fallacy".'

pavlova. This dessert consisting of meringue, whipped cream and fruit (often strawberry), was created in the Antipodes (places and dates vary, but it was current in New Zealand by 1927) as a sort of compliment to Anna Pavlova, the Russian-born ballerina (*d* 1931). The concoction may resemble the spread-out skirts on a ballerina's tutu.

pay through the nose, to. Meaning 'to pay heavily', one possible explanation for the origin of the phrase lies in the 'nose' tax levied upon the Irish by the Danes in the ninth century. Those who did not pay had their noses slit. Known by 1672.

> Trackside advertising brings in tens of thousands of pounds a week. TV and radio pay through the nose to cover games live or in highlights packages.
> *Daily Record* (1 February 1995)

> A wide smile like Julia Roberts' is much sought after – and some people will pay through the nose for a set of gleaming teeth like hers.
> *Sunday Mirror* (26 March 1995)

payola. A term used in the 1950s to describe a bribe to persuade radio disc jockeys to play records. The idea goes back to the 1930s at least, to describe various forms of inducement in the record and music publishing business. The word is formed, clearly, from 'pay' as in 'pay-off' plus '-ola', a suffix familiar in the music business from such terms as 'pianola' and 'Victrola'.

Variants include 'plugola' (purchased plugging of specific records on radio) and 'royola' (extra royalties available for corrupt disc jockeys who plug certain records). 'Payola' has also progressed to refer to bribing outside the record and music businesses.

The word 'plug' in this context seems to derive from an association with trickery that began when counterfeit coins were 'plugged' or filled up with base metal.

peace dividend. A benefit bestowed by the cessation of hostilities – e.g. the fact that savings can be made by the withdrawal of troops and reduction of arms expenditure when an atmosphere of tension no longer obtains. The phrase was coined at the time of the collapse of communism in eastern Europe in 1989, which meant that, for example, the presence of American troops in western Europe was no longer necessary. The phrase was also applied to Northern Ireland during the IRA ceasefire (1994–6).

> There is only one obvious solution: the long-term diversion of funds from military to peaceful spending; the so-called 'peace dividend'.
> *Observer* (24 December 1989)

> He turned to an elegant blonde lady ... 'You must meet this man. He's the most important man in the Government. He's producing the peace dividend.'
> Alan Clark, *Diaries* (1993)

The idea may have been formulated, though not expressed in this phrase, at the end of the Vietnam War in the early 1970s.

Peach Melba. This dessert consists of peaches in vanilla-flavoured syrup on top of ice cream and coated with raspberry sauce. It was named after Dame Nellie Melba, the Australian opera singer, who was staying at the Savoy Hotel in London in 1892 when the chef, Auguste Escoffier, created this dessert for her. It was served as though between the wings of a swan – alluding to *Lohengrin*, in which she was appearing at Covent Garden. In 1897, Escoffier also invented **Melba toast** (made with extremely thin bread), though the name was applied by M.L. Ritz. (Melba was born Helen Mitchell. For her stage name she adapted a portion of Melbourne, her home town.)

pear-shaped. Out of control, chaotic. Because it is a collapse from the perfect sphere. Known by the mid-twentieth century.

Pecksniff. Seth Pecksniff is the hypocritical character in *Martin Chuzzlewit* (1843–4) by Charles Dickens. He is an oily man, 'fuller of virtuous precepts than a copybook', who behaves in a manner contrary to a 'moral man'. Hence the word **Pecksniffian** and other derivatives.

Peeping Tom. A voyeur of any kind. Derived from the name of Tom the Tailor who was struck blind because he peeped when Lady Godiva rode by. In the legend, Lady Godiva's husband, the Lord of Coventry, only agreed to abolish some harsh taxes if she would ride naked through the town. The townspeople responded to her request that they should stay behind closed doors – all except Peeping Tom. This element of the story was probably grafted on to the record of an actual happening of the eleventh century. Recorded use by 1796. *Peeping Tom* was the title of a film (UK, 1959), about a man who films his victims while murdering them.

peg. *See* TAKE DOWN A …

Peniel. Name given to chapels. In Hebrew, the name means 'the face of God' and commemorates the place where Jacob wrestled with an angel (Genesis 32:20) in order to receive a blessing.

penny has dropped. Realization has dawned. The implications of a situation have belatedly been understood. Known by the 1940s. From the workings of a slot machine in which it takes a certain amount of time for a coin to operate.

> The penny had begun to drop before the present fuel crisis.
> *The Times* (1 December 1973)

perestroika. Restructuring – one of the Russian words that passed into English during the final years of Soviet communism in the

1980s. President Leonid Brezhnev used the word in a speech to the 26th Party congress in April 1979, but Mikhail Gorbachev, who was to become President and Communist Party leader, introduced the concept in a speech to the 27th Party Congress in February/March 1986. He also published a book entitled *Perestroika* in 1987. The term came to be applied to other fundamental reforms, unconnected with Soviet communism.

> Perestroika in publishing takes many forms, but it did not take the form of Bell & Hyman 'buying' Allen & Unwin ... The two companies merged their publishing interests and became Unwin Hyman.
> *Publishing News* (23 October 1987)

> As Frank Field knows, you can't get perestroika overnight, particularly when your route to reform requires the assent of the very institutions which need reforming.
> *Guardian* (28 June 1990)

Perils of Pauline, The. Name given to a classic cinema serial (1914 onwards) in which Pearl White portrayed a girl, Pauline, who was always getting into hair-raising scrapes and getting rescued.

phooey. Expression of disbelief and rejection. Known by 1929 in the US, it was popularized in the 1930s by the American journalist and news broadcaster Walter Winchell. It probably derives from the Yiddish/German *pfui*.

photo opportunity. An 'event' prepared solely so that it will attract the media cameras and thus publicity for the subject of the photocall. Given the contrivance involved – it is a form of **pseudo-event** (*see* PSEUD) – it is surprising how the media invariably fall for it. Said to have been raised to an art form by Ronald Reagan's advisers when he was US President.

> Heseltine visits ... tend to be one long photo-opportunity ... Whatever the occasion you could be sure it would produce pictures and copy.
> *Listener* (16 January 1986)

> They operate in the slick new tradition of political handlers, whose job is to reduce a campaign to photo ops and sound bites.
> *Time* Magazine (21 November 1988)

pidgin. Jargon made up of mainly English words but arranged according to Chinese methods and pronounced in a Chinese way.

It arose to facilitate communication between Chinese and Europeans at seaports and has nothing to do with 'pigeon'. Rather, it is the Chinese pronunciation of 'business', although now 'pidgin' can be formed from any two languages and is not restricted to Chinese and English. Known by 1826.

pink. *See* SHOCKING . . .

pissed as a newt. Very drunk. Recorded by 1957. Partridge/*Slang* gives various metaphors for drunkenness from the animal kingdom – 'pissed as a coot/rat/parrot' among them. None seems particularly apposite. And why 'newt'? Could it be that the newt, being an amphibious reptile, can submerge itself in liquid as a drunk might do? Or is it because its tight-fitting skin reflects the state of being 'tight'?

We may never know, though the alternative (and, according to Partridge, original) expression 'tight as a newt' has a pleasing sound to it. Folk expressions have been coined with less reason. (Partridge's reviser Paul Beale wrote in December 1987: 'The great thing about newts is the characteristic they share with fishes' arse'oles: they are watertight. And you can't get tighter than that!')

There is any number of other explanations, most based on mishearings of words.

pizzazz. Vitality of personality, zest. Of no very obvious etymology. The coinage has been attributed, somewhat dubiousy, to the fashion journalist Diana Vreeland (as in the *Independent on Sunday*, 8 April 1990). Known since the late 1930s.

> Pizazz [*sic*] to quote the editor of the Harvard *Lampoon*, is an indefinable dynamic quality, the *je ne sais quoi* of function; as for instance, adding Scotch puts pizazz into a drink.
> *Harper's Bazaar* (March 1937)

planet earth (sometimes **Planet Earth**). Portentous term for the planet on which man lives. Known by 1965.

> We should simply seek to make a mark in the universe . . . that some other civilisation will detect and so know there is . . . sophisticated life on planet Earth.
> Len Deighton, *Tinker Tailor Soldier Spy* (1976)

play fast and loose, to.   To mess another person about, to resort to deceit, to act in a slippery fashion. The expression was known by 1557, as was a game called Fast-and-Loose – though which came first is hard to say. The game, also called 'Pricking the Belt', was an old fairground trick akin to 'Find the Lady' (the so-called Three-Card Trick). The victim was incited to pin a folded belt to the table. The operator would then show that the belt was not (held) 'fast' but 'loose'. So the victim would lose the bet.

Plimsoll.   (1) Name given to the load-line on the hull of a ship and so called after Samuel Plimsoll, the MP for Derby, to whose agitation the Merchant Shipping Act of 1876 was due (*OED2*). (2) In the plural, **plimsolls**, the name given to rubber-soled canvas shoes. There appears to be some connection with the MP but this word has not been found in print before the Army and Navy Stores Catalogue for 1907. Possibly the band of rubber put round the shoes to keep the water out was somehow reminiscent of the the Plimsoll line round a ship.

plonk.   A word for 'cheap wine' probably first used in Australia (by 1919). The *OED2*'s earliest contextual usage – in the form 'plinketty plonk' – dates from 1930. It may reflect the sound of a cork being drawn out of a bottle or come from *vin blanc*, the French for 'white wine'.

ploughman's lunch.   The coinage of this term for a meal of bread, cheese and pickle, though redolent of olden days, was in fact a marketing ploy of the English Country Cheese Council in the early 1970s. *The Ploughman's Lunch* was then the title of a film (UK, 1983), about how history gets rewritten.

poison(ed) dwarf.   A name given to any unpleasant person of small stature. According to episode one of the ITV series *The World at War* (1975), this was a popular German nickname in the late 1930s for Hitler's diminutive propaganda chief, Joseph Goebbels. The German *Giftzwerg* is defined by the Collins German dictionary as 'poisonous individual; spiteful little devil'. In Wagner's *Das Rheingold* (1869), however, Wellgunde calls Alberich '*Schwefelgezwerg*' (literally 'sulphurous dwarf'). Knowing how a Wagnerian phrase like 'night and fog' was adapted in the Nazi era, this seems a likely source for the phrase.

> The regiment involved in the unhappy events at Minden some 30 years ago, which provoked the local inhabitants to nickname its soldiers 'The Poison Dwarves' was The Cameronians (The Scottish Rifles).
> *Independent on Sunday* (5 July 1992)

Compare, from John Osborne, *Almost a Gentleman* (1991): 'Ronald Duncan (dubbed "the **Black Dwarf**" by Devine and Richardson, because of his diminutive height and poisonous spirit) . . .' Sir Walter Scott published *The Black Dwarf* in 1816.

Pollyanna. The name for an (excessively) optimistic person comes from the heroine of *Pollyanna*, a novel (1913) by Eleanor Porter.

> I should not like to hold stock in a company with Pollyanna as president.
> *Collier's* Magazine (11 June 1921)

pom(my). Meaning 'an Englishman' in Australian usage ('pommy bastard', 'whingeing poms') this was established by 1912. It is possibly from a melding of 'pomegranate' and 'immigrant'; or from the French *pomme* ('apple') – compare LIMEY; or from an acronym stamped on the shirts of convict settlers, POHMS ('Prisoners Of Her Majesty').

poodlefaker. Denoting a man who cultivates the society of women, this is an Anglo-Indian services term describing a type of man to be found in the hill stations and alluding to lap-dogs. Known by 1902.

poof. *See under* GAY.

Poona. *See* WHEN I WAS IN . . .

poor little rich girl. Phrase used about any young woman whose wealth has not brought her happiness. *The Poor Little Rich Girl* was the title of a novel (1912) by the American writer Eleanor Gates, filmed (US, 1917) starring Mary Pickford, remade (US, 1936) with Shirley Temple. It is the story of a rich society girl who lives an isolated life and is kept apart from her parents. Later, the title of a song (1925) by Noël Coward.

Popemobile. Popular name for a type of vehicle used by a Pope, especially on his foreign tours. With bullet-proof glass and a prominent viewing platform, it was introduced by John Paul II in 1979. The name was based on 'Batmobile', the vehicle used by the character Batman in strip cartoons, TV and cinema shows.

porridge. The term 'porridge' for 'time spent in prison' has been current since the 1950s at least. It is supposedly from rhyming slang 'borage and thyme' (time). The porridge-stirring connection with the (more American) expressions 'stir' (meaning 'prison'), 'in stir' (in prison) and 'stir crazy' (insane as a result of long imprisonment) may just be coincidental. These terms are said to derive from the Anglo-Saxon word *styr*, meaning 'punishment', reinforced by the Romany *steripen*, meaning 'prison' (*DOAS*). On the other hand, if porridge was once the prisoner's basic food – and it was known as 'stirabout' – it may be more than coincidence that we have here. *Porridge* was the title of a BBC TV comedy series (1974–7) about prison life. In *Something Nasty in the Woodshed* (1976), Kyril Bonfiglioli provides another angle: '"Porridge"... means penal servitude. There is a legend ... that if ... on the last morning of your "stretch", you do not eat up all your nice porridge, you will be back in durance vile within the year.'

posh. The mythical etymology for this word meaning 'smart; grand' is that it is an acronym for '*P*ort *O*ut *S*tarboard *H*ome', as the requirement for the most desirable staterooms on ships travelling to and from British India. The P&O Line, which was the principal carrier, has no evidence of a single POSH booking, nor would it have made much difference to the heat of the cabin which side you were on. *OED2* has no citations before the twentieth century. However, meaning 'dandy' or 'money' the word was nineteenth-century thieves' and especially Romany slang. It is not hard to see either of these meanings, or both combined, contributing to what we now mean by 'posh'.

possession is nine points of the law. (Out of a possible ten points): in a dispute over ownership of property, the present owner is in the strongest position. An alternative: 'Possession is nine-tenths of the law'. An earlier version: 'Possession is eleven points of the law (i.e. out of a possible twelve) is quoted in Jonathan Swift's *Polite Conversation* (1738).

The original nine points of the law were said to be: 1) a lot of money; 2) a lot of patience; 3) a good cause; 4) a good lawyer; 5) a good counsel; 6) good witnesses; 7) a good jury; 8) a good judge; 9) good luck. Sometimes only eight points have been listed.

post-war bulge.   *See under* BABY BOOMER.

pot.   *See* GO TO . . .

potboiler.   A work of literature or art composed chiefly with the aim of keeping the pot boiling = keeping the author or artist in funds and thus alive, and probably of no great merit. Known by 1864.

poverty of ambition/aspirations.   'The real tragedy of the poor is the poverty of their aspirations' is a saying attributed to Adam Smith in this form in *c.*1960, but unverified. Since 1987, however, it has frequently been attributed to Ernest Bevin, the British Labour minister, though with no precise source as yet (also to Aneurin Bevan, though with even less backing) and any number of subjects – the poor, the working class, Britain, the trade unions.

> There was a marvellous remark by Ernest Bevin when he said that what characterized Britain was a poverty of aspiration – and it's true.
> *The Times* (19 May 1987)

Sometimes the word 'ambition' is substituted.

> John Edmonds, secretary of GMB, the general union, recalled Ernest Bevin's observation 50 years ago that the greatest failing of Britain's trade unions was their poverty of ambition which made them set their sights too low.
> *Guardian* (6 September 1990)

> My family were the same as any other working class family in those days; they suffered from what I shall call the poverty of ambition.
> Sir Bernard Ingham, *The Times* (18 May 1991)

> Only the Morgan Motor Company refused to follow his advice to expand – a course of action which Sir John [Harvey Jones] cites as evidence of the poverty of ambition of small and medium-sized British companies.
> *Financial Times* (21 April 1993)

powder one's nose, to. To go to the lavatory (mostly female use). Known by 1921. In a Cole Porter song by 1930.

powers that be. Now used to describe any form of authority exercising social or political control, this phrase derives from Romans 13:1: 'Let every soul be subject unto the higher powers. For there is no power but of God: the powers that be are ordained of God.' The New English Bible has: 'the existing authorities are instituted by him.'

The Powers That Be
Title of book by David Halberstam (1979)

prays. *See* FAMILY THAT . . .

prestigious. Now meaning 'having prestige', originally this word meant quite the opposite: 'cheating, deceptive, illusory'. Compare 'prestidigitation' ('juggling, trickery'). But that meaning slips easily into the idea of 'dazzling', and has done so. First meaning by 1546, second by 1913.

private eye. Although it is true that a private investigator's job consists of keeping an eye on people, there may be more to it than that. The term could derive from 'private investigator' or from the wide-open 'eye' symbol of the Pinkerton detective agency, founded in Chicago (1850). It went with the slogan 'We never sleep' and was referred to as the 'Eye' by criminals and others. The full phrase seems to have emerged in the 1930s and 40s, particularly through the fiction of Raymond Chandler and others. The British satirical and investigative magazine *Private Eye* was first published in 1961.

propose/drink a toast, to. At one time a piece of spiced toast would be put in a glass of wine in order to improve the flavour or to collect the sediment. From this word 'toast' came to be identified with the drink. Equally, the mention of a lady's name to accompany the gesture was supposed to flavour a bumper as spiced toast did a drink. Known by 1700.

ps and qs. *See* MIND YOUR . . .

psephology. The study of political elections. Known by 1952 and said to have been coined by R.B. McCallum, an Oxford don, from the Greek word representing the pebble which the Athenians dropped into the urn to vote.

pseud. Referring to a pseudo-intellectual person, this word is sometimes thought to have been a *Private Eye* coinage because of the 'Pseud's Corner' feature (from 1968 onwards). But the prefix 'pseudo-' for 'counterfeit; spurious' is very old indeed (it is a Greek prefix), and Daniel J. Boorstin in *The Image* (1960) had used the term **pseudo-event** for an occasion laid on solely for the purpose of attracting news coverage. 'Pseud' existed as a word in 1962.

pull out all the stops, to. To execute some task with vigour, energy or emotion, to make every effort. From the action of an organist who, when pulling out all the organ-stops, is enabled to play with the greatest volume of sound. Known since 1865.

pull the other one! Do you take me for a fool – an expression of disbelief. Part of a longer phrase, 'Pull the other one, it's got bells on', probably referring to the bells on a jester's, or fool's, costume. Recorded by 1966.

pull the wool over someone's eyes, to. When wigs were commonly worn, they were sometimes referred to as wool (because of the resemblance, particularly the curls). Thus to pull the wool over people's eyes was to pull wigs over their eyes and render them incapable of seeing. Hence also the modern meaning of 'to hoodwink'. 'To pull the wool etc.' would seem to be a phrase of American origin and was in use by 1859.

punchline. The last line of a joke or the last line or keyline of a sketch, play or song. Bob Monkhouse, the British comedian and student of humour, was quoted in *Radio Times* (August 1983) as believing 'it was Fred Allen who invented the word "punchline". He called it the gag that got you right in the belly.' Lesser varieties, he said, included the low joint-laugh, which provides a squeal rather than a laugh.

'We once used "pay-off" as a British synonym, but this became associated with bribery and corruption, and so was discreetly dropped from the comic vocabulary.'

This could well be the case and the word is certainly of American origin but the attribution to Allen (1894–1956) is somewhat doubtful. The *OED2* provides a citation from *Variety* in 1921 (by which time Allen can hardly have got going as a comedian – and certainly not on American radio where he made his name.) Perhaps it was one of *Variety*'s own famous coinages – though it probably came from within vaudeville rather than from the reporters of it.

pup.   *See* SOLD A . . .

push comes to shove.   *See* WHEN . . .

push the envelope, to.   To take a risk. Suddenly popular in the mid-1990s, though the allusion is not clear. Drug-taking?

> Messrs E & V want you to know that if you thought *Basic Instinct* was pushing the envelope, this year's trendy phrase for taking a risk, *Showgirls* is, according to the publicity material, 'pushing the edge of the envelope'.
> *Sunday Times* (10 September 1995)

> This film, set against the background of the Mexican Revolution, aroused enormous controversy over the extent of the violence, which pushed the already bulging envelope out still further.
> Simon Rose, *Classic Film Guide* (1995)

put a sock in it!   'Shut up!' 'Shut your mouth!' addressed to a noisy person. Neil Ewart in *Everyday Phrases* (1983) confidently asserts that this dates from the days of the wind-up, 'acoustic' gramophones where the sound emerged from a horn. With no electronic controls to raise or lower the volume, the only way to regulate the sound was to put in or take out an article of clothing, which deadened it. (Presumably, mutes as stuck in the horns of brass instruments were not supplied.)

The *OED2* has a citation from 1919 – an explanation of the term from the *Athenaeum* journal – which suggests the phrase was not widely known even then.

The gramophone explanation is not totally convincing. Partridge/*Slang* compares the earlier expression '(to) put a bung in it' – as in a bath or leak. Why shouldn't a sock inserted in the human mouth be the origin? After all, a sock in the jaw would be the next best thing.

put a spoke in someone's wheel, to. Meaning 'to prevent someone from doing something' this is an odd expression if one knows that bicycle wheels already have spokes in them. Here, however, what is evoked is the days when carts had solid wheels and no spokes in the modern sense. The spoke then was a pin which could be inserted into a hole on the wheel to act as a brake. The *OED2* believes that, while the expression has been known since 1583, 'spoke' may be a mistranslation of a Dutch expression including the word *spaak*, meaning 'bar, stave'.

put 'em/them up! Challenge from someone with a gun, meaning 'put your hands up', but originally in boxing where the challenge meant 'raise your fists' before a fight. Known in the first sense since *c*.1860 and in the second since 1923.

> The idea of using the Ugly Sisters to represent topical characters or types is by no means new. In 1897, we find a Thisbe who ... has taken lessons from Eugene Sandow, the strong-man who ... is 'disposed to challenge all and sundry to "put them up".'
> Gerald Frow, *Oh, Yes It Is!* (1985)

put on (the) dog, to. Meaning 'to put on airs, fine clothes', this is a US expression dating from the 1870s, probably from among college students (especially at Yale) who had to wear stiff, high collars (jokily known as 'dog-collars') on formal occasions.

put one's dukes/dooks up, to. To put one's fists up as though preparing for a fight. Describing a summit between Soviet and US leaders, *Time* Magazine (20 October 1986) stated: 'Reagan and Gorbachev both came to office not with their hands outstretched but with their dukes up.' If 'dukes' means 'fists', why so? One theory is that because the 1st Duke of Wellington had such a large nose, a 'duke' became a synonym for one. Then, so this theory goes, a man's fist became a 'duke buster'. In time this was shortened, and fists became 'dukes'.

The *Morris Dictionary of Word and Phrase Origins* (1977) prefers another theory: that the use derives from Cockney rhyming slang, viz. 'Duke of York's' ('forks' meaning 'fingers' – standing for the whole hand or fist). *OED2* has the expression by 1874. Winston Churchill neatly played on the phrase in a public speech about House of Lords reform on 4 September 1909: 'In the absence of any

commanding voice, the Tory party have had to put up their "dooks".'
A report of the speech adds: 'Great laughter and a voice: "What
about your grandfather?"' (Churchill's grandfather was the Duke of
Marlborough).

put one's shoulder to the wheel, to.   To make extra effort to
start and/or complete a task – obviously from the acting of shifting
a wheeled vehicle that has become stuck and requires, in addition
to any horse-drawn effort, a human shove to free it. Known by
1692.

> Putting your shoulder to the wheel when the coach gets into the mud.
> That's what I've been doing all my life.
> Anthony Trollope, *The Small House at Allington*, Chap. 46 (1864)

put the kibosh on something, to.   Meaning 'to squelch; put an
end to; spoil; veto', this expression was current by 1884. It possibly
comes from the Gaelic *cie bais*, meaning 'cap of death', but it is also
known in Yiddish. An extraordinary (and unverified) explanation is
that 'kibosh' was the name of the black cap worn by a British judge
when pronouncing sentence of death.

> For Belgium put the kibosh on the Kaiser;
> Europe took a stick and made him sore.
> Song, 'Belgium Put the Kibosh on the Kaiser' (*c.*1914)

put the screws on, to.   Meaning 'to apply pressure on someone
to do something', 'screws' here is short for 'thumbscrews', the
ancient and medieval method of torturing prisoners. Known by
1834. This could be why prison guards have been nicknamed 'screws',
although another explanation is from screw meaning 'key'. Gaolers
were sometimes known as 'turnkeys', as this was their most significant
function.

Q

quango. The acronymous name of a type of statutory body set up outside the Civil Service but appointed and financed by central government seems to have originated in the US in the 1960s. It became popular in the UK in the 1970s, standing for '*QU*asi-*A*utonomous-*N*on-*G*overnmental-*O*rganization', though sometimes 'National' has been substituted for 'Non-Governmental'.

quarter. *See* GIVE/GRANT NO . . .

queer the pitch, to. To ruin a plan or prospects. The pitch here is as in 'sales pitch' rather than 'football pitch'.

quiet revolution. A subtle change which does not draw attention to itself. The phrase was written by Barry Day, a speechwriter for the British Prime Minister Edward Heath who, shortly after his election, said in a Conservative Party Conference speech (October 1970): 'If we are to achieve this task we will have to embark on a change so radical, a revolution so quiet and yet so total, that it will go far beyond the programme for a parliament to which we are committed and on which we have already embarked, far beyond the decade and way into the 80s.'

> What we have had is a Quiet Revolution, people starting to tell pollsters that, well, Betty Boothroyd would make a very nice Madam President, and maybe the Royal Family would not be missed after all.
> Polly Toynbee, *Radio Times* (22 July 1995)

quisling. Meaning 'a traitor' – from the name of Vidkun Quisling, former Minister of Defence in Norway who supported the invasion of his country by the Germans in 1940. He headed a puppet government under the Nazi occupation. After the German defeat he was tried and executed in 1945. Chips Channon wrote in his diary (8 May 1940): 'We watched the insurgents file out of the

Opposition [in the House of Commons lobby] ... "Quislings", we shouted at them, "Rats". "Yes-men", they replied.'

quiz. It is said this word came into use in the 1780s when Mr Daly, a Dublin theatre manager, had a bet that he could introduce a new word into the language within twenty-four hours. Somehow he came up with this word and had it chalked all over Dublin. *OED2* dates the word at 1782 with the now rare meaning 'an odd or eccentric person, in character or appearance', but it is not far from the Latin interrogative pronoun *quis* ('who?' *or* 'what?') and also resembles the second syllable of the word 'inquisitive' (from the Latin *inquisitere*, to acquire) which was current by the sixteenth century.

R

R in the month. *See* DON'T EAT OYSTERS ...

radar. So familiar is this word now that it is worth remembering it has a down-to-earth derivation. It is made up of the first part of the word '*ra*dio' and the initial letters of '*d*irection *a*nd *r*anging'. The word was established – along with the invention – during the first two years of the Second World War. The device was the brain-child of Sir Robert Watson-Watt who had developed it in 1933–5.

rag. *See* CHEW THE ...

rain cats and dogs, to. Meaning 'to rain extremely heavily'. Known by 1738, though there is a 1652 version: 'Raining dogs and polecats'. There is no very convincing explanation for this phrase. According to the *Morris Dictionary of Word and Phrase Origins* (1977), it comes from the days when street drainage was so poor that a heavy rain storm could easily drown cats and dogs. After the storm people would see the number of dead cats and dogs and assume they had fallen out of the sky. *Brewer* suggests, on the other hand, that in northern mythology cats were supposed to have great influence on the weather and dogs were a signal of wind, 'thus cat may be taken as a symbol of the downpouring rain, and the dog of the strong gusts of wind accompanying a rain-storm'.

rain-check. *See* TAKE A . . .

raise Cain, to. Meaning 'to make trouble, a fuss, a disturbance', the allusion here is to the biblical Cain ('the first murderer') who killed his brother Abel (Genesis 4:2–8). A person who makes trouble, 'raises the spirit' of Cain by doing so. Known by 1840.

raspberry. *See under* BRONX CHEER.

raunchy. There are two meanings to this word, both from the US. One is 'disreputable, dirty, grubby' (and may come from the word 'ranchy', as from 'ranch'). The other, more common, describes an aspect of sexuality that is a little hard to pinpoint. It evokes elements of earthiness and suggestiveness, though it can be used to describe anything that excites sexual feelings. It was much used in this sense in the early 1960s, though there was a song 'Raunchy' in 1958.

read it here first. *See* (AND REMEMBER) YOU . . .

read the riot act, to. The meaning of this phrase is 'to make strong representations about something; express forcibly that something must cease'. The actual Riot Act passed by the British Parliament in 1714 (and finally repealed in 1973) provided for the dispersal of crowds (defined as being of more than 12 persons) by those in authority. The method used was for someone to stand up and, literally, read out the terms of the Act so that the rioters knew what law they were breaking. Known by 1795.

real McCoy. Meaning 'the real thing; the genuine article', the phrase *possibly* derives from 'Kid' McCoy, a US welterweight boxing champion in the late 1890s. When challenged by a man in a bar to prove he was who he said he was, McCoy flattened him. When the man came round, he declared that this was indeed the 'real' McCoy. 'Kid' McCoy apparently promoted this story about himself.

However, Messrs G. Mackay, the Scottish whisky distillers, were apparently promoting their product as 'the real *Mackay*' in 1870, as though alluding to an established expression. This could have derived from the Mackays of Reay in Sutherland claiming to be the principal branch of the Mackay clan. Robert Louis Stevenson used this version in an 1883 letter.

Recording Angel. Referring to an angel who keeps a record of every person's good and bad deeds, this was a concept known by 1761 (in Sterne's *Tristram Shandy*), but is not mentioned as such in the Bible.

> She had not convinced me. If the recording angel had come down from heaven to confirm her, and had opened his book to my mortal eyes, the recording angel would not have convinced me.
> Wilkie Collins, *The Woman in White*, First Epoch, Chap. XI (1860)

red herring. A diversionary or misleading device to divert attention from the real question, especially (say) in a fictional murder hunt. From the device used to encourage dogs to follow a scent (1686). 'To draw a herring across the track/trail' was an expression known in the US and UK by the 1880s.

red tape. Referring to delay caused by bureaucrats, the allusion, dating from the eighteenth century, is to the ribbons that lawyers and other public officials still use to bind up their papers (although they look more pink than red).

red-handed. *See under* CAUGHT IN THE ACT.

red-letter day. Denoting a special day, because in almanacs and old calendars, feast days and saints' days were often printed in red rather than black ink. The *OED2*'s earliest citation is from 1704 in the US.

religion. *See* GET . . .

ride. *See* TAKE SOMEONE FOR A . . .

rigmarole. Fuss, palaver, lengthy procedure. At the Public Record Office in London you will still find the 'Ragman Roll', a sequence of documents joined together to form a sheet some 12 m (40 ft) long and dating from 1296. Each document was a pledge of loyalty by Scottish noblemen to King Edward I (1272–1307). This use of 'ragman roll' conveys the idea of a catalogue. The term was also used to describe the Hundred Rolls submitted to Edward in 1274–5. Because of the many seals hanging from them, they had a ragged appearance.

Since the eighteenth century, a 'rigmarole' has been used to describe a rambling tale or yarn. Could it be derived from the earlier term? Nobody is too sure.

ringer. *See* DEAD ...

riot act. *See* READ THE ...

Ripper. *See* JACK THE ...

ritzy. (1) Smart, glamorous, ostentatiously rich. (2) Flashy, pretentious. The adjective derives from the surname of César Ritz, the Swiss-born hotelier (1850–1918) who established luxury hotels in Paris, London, New York and elsewhere at the turn of the century. Allusions were being made to his name in such coinages by 1910–11.

river. *See* SOLD DOWN THE ...; SEND SOMEONE UP THE ...

road rage. The phenomenon of ordinary drivers of motor vehicles being transformed into violent and abusive people by the behaviour of other motorists on the road. The phrase was apparently coined by a writer in the *Los Angeles Times* in 1984 when a pick-up truck driver shot dead the driver of a Cadillac car who cut him up on the main 405 freeway in Los Angeles. The term became widely known in the UK in 1995–6 when measures to combat it were urged – including roadside counselling by psychotherapists.

road to Damascus. The occasion of a change of heart, conversion or sudden realization; a turning point. From St Paul's conversion, on the road to Damascus, to a fervent belief in Christ, as described in Acts 22 – the occasion when he **saw the light** ('suddenly there shone from heaven a great light round about me'). Previously he had been a Pharisee persecuting the Christians.

It is easy to imagine Madonna's biographer, poring over her possessions, years after her death, hoping to arrive at a biographical Damascus ... and finds no porn at all.

Independent on Sunday (11 April 1993)

Traffic jam to Damascus. Everyone should try it at least once. The trendiest have several. Conversions, that is. Peter Popham reports.

Headline and byline, *Independent* (20 October 1995)

Roaring Twenties.   The decade label for the 1920s had established itself by 1939, reflecting the heady buoyant atmosphere in certain sections of society following the horrors of the First World War. The adjective 'roaring' meaning 'boisterous, riotous, noisy', had previously been applied to the 1850s and, in Australia, to the 'roaring days' of the gold-rush. The same meaning occurs in the expression 'roaring drunk'. The 1940s do not appear to have been given a label, least of all **Roaring Forties** – that term had already been applied to parts of the oceans between 40 degrees and 50 degrees south where strong westerly winds blow.

roast/roost.   *See* RULE THE ...

rock and a hard place.   *See* BETWEEN A ...

rock'n'roll.   This name for a type of popular music was first popularized by Alan Freed, the US disc jockey, who is generally credited with first discovering and promoting it. In 1951, he was hosting *Moondog's Rock'n'Roll Party* on a radio station in Cleveland, Ohio. It was not until he moved to New York City in 1954, however, that the term took hold. Earlier, in 1934, there had been a song by Sidney Clare and Richard Whiting with the title 'Rock and Roll' in the film *Transatlantic Merry-Go-Round*, referring to a ship's movements. Even earlier, the phrase may also have been Black English slang for the sexual act.

ropes.   *See* KNOW THE ...

round robin.   A letter where the responsibility for sending it is shared by all the signatories (known in the British Navy by 1730). In France, in the same century, petitioners would sign their names on a ribbon whose top was joined to its bottom. This was to prevent a situation where the first signatory on the list might be singled out for punishment. Nowadays, the term is often applied to a letter of protest with signatures not arranged in any special way, except perhaps alphabetically.

The term has nothing to do with the bird. 'Round' is from French *rond* and 'robin' is a corruption of French *ruban*, meaning 'ribbon'.

round up the usual suspects. *See under* USUAL SUSPECTS.

roundabouts and swings (or **swings and roundabouts**). An expression of acceptance of life's fluctuating fortunes, from the modern proverb, 'What you lose on the swings you gain on the roundabouts' – a fairground metaphor, apparently first formulated by Patrick R. Chalmers in 'Roundabouts and Swings' in *Green Days & Blue Days* (1912): 'What's lost upon the roundabouts we pulls up on the swings.'

royal 'we'. King Richard I is believed to have been the first monarch to use the royal 'we' (in Latin) – as a way of showing that he did not simply rule for himself but on behalf of his people. Before this, when Roman consuls *shared* power, it was appropriate for each of them to speak in this collective manner.

Some monarchs seem to have been more prone to using it than others. As is obvious from her alleged expression, 'We are not amused', Queen Victoria was one who did, but nevertheless her letters and journals are just as full of the first person singular.

However, when non-royals like Margaret Thatcher start saying things like 'We have become a grandmother' (as she did to widespread guffaws in March 1989), it is clearly time for the rest of us to desist. The actual term 'royal we', as opposed to the usage, is comparatively recent (by 1931).

rubber! An abusive term for a starer or gaper, from the American 'rubbernecker'. In Theodore Dreiser's *Sister Carrie* (1900), he twice allows characters (male and female) to use the term 'Rubber!' about each other, as a mildly abusive epithet. The setting is a Chicago shoe factory in 1889. Frank Loxley writes (1996): 'I recall my History Master telling the following joke – it must have been in 1940. In the New York subway sat a woman with a rather strange-looking baby. The man opposite could not keep his eyes off it. After he had been staring at the child for a while, the woman snapped, "Rubber!" The man replied, "Oh, I'm sorry, I thought it was real." My teacher explained that in America "Rubber!" was short for "Rubbernecker", i.e. a starer or gaper.' This is confirmed by Webster's Second and Third International Dictionaries, finding it just before the turn of the century.

Rubicon. *See* CROSS THE . . .

ruddy. *See* FLAMING NORA!

rule of thumb. A rule taken from experience, not theory. This refers either to the use of a thumb's width as a rough and ready means of measurement or to the use of a thumb for dipping into liquids to test them. Known by 1692.

rule the roost, to. Meaning 'to lord it over others', this possibly derives from the image of a cock's behaviour towards hens on the roosting perch. The existence of the (probably) earlier expression 'to **rule the roast**' – presiding as the head of the dinner table (as in Shakespeare, *Henry VI, Part 2*, I.i.108, 1590) – may point to a more likely source (though just possibly the two phrases developed side by side).

run the gauntlet, to. An expression meaning 'to endure something of a prolonged, testing nature, to be attacked on all sides', this has nothing to do with the type of glove but is from the Swedish *gatlop* or *gatloppe* which means 'lane run'. It carries the idea of someone having to run as a punishment (in the military) between two lines of tormentors. The literal use was recorded in English in 1676, but the transferred sense 15 years earlier.

> He claps not only himself but his old-fashioned wife on my back . . . and then, I suppose we are to run the gauntlet through all the rest of the family.
> Oliver Goldsmith, *She Stoops to Conquer* (1773)

S

sack. *See* GET/BE GIVEN THE ...

safety first. A slogan that was apparently first used in the US in connection with railroad safety. In the UK of the 1890s, this was also the original use of the slogan when a railway notice declared: 'The Safety of the Passengers is our First Concern'. First recorded use of the phrase in the UK was, however, in 1873 – 'A system that would go on the motto of safety first' (*Cassell's Magazine*).

In 1915, it became the motto of the National Council for Industrial Safety in the US. In 1916, the London General Bus Company formed a London 'Safety First Council'. The 1922 British General Election saw the phrase in use as a political slogan for the Conservatives. Again, in 1929, it was the Tory slogan under which Stanley Baldwin fought for re-election, but it proved a loser. In 1934, the National Safety First Association was formed, concerned with road and industrial safety, and it is in this connection that the slogan has endured.

Sally Lunn. A tea-cake named after a pastry-cook who sold them in Bath during the eighteenth century, or from the French *soleil lune* ('sun and moon' cake). Known by 1780.

salt. *See* TAKE SOMETHING WITH A GRAIN OF ...; WORTH ONE'S SALT ...

Sam Hill. *See* WHAT IN THE ...

sandboy. *See* AS HAPPY AS A ...

sandwich. This snack, originally of beef between two slices of bread, was invented by John Montagu, 4th Earl of Sandwich (1718–92) who, being a committed gambler, disliked having to stray from the table for such small matters as eating. He once played for twenty-four hours non-stop. Known by 1762. The Sandwich Islands in the Pacific (now part of Hawaii) were named by Capt. Cook after him rather than the food.

sandwich men. Carriers of portable advertisements. Obviously, there is a resemblance – the men are sandwiched between the two boards – but Charles Dickens has been mentioned as inventing the phrase. The earliest citation in the *OED2* is 1890, however.

savvy. Meaning 'do you understand?', when addressed to foreigners or to people who may not be very bright. One's first thought is that this must be a contraction of French *savoir-faire* [knowing how to do] or *savez-vous?* [do you know?] and, indeed, another meaning of the word 'savvy', as a noun, is 'knowingness, understanding, nous, gumption.'

There is a common root, but in fact the word in this form comes to us – probably via the US (where it was established by the mid-nineteenth century) – from the Spanish *sabe usted* [you know]. In Spanish, *b* and *v* sound very similar.

'Savvy', as we have it, is from a Negro- and Pidgin-English version of this Spanish. Recorded in precisely this form, 1897.

scarper, to. To run away, 'do a bunk'. Possibly from the Italian *scappare*, to escape. Known by 1846. A link has also been suggested to Scapa Flow, the British naval base in the Orkneys where German vessels were scuppered at the end of the First World War in 1919. From this event, 'Scapa' became Cockney rhyming slang for 'to go'.

scenery is better. *See* BECAUSE THE . . .

Scott. *See* GREAT . . .

scratch. *See under* UP TO SNUFF.

scratch'n'sniff. Name for a gimmick used originally in the cinema whereby audience members scratched cards to release smells appropriate for the scene they were watching. American origin, early 1980s? The first 'scratch'n'sniff' opera production may have been *The Love for Three Oranges* at the English National Opera in 1989.

Using the latest refinements in tasteless high technology, Revlon is bringing out a new scratch'n'sniff range of advertisements in America's national women's magazines, under the copy line, 'Where does Joan Collins become a Scoundrel?'
Today (1 April 1987)

screws. *See* PUT THE . . .

sea change. *See* SUFFER A . . .

see Naples and die. Old Italian saying suggesting that once you have been to Naples there is nothing more beautiful to be seen on earth or, more ominously, a warning dating from the time when the city was a notorious centre for typhoid, cholera and other diseases. This extract dated 3 March 1787 from Goethe's *Italian Journey* would seem to support the first origin: 'I won't say another word about the beauties of the city and its situation, which have been described and praised so often. As they say here, "*Vedi Napoli e poi muori!*" "See Naples and die!"'

see the light. *See under* ROAD TO DAMASCUS.

see you on the green. A theatrical slang expression meaning 'I'll see you on the stage'. Has it something to do with 'Green Room', the usual name given to the actors' retiring room? Apparently not, it is simple rhyming slang: 'greengage' = stage. Recorded by 1931. Sometimes 'the greengage' is used in full to mean 'the stage'.

seen better days. *See* HAVE . . .

segue (pronounced 'segway'). In broadcasting and musicians' jargon, this word is used to mean that you will go from one piece of music to another, or from one record to another, without a spoken link. A radio producer might say, 'We'll *segue* from the Sinatra to the "Nuns' Chorus". . .' Known in this sense by 1937.

DOAS provides a rare use in another context, with the meaning simply 'to go'. 'When I sagway [*sic*] up to the roadside abbatoir, and order the concentric waffle' (Arthur Baer, newspaper columnist, 1947).

It comes from the Italian word meaning 'follow' and has been used as a written instruction in music since at least the eighteenth century. Clearly broadcasters have adopted the musicians' use. *Variety*, the American showbiz paper, also uses it to mean that one thing leads to another.

self-fulfilling prophecy.   Anticipation of an outcome which only serves to bring it about. Coined by R.K. Merton in *Social Theory and Social Structure* (1949): 'The self-fulfilling prophecy is, in the beginning, a *false* definition of the situation evoking a new behavior which makes the originally false conception come *true*.'

> Panic buying of spirits ... caused largely by forecasts of the shortage – a self-fulfilling prophecy.
> *The Times* (7 December 1973)

sell-by date.   A date marked on perishable products, especially foodstuffs, by which time they should have been sold or else they would be unfit for consumption. Used in shops and markets in the UK from 1972. Also figuratively to describe anything that is old or out-of-date.

> Socialism: the package that's passed its sell-by date.
> *Daily Telegraph* (13 March 1987)

send someone to Coventry, to.   Meaning 'to refuse to speak to a person', this expression may have originated in the old story of soldiers stationed in Coventry who were so unwelcome that the citizens carried on as if they did not exist, alternatively that if women talked to the soldiers, they were ostracized. Another version comes from the Civil War in England in the seventeenth century. When captured Royalists were sent to Coventry, a strongly Roundhead (Parliamentary) town, they were bound to be ignored. Evidently, the Roundheads sent doubtful or useless officers or soldiers to the garrison at Coventry.

This is possibly supported by a passage in Clarendon's *History of the Rebellion* (VI:83, 1702–4): '[Birmingham] a town so wicked that it had risen upon small parties of the King's [men], and killed or taken them prisoners and sent them to Coventry.'

'The expression is used also in America: "Send them into ever-lasting Coventry" – Emerson's essay, "Manners"' – according to *Benham's Book of Quotations* (1948).

send someone up the river, to.   To imprison. Because Sing Sing gaol lies up the Hudson River from New York City. Known by 1891.

> I done it. Send me up the river. Give me the hot seat.
> *Chicago Daily News* (5 March 1946)

set one's cap at, to.   To try earnestly to attract someone's favours, especially romantic or sexual ones. Possibly a reference to a woman wearing beguiling headgear with a view to getting her man. Or possibly a mistranslation of the French nautical expression *mettre le cap à* [to head towards]. Known by the early nineteenth century.

> 'You will be setting your cap at him now, and never think of poor Brandon.'
>   'That is an expression, Sir John,' said Marianne warmly, 'which I particularly dislike. I abhor every commonplace phrase by which wit is intended; and "setting one's cap at a man" and "making a conquest," are the most odious of all.'
> Jane Austen, *Sense and Sensibility* (1811)

set the people free.   Slogan used by the British Conservative Party which helped it regain power, with Winston Churchill as Prime Minister, in the 1951 General Election. In a radio broadcast (3 May 1952), Churchill returned to the theme: 'We think it is a good idea to set the people free ... from the trammels of state control and bureaucratic management.' It was based on a patriotic song of the Second World War.

Many years later, in a House of Commons debate on the Rates Bill, Edward Heath recalled how he had entered the House in 1950 having fought an election on Mr Churchill's theme that Conservatives were to set the people free. 'It was not a theme,' he said, 'that we were to set the people free to do what we tell them' (17 January 1984).

seven bells.   *See* KNOCK ...

seven year itch.   The urge to be unfaithful to a spouse after a certain period of matrimony. The *OED2* provides various examples of this phrase going back from the mid-twentieth to the mid-nineteenth century, but without the specific matrimonial context. For example, the 'seven year itch' describes a rash from poison ivy which was believed to recur every year for a seven-year period. Then one has to recall that since biblical days seven-year periods (of lean or fat) have had especial significance, and there has also been the Army saying, 'Cheer up – the first seven years are the worst!'

But the specific matrimonial meaning was not popularized until the phrase was used as the title of George Axelrod's play (1952) and then film (1955). 'Itch' had long been used for the sexual urge but, as Axelrod commented on BBC Radio *Quote ... Unquote* (1979): 'There was a phrase which referred to a somewhat unpleasant disease but nobody had used it in a sexual [he meant 'matrimonial'] context before. I do believe I invented it in that sense.'

'Itch', oddly, does not seem to have been used in connection with venereal diseases. Nonetheless, there is this from *W.C. Fields: His Follies and Fortunes* (Robert Lewis Taylor, published as early as 1950): 'Bill exchanged women every seven years, as some people get rid of the itch.'

seven years of (bad) luck. The penalty for breaking a mirror. According to Robert L. Shook in *The Book of Why* (1983), this superstition began with the Romans who believed life renewed itself every seven years (one is also told that the skin on the human body renews itself every seven years). 'Since a mirror held a person's image, when it was broken, the health of the breaker – the last person to look into it – was also broken.' The specific term of seven years for this accident has been recorded as a superstition since the mid-nineteenth century.

sexual chemistry. In the period prior to the start of TV-am, the British breakfast television station, in 1983, David Frost talked about hoped-for new approaches to on-screen presentation. He either invented the phrase 'sexual chemistry', or merely endorsed it when it was suggested to him by a reporter, to describe what it was important for Frost and his colleagues to have: 'The chemistry thing is really important ... chemistry – sexual or otherwise – that is important.'

'Personal chemistry' to describe the attraction between two people had long been remarked where it existed in other walks of life. 'Remember the nauseating way Margaret Thatcher turned into a lovesick girl during Gorbachev's visit here and all that talk in the press of "personal chemistry"?' (*Guardian*, 7 June 1989). George Bernard Shaw in *You Never Can Tell* (1898) had earlier had: 'Not love: we know better than that. Let's call it chemistry . . . Well, you're attracting me irresistibly – chemically.'

shake/show a leg, to. 'Shake a leg' means either 'to dance' (by 1881) or (in the US) 'to hurry up' (by 1904). 'Show a leg' (meaning 'to get up out of bed in the morning or get a move on') dates from the days when women were allowed to spend the night on board when ships of the Navy were in port. Next morning at the cry: 'Show a leg!', if a woman's leg was stuck out of a hammock, she was allowed to sleep on. If it was a man's, he had to get up and on with his duties. No citation for this use before 1854, however.

shape. *See* LICK INTO . . .

sheets. *See* THREE . . .

'Shine on Harvest Moon'. This was the title of a song (1908) by Nora Bayes and Jack Norworth. The harvest moon seems particularly bright between 15 and 20 September, thus enabling farmers to bring in their crops by moonlight, should they need to. An ITV series was subsequently (1982–5) entitled *Shine on, Harvey Moon*.

shirtlifter. Now what does this word mean? First encountered in the late 1970s when it was being used to describe a meal made up of lentils and beans and other currently fashionable fibre-full ingredients. The net result would be a good deal of farting on the part of the diners, lifting the shirts of those who happened to be wearing them.

However, 'shirtlifter' was then found being used to describe a male homosexual, i.e. one who lifts the shirt of another man in the course of obtaining his pleasure (though Partridge, curiously, hears it as rhyming slang for 'poofter'). The *OED2* labels this as Australian slang, yet it is commonly used elsewhere. The *OED2*'s earliest citation is from 1966.

It has also been used to describe anything (a pornographic book or film) that would cause a man to have an erection.

> 'Gay' was a perfectly useful word which I dropped into my ordinary conversation at least three times a day until the shirtlifters got hold of it.
> *The Times* (14 May 1992)

shit list. *See under* HIT LIST.

shocking pink.   A coinage of the Italian fashion designer Elsa Schiaparelli (1896–1973). She used it in February 1937 to describe a lurid pink she had created (or 'crude, cruel shade of rose', as someone put it). As such it made a pleasant change from alliterative coinages and has undoubtedly stuck. In her autobiography, entitled, understandably, *Shocking Life*, Chap. 9 (1954) she notes that her friends and executives warned her off creating a 'nigger pink' but 'the colour "shocking" established itself for ever as a classic. Even Dali dyed an enormous stuffed bear in shocking pink'.

shoulder.   *See* GIVE SOMEONE THE COLD ...; HAVE A CHIP ON ONE'S ...; PUT ONE'S ...

shouting.   *See* ALL OVER BAR THE ...

shove.   *See* WHEN PUSH COMES TO ...

show a leg.   *See* SHAKE A ...

show must go on.   Originally a circus phrase, though no one seems able to turn up a written reference much before 1930. It was the title of a film in 1937 and of an Ira Gershwin/Jerome Kern song in *Cover Girl* (1944). *Punch* (13 April 1938) showed a reluctant bridegroom in the church porch, with the caption: 'Come, come Benedict – the show must go on!' In 1950, the phrase was spoken in the film *All About Eve* and, in the same decade, Noël Coward wrote a song which posed the question '*Why* Must the Show Go On?'

shrinking violet.   A timid, shy person. From the customary role of the violet flower symbolizing modesty. Known by 1915.

shufty.   *See* TAKE A ...

sick as a parrot.   *See under* OVER THE MOON.

sideburns (or **sideboards**).   Denoting short strips of hair in front of the ears. Not to be confused with **burnsides**, the style of beard (whiskers, moustache but shaven chin) worn by General Ambrose

E. Burnside (1824–81) who fought in the American Civil War. However, the syllables of 'burnsides' were transposed to form the new word 'sideburns' by 1887. Burnsides came first.

significant other. The person with whom one is having a relationship or to whom one is actually married – though whom, for some reason of political correctness, one does not wish to describe in terms of dependency or dominance. Of American origin, since the mid-1980s.

> We are envious when we feel that the significant other has all the power. We feel envy in a relationship of one to one, jealousy in a relationship of one to two. When one partner in an alliance has all the power the other, however apparently loved and cherished, feels envy.
> *Sunday Times* (19 January 1986)

> After all, the business is becoming much more dangerous with Aids. But it seemed a little tactless to take this up with Sharon as she was by now heavily entangled with my significant other person.
> *Sunday Times* (2 November 1986)

> If there's anything I can stand less than the term Significant Other it's hearing its defence mounted in unblushing terms of political correctness.
> *The Times* (14 May 1992)

silhouette. An outline or profile, originally of a person in portrait form. The name comes from that of Étienne de Silhouette (1709–67) who was the Controller-General (finance minister) to Louis XV of France. But how one led to the other is not clear. One suggestion is that his tenure of office was extremely short – only eight months – and that it seemed to pass 'as a fleeting shadow – as a silhouette'. Another is that he was 'associated with policies of retrenchment, and these cheap cut-out portraits gained their name by association with ideas of cheapness and economy' (Edwin Radford, *To Coin a Phrase*, 1974).

It is also said that Silhouette himself practised the art of making silhouettes and decorated the walls of his chateau with them. The word was known in English by 1798.

sincere. Pure, genuine. The word is derived from the Latin word *sincerus*. The *OED2* sternly states that 'there is no probability in the old explanation' that it comes from *sine cera*, 'without wax'.

sing. *See* I . . .

sirloin. The upper, choicer part of a loin of beef. The word would seem to derive from French *sur* [over] and *longe* [loin]. However, the fanciful etymology of an English king knighting a loin of beef – to commend it – hence making it 'Sir Loin' was in circulation by 1655. This version involved Henry VIII, but James I and Charles II have also become embroiled. The word was known however by 1554 in a way that proves it convincingly predates all these characters, maybe even Henry VIII.

skiffle. According to Chris Barber, the British jazz musician, quoted in *Radio Times* (11 February 1984), 'The term "skiffle" occurs only twice on old records – a 1929 sampler on the Paramount label, featuring various blues artists and made to sound like a party, called "Home Town Skiffle", and there's a record made in the 1940s by Dan Burley's Skiffle Boys . . . So we assume that "skiffle" must have been part of the jazz terminology of the time.'

The *OED2* concurs with the American jazz origin of the phrase and finds a 1926 jazz title, *Chicago Skiffle*.

In Britain, the skiffle craze occurred in the 1950s. It was do-it-yourself music, often played on improvised instruments like tea-chest double basses and washboards.

But the word itself remains a mystery. In Black American usage, a 'skiffle' was a rent party where guests contributed to the host's rent bill. These were popular at the time of the Depression and perhaps such makeshift music was played at them. All one can say for certain is that the word sounds like something improvised – a skiffling, shuffling thing.

skin. *See* GET UNDER SOMEONE'S . . .

sky's the limit. There is no upper limit of opportunity, especially of money to be earned or spent. There are no constraints on any activity. Known by 1920.

> Mr Bryhn said it was up to the successful bidder exactly how to gain most benefit from their space advertisement. 'The sky's the limit, there are endless possibilities,' he said.
> *Independent* (12 August 1995)

'I would never do anything involving children being beaten or people suffering from Aids or cancer,' De Caunes says in his defence. 'But otherwise I'd say the sky's the limit.'
Independent (17 February 1996)

slap. Make-up, usually in the theatrical sense. 'Get your slap on', means 'get your make-up on, get ready to do something'. 'Covered in slap', means 'wearing too much make-up', and so on. A simple derivation from the act of slapping on grease, the old form of theatrical make-up. Known by the mid-twentieth century.

slightly foxed. A term used in second-hand bookselling to denote a work for sale that is slightly soiled by discoloration but has no major damage to it. From the original use of the phrase to describe reddish-brown or brownish-yellow stains on a book or print. In use by 1847. Also figuratively about anything less than good.

> The rest of the concert consisted of Elgar's 'Cockaigne' Overture and the quintessential Holst, Egdon Heath – both carefully sympathetic, a bit over-literal and prosaic, slightly foxed by small fluffs – and the Brahms Double Concerto.
> *Financial Times* (12 September 1983)

sling one's hook, to. To go/run away. 'Sling your hook' has been defined as 'a polite invitation to move on'. This British slang expression dates from the nineteenth century (recorded by 1874) but no one seems too sure where it comes from. One reasonable explanation is that 'hook' in this context means 'anchor', so it means the equivalent of slipping or weighing anchor. *The ABZ of Scouse* (1966) suggests rather that the reference is to a Liverpool docker's loading hook.

Sloane Ranger. A posh, upper-class woman, of good family, living (originally) in the Sloane Square area of London. The joke allusion is, of course, to the Western character, the Lone Ranger. The term was invented in 1975 by the magazine *Harpers & Queen*, and when the Princess of Wales ('Supersloane') entered public life in 1981, the term became much more widely understood.

The coinage has been attributed to the style writer Peter York but was apparently coined by Martina Margetts, a sub-editor on the magazine.

slush fund.   A (probably) illegal stash of money used (perhaps by a politician) to pay off people. William Safire in *Safire's Political Dictionary* (1978) says the word is probably 'derived from the Swedish *slask*, meaning wet, or filth. Naval vessels would sell the slush and other refuse on board; the proceeds went into a fund to purchase luxuries for the crew. Later this practice was extended to war-damaged equipment as well.' Known in this sense by 1839.

Robert L. Shook in *The Book of Why* (1983) specifically defines the slush as grease from the cook's galley which was used to lubricate the masts. 'Whatever was left over was sold, and the money put into a fund for the enlisted men.' Both meanings were established by the end of the nineteenth century – the political one via the US.

> A dawn barrage was launched on the already heavily bombarded reputation of Pavel Grachev, Russia's defence minister, yesterday, with front-page accusations linking him to a secret hard-currency slush fund in a German bank.
>
> *Guardian* (4 February 1995)

small beer.   Something unimportant, inconsequential, trivial. Originally this meant 'weak' beer, but the newer meaning derives from a number of references in Shakespeare, notably *Othello*, II.i.160 (1604): 'She was a wight, if ever such wight were .../To suckle fools, and chronicle small beer.'

smarty boots.   Derogatory term for a clever person. It was Virginia Woolf's nickname for the critic and writer Cyril Connolly (referred to by Evelyn Waugh in a published letter of 5 January 1946). Possibly of US origin. It may or may not have been preceded by the also possibly US original **smarty pants**.

snap a wrist!   *See under* BREAK A LEG!

snob.   One who aspires to a higher social position in order to look down on those below. This is but one of many meanings of the word and can only be pinpointed at the time of Thackeray's *Book of Snobs* (1848). Sixty years before this, a snob was a shoemaker or cobbler. Could the idea of polishing the boots or, indeed, the licking the boots of other people possibly have led to the later meaning?

Another origin is from the practice at Oxford and Cambridge Universities of new undergraduates having to register not only their names but also their ranks. Nobles put what they were; those who weren't put *sine nobilitae* [without nobility]. This was then contracted to 'snob' to describe those of these lower orders who, nevertheless, tried to cultivate their betters. Compare POSH.

snook(er).   *See* COCK A SNOOK.

snuff.   *See* UP TO . . .

soap (opera).   This type of seemingly endless melodramatic serial was first broadcast on radio, then on TV, in the US. By the late 1930s, they were being referred to as 'soap operas' or 'soaps' or 'soapers' because the original sponsors were soap manufacturers. A critic writing in 1938 makes this clear – although he chooses a variation on the term: 'These fifteen-minute tragedies . . . I call them "soap tragedies" because it is by the grace of soap that I am allowed to shed tears for these characters who suffer so much from life.'

The word 'opera' is part of the expression, following the example set by 'horse opera', meaning a cowboy film, a term in use by 1927.

sock.   *See* PUT A . . .

sod this for a game of soldiers.   *See* BEGGAR THIS . . .

Sod's Law.   *See under* MURPHY'S LAW.

soft shoe shuffle.   A kind of gliding dance in which the performer gently scrapes the floor with the sole of the shoe. An alliterative invention, building upon the adjectival 'soft shoe' to describe a type of tap-dance without metal plates on the shoe. The latter phrase may have been in use by about 1905.

sold a pup, to be.   To be sold something that is worthless, to be cheated. Presumably from the act of selling a small dog when a larger, trained animal is expected. From fairground practice. Well-established by 1901. Compare LET THE CAT OUT OF THE BAG.

sold down the river, to be.   Meaning 'to be betrayed', this expression is of US origin. In the South, after 1808, it was illegal to import slaves, so they were brought down the Mississippi to the slave markets of Natchez and New Orleans. Hence, if a slave was 'sold down the river', he lost his home and family. The saying particularly relates to the practice of selling troublesome slaves to the owners of plantations on the lower Mississippi where conditions were harsher than in the Northern slave states. Mark Twain's novel *Pudd'nhead Wilson* (1894) is dominated by this theme and the expression occurs in it some 15 times, e.g.: '"Very good," said the master, putting up his watch, "I will sell you *here*, though you don't deserve it. You ought to be sold down the river."'

son et lumière (French, 'sound and light'). A type of entertainment, usually performed in a historical setting, in which the story of the place is told through the use of a (recorded) soundtrack and lighting effects. It is said to have been devised by a French architect, Paul Robert-Houdin, and first presented at Chambord in 1952. The first place to be given the treatment in Britain was the Royal Naval College at Greenwich in 1957. Now it would be hard to think of any major tourist site around the world which has not been subjected to this frequently disappointing but sometimes evocative procedure.

son of a gun. Nowadays, this is an inoffensively jocular way of addressing someone. However, in seafaring days, if a pregnant woman somehow found herself upon a warship and was ready to go into labour, the place traditionally made available to her was between two guns. If the father was unknown, the child could be described as a 'son of a gun'. Known by 1708. Partridge/*Slang*, however, quoting an 1823 source, defines the term as meaning a '*soldier*'s bastard', so perhaps there was an Army equivalent of the space made available.

song. *See* GO FOR A . . .

sophomore. A student in his or her second year at an American university (after being a 'freshman' in the first year). Known by 1726. The Greek *sophos* means 'wise' and *moros* means 'foolish'. So a second-year student is half-way between ignorance and wisdom. Well, that is more or less the idea. The *OED2* clings to an obscure definition relating the word to *sophom* ('sophism') plus *or*. Earlier, by 1688, the word was in use at Cambridge University to describe a student in the second year.

Sophomoric means 'pretentious, bombastic, foolish'.

sorry sight. *See* IT IS A ...

SOS. The emergency morse code signal, represented by the dots and dashes for the letters SOS, does not actually stand for anything, least of all 'Save Our Souls', as commonly supposed. The letters were chosen because they were easy to send in an emergency. Until about 1910, the Morse cry for help was 'CQD'. Other acronyms have been devised to suit the letters SOS: e.g., '*Si Opus Sit*' (which, in medicine, means 'give relief where necessary'), 'Slip On Show', 'Same Old Slush/Story/Stuff' and 'Short Of Sugar'.

soundbite. A very short extract from a speech or interview used in a television news programme. Originating in American broadcasters' jargon (compare 'clip'), the word is now used to suggest that meaning and context are often lost in the process and that it is a worthless activity for politicians and similar public figures to speak in soundbites in the hope that they will thereby acquire media coverage for themselves. Known in the US by 1980, in the UK somewhat later, especially after its wide use in the American presidential election campaign of 1988.

> 'Gaffe'... [is] monosyllabic, which is a help of course, to the Editor; and, to them, it signifies 'soundbite', or 'unpalatable truth'.
> Alan Clark, *Diaries* (entry for 18 November 1986)

sour grapes. Explanatory phrase given for the behaviour of anyone who affects to despise something because he knows he cannot have it. The source is Aesop's fable of 'The Fox and the Grapes' in which a fox tries very hard to reach some grapes but, when he is unable to do so, says they looked sour anyway. Phrase known by 1760, though the story was being quoted by the thirteenth century.

sow one's wild oats, to. A wild oat is a common weed, so for anyone to sow it means that (usually) he is doing something useless or worthless. Hence, the expression is employed to describe behaviour prior to a man's 'settling down'. In use by 1576. Quite how much implication there is of him wasting his semen in unfruitful couplings is hard to judge, though the expression often has reference to sexual dissipation. Perhaps this connotation has increased with the popularity of such expressions as 'getting one's oats' (for having sex).

spade.   *See* CALL A . . .

Spaghetti Western.   A film about the American West made by an Italian director (and often filmed in Spain . . .) Chiefly made in the 1960s, these cheaply produced Westerns were principally directed by Sergio Leone, through whom Clint Eastwood achieved international stardom in such films as *A Fistful of Dollars* (1964) and *The Good, the Bad and the Ugly* (1967). The coinage of the term – in use by 1969 – has been ascribed to the British writer, Christopher Frayling. The term 'Sukiyaki Western' for Japanese-made films of this type does not seem to have caught on.

> I've heard of Spaghetti Westerns but never of Spaghetti Scotsmen.
> Margaret Thatcher (on David Steel's candidacy for an Italian seat in the European Parliament), *Independent* (17 June 1989)

Spanish practices.   *See* OLD SPANISH CUSTOMS . . .

spic.   This pejorative term for Spanish-speaking people sounds like a contraction of 'Spanish-speaking' or 'hispanic'. The journal *American English* suggests rather that the word comes from 'spiggoty', an abusive term for Spanish speakers in Central and South America (*c.*1900). When the Panama Canal was being constructed (1901–4), Panamanians would say: 'No spikee de English' and 'spikee de' became 'spiggoty'. *DOAS* adds that, in the US 'spic' has also been applied to Italians or Italian-Americans and derives from 'spaghetti . . . reinforced by the traditional phrase "No spika da English".' Rodgers and Hart had a song (1939) called 'Spick and Spanish'.

spill the beans, to.   To divulge information inadvertently. This has been traced back to the ancient Greeks who held secret ballots for membership of clubs by using beans. A white bean was a 'yes' vote, a brown bean a 'no' vote. The beans were counted in secrecy so that a prospective member would know how many people voted for or against him. If the jar containing the beans was knocked over, that secret might get out.

This is a very elaborate explanation, but the phrase only entered American speech (from whence it passed into English generally) early in the twentieth century. Why did it take so long?

Another possible explanation is that gypsy fortune tellers in Turkey do not have crystal balls, neither do they read tea leaves. One of the many ways they tell fortunes is to spill beans out of a cup and interpret the resulting pattern.

spin doctor.   A public relations practitioner or political aide who puts a positive interpretation upon events, usually in the political sphere, by briefing journalists and correspondents. Out of the US in the mid-1980s, particularly during the 1988 presidential election, and taken from the game of baseball where spin has to be put on the ball by a pitcher to make it go where it is wanted.

> The spin doctors, the PR generals, argued after the Reykjavik talks that Reagan still stands by Star Wars and within reach.
> *Newsweek* (27 October 1986)

> The theme of the two men having talked bluntly yet courteously ... is likely to be stressed further by Reagan Administration 'spin doctors' who will try to present the summit in a favourable light in the days to come.
> *Daily Telegraph* (11 December 1987)

spitting image.   An exact likeness. Used as the title of a British TV comedy series (from 1984) using puppets to satirize current events. Given the venom involved in *Spitting Image*, it might be thought that any spitting had to do with saliva. The theories are, however, that the phrase is a corruption of 'speaking image' or 'splitting image' (two split halves of the same tree which provide an exact likeness), or a Black Southern US pronunciation of 'spirit and image' (which a true likeness might have). Current by 1901 and – as 'the spit of someone' by 1894.

spiv.   A man who lives by his wits, possibly working on the blackmarket, and noted for his flashy apparel. Known by 1934. Probably deriving from 'spiffy', a nineteenth-century English slang term for a smartly dressed man, a swell. That it is back-slang for 'VIPs' (Very Important Persons) may politely be doubted.

splice the main brace, to.   Meaning 'to have a drink', the expression comes from a comparison between the reviving effect of alcoholic drink and repairing or strengthening the mainbrace on board ship, where the mainbrace is the rope for holding or turning one of the sails. As used in the Royal Navy itself, the expression refers to the rare occurrence of an extra tot of rum all round – and known in this sense by 1805.

Spode's Law. *See under* MURPHY'S LAW.

spoke. *See* PUT A . . .

spoof. A send-up, take-off, skit. Known in this sense since 1958. Probably derived from the earlier use of the word to describe a nineteenth-century card game which involved hoaxing and a turn-of-the-century name for 'hoax' and 'humbug'.

spoonerism. The accidental transposing of the beginnings of words, named after Rev. William Spooner (1844–1930), Warden of New College, Oxford. The word had been coined by 1885 and many of his reported efforts must be apocryphal. 'In a dark glassly' and 'a half-warmed fish' are two of the more likely ones. 'Kinquering Congs Their Titles Take' – announcing the hymn in New College Chapel (1879) – sounds reasonable, but 'Sir, you have tasted two whole worms; you have hissed all my mystery lectures and been caught fighting a liar in the quad; you will leave Oxford by the next town drain', seems utterly contrived. Had he been an ornithologist, Spooner might well have described himself as a word-botcher.

spots off. *See* KNOCK . . .

sprauncy. Spry, smart, perky in appearance or voice. Known by 1957. Possibly related to the English dialect word *sprouncey* = cheerful. Could 'spry' be a simple contraction of 'sprauncy'? Yes, except that it appears to have been known long before.

sprog. A child. Known since 1945 and originally nautical slang clearly derived from services' use of the word to describe a new recruit. But why sprog? Well, 'sprag' was a word for a lively young fellow by 1706 but, again, there is no obvious reason for this.

square. Out of touch with popular trends – originally in relation to jazz in the US (known by 1946). In *The Neophiliacs* (1969), Christopher Booker pointed out the similarity with a coinage of the 1770s when the word was used to describe those who still affected square-toed shoes after they had gone out of fashion.

square one. *See* BACK TO . . .

squire. Mode of address, self-consciously archaic. Noticed in the mid-1970s, especially in the English Midlands. The *OED2* has this as 'a term of polite address to a gentleman not formally a squire. More recently, a jocular or familiar address to another man, not necessarily of different status', and has citations back to 1828.

> At a garage in Paddington I overheard a very sleek young man . . . ask the attendant to 'fill both tanks up'. 'Blimey, squire,' was the reply, 'you going all the way to Marble Arch?'
> *Listener* (22 February 1968)

stalking horse. A device used in hunting to get close to game which apparently sees no danger in a four-legged beast (and recorded since 1519). The wooden horse at Troy was an even more devastating form of equine deception.

Also used figuratively: 'He uses his folly like a stalking horse and under the presentation of that he shoots his wit' – Shakespeare, *As You Like It*, V.iv.105 (1598). Since the mid-1800s in the United States, the phrase has been used in politics about a candidate put forward to test the water on behalf of another candidate. Latterly in Britain (since about 1989) the term has been applied to an MP who stands for election as leader of a party with no hope of getting the job. The stalking horse's role is to test the water on behalf of other stronger candidates and to see whether the incumbent leader is challengeable.

stand up and be counted, to. To declare openly one's allegiance or beliefs. American origin. From the *Hartford Courant* (Connecticut, 12 August 1904): 'Another democratic paper, the "Sacramento Bee", follows the example of the "Chicago Chronicle" and stands up to be counted for Roosevelt.'

Stand Up and Be Counted was the title of a film (US, 1971) about a woman journalist who becomes involved in Women's Lib. In 1976, the British-based entertainer Hughie Green brought out a record entitled 'Stand Up and Be Counted' in which he quoted Churchill, lambasted the then Labour Government (by implication) and told the nation to pull its socks up.

star. *See* YOU'RE A . . .

starboard. The right-hand side of a ship or boat, as you face forward. The Anglo-Saxon words *steor* and *boord* meant 'rudder' and 'side', respectively. So, the *steorboord* was the side of the ship on which the rudder was positioned. The other side was probably called the *port* side because it was the side that was against the harbour (which the starboard could not be because of the rudder). Originally, this side was known as the 'larboard' (possibly meaning 'loading board') but was changed to avoid confusion.

steal a march on someone, to. To gain an advantage over someone by acting earlier than expected. If one army wished to gain advantage over another, it could march while the other one slept, hence it would 'steal a march' on its opponent. Known by 1771.

steal another's thunder, to. Meaning 'to get in first and do whatever the other wanted to make a big impression with', particularly with regard to ideas and policies. Known by 1900. The expression is said to derive from an incident involving the dramatist John Dennis (1657–1734). He had invented a device for making the sound of thunder in plays and had used it in an unsuccessful one of his own at the Drury Lane Theatre, London. Subsequently, at the same theatre, he saw a performance of *Macbeth* and noted that the thunder was being produced in his special way. He remarked: 'That is *my* thunder, by God; the villains will play my thunder, but not my play.'

Stella Maris. A Latin name for the Virgin Mary meaning 'star of the sea' and used of her as a protectress or guiding spirit. Allusive use since the mid-nineteenth century. The Virgin Mary was so named through the mistaken belief that 'sea-star' was the meaning of the Hebrew name Miriam (or Mary).

stetson. Name of a cowboy's hat. John B. Stetson (1830–1906) was the man who originally created the characteristic broad-brimmed, high-crowned cowboy hat. His hat-producing company was founded in Philadelphia in 1865. Known as such by 1900. Sometimes the hat is referred to by the nickname 'John B.'

As for the phrase 'ten-gallon hat' for a particular type of cowboy hat, this refers not to its literal capacity but to its usefulness, when necessary, as a means of carrying water. Known by the 1920s.

stick it, Jerry! A phrase from a sketch involving Lew Lake, a Cockney comedian of the early 1900s. Playing a burglar, he would say it to his companion when they were throwing missiles at policemen pursuing them. Based on 'stick at it', the phrase of encouragement, originating in the early years of the twentieth century. It was popular during the First World War but, apparently, this is not how the name 'Jerry' came to be applied to refer to Germans. As simply 'Stick it!' the phrase appears in a *Punch* cartoon on 2 January 1918.

stickers. *See* BILL . . .

stir one's stumps, to. To walk or dance briskly – and latterly to bestir oneself to action of any kind. Known since 1559. 'Stump' here means leg, as it has done since at least the fifteenth century.

stitch in time saves nine. A small repair to clothing now may avoid the necessity of having to make a larger repair at a later date; or, figuratively, prompt action now will save serious trouble later on. A proverbial expression known by 1732. The *Concise Oxford Dictionary of Proverbs* (1982) suggests that 'nine' is merely to give assonance to the couplet (in which the saying is sometimes displayed).

stone broke (sometimes **stony-broke**). Hard-up, ruined. Known by 1886. This expression is said to refer to the custom of breaking up a craftsman's stone bench when he failed to pay his debts.

stool pigeon. A policy spy or decoy. American origin, from the original meaning of the term, a decoy-bird – after the practice of tying or fixing a pigeon to a stool in order to attract other pigeons to it. They were then shot. First sense known by 1825, second by 1906.

stop me if you've heard this. Preliminary remark to the telling of a joke. Current by the 1920s: 'Stop me if you've heard it before, won't you?' – *Punch* (28 January 1925 and several times shortly thereafter).

> Surely, if Mr Lewis in outlining his plot to some friend, had only said, 'Stop me if you've heard this,' more than two hundred pages of *Dodsworth* need never have been written.
>
> Dorothy Parker in the *New Yorker* (16 March 1929)

stops.   *See* PULL OUT ALL THE . . .

straight from the horse's mouth.   To hear something directly from the person concerned and not garbled by an intermediary. The horse itself is not doing any speaking, of course. A horse's age can be judged best by looking at its teeth (which grow according to a strict system). So, if you are buying a horse, you do better to look at its teeth than rely on any information about its age that the vendor might give you. Known by 1928. *The Horse's Mouth* was the title of a novel by Joyce Cary (1944).

streets paved with gold.   *See* FIND THE . . .

strict tempo.   There is nothing new about the idea of *a* strict tempo in music. The *OED2* finds the term *tempo giusto* in 1740. But used, especially from the 1950s onwards, to mean a type of ballroom dancing to such a strict beat, the coinage is that of Victor Sylvester (1902–78). This ballroom dance instructor and orchestra leader was notable for his distinctive enunciation of the strict foxtrot tempo: 'slow, slow, quick, quick, slow'.

striving mightily.   A florid expression for great endeavour. It appears to have originated in Shakespeare, *The Taming of the Shrew*, I.ii.276 (1592–3): 'And do as adversaries do in law,/Strive mightily, but eat and drink as friends.'

stroking session.   An informal meeting at which an attempt is made to persuade and win over somebody – a political opponent, say – to your cause. The term emerged from the White House occupancy of President Richard Nixon and was known by 1973. The choice of the word 'stroking' may have a sexual connotation. Sometimes envoys would be sent on a **stroking mission**.

> President Nixon, revolted by such direct methods, preferred what he called 'stroking,' a process of jawboning so sweet to the strokee's earbones that the victim fell into a hypnotic state in which he could be deboned without realizing it.
> Russell Baker, *New York Times* (4 April 1978)

> As if the 'stroking missions' were not enough, Nixon began to write Lon Nol a series of warm optimistic letters.
> William Shawcross, *Sideshow* (1986)

stumps. *See* STIR ONE'S ...

Sturm und Drang. German for 'storm and stress' – the name given to the German literary movement of the late eighteenth century which chiefly consisted of violently passionate dramas by the likes of Goethe and Schiller. Said to have been applied by Goethe himself. Derived from the title of a tragedy (1776) written by Maximilian von Klinger.

subtext. *See under* HIDDEN AGENDA.

suck eggs. *See* DON'T TEACH YOUR GRANDMOTHER TO ...

suffer a sea change, to. To undergo a significant change, meta-morphosis. Now a grandiloquent and irrelevant way of saying 'change', whereas originally it meant specifically a change wrought by the sea. It alluded to the line from Shakespeare, *The Tempest*, I.ii.401 (1612) where Ariel sings 'Suffer a sea-change into something rich and strange.'

> I sensed, as apparently Jim Callaghan also sensed in the course of the campaign, that a sea change had occurred in the political sensibility of the British people. They had given up on socialism – the thirty-year experiment had plainly failed – and were ready to try something else. The sea change was our mandate.
> Margaret Thatcher, *The Downing Street Years* (1993)

> Anne Simpson, director of PIRC, said: 'I believe that if we win, it will bring about a sea-change in pay policies. If we can put down a marker, I think other companies will take note.'
> *The Times* (8 April 1995)

suit. *See* MAN IN A GREY ...

summer of love. The summer of 1967 – a retrospectively applied phrase for what may have been the highpoint of the Sixties, at least in terms of the Hippie, Flower Power, 'Love' generation concerned with drugs and pop music.

> It was ... the summer of '67, 'the summer of love', when the Beatles' now classic *Sgt Pepper's Lonely Hearts Club Band* was released.
> Blurb, Derek Taylor, *It Was Twenty Years Ago Today* (1987)

summit conference/meeting. A meeting of the chief representatives of anything, usually political leaders of major world powers. 'It is not easy to see how things could be worsened by a parley at the summit, if such a thing were possible' – Winston Churchill, quoted in *The Times* (15 February 1950). This is apparently the genesis of the 'summit' concept.

Sun King (French, *Le Roi Soleil*). Name given to Louis XIV, King of France (1643–1715) on account of his having once worn a sumptuous 'sun' costume when he danced in the *Ballet de la Nuit*, a court masque, at the age of fifteen. There was a popular engraving of it, and the name easily reflected the brilliancy that was to characterize his court. Also said to derive from a heraldic device he used.

sunrise industries. New and expanding industries. These were much talked about in the 1980s in comparison with 'sunset industries'. The image is a simple one. Sunrise industries are on the way up, sunset industries are on the way down. The term 'sunrise' does not mean that people have to get up early to go to work in them.

President Reagan, in his January 1984 State of the Union message, paid tribute to the 'entrepreneurs and risk-takers in the "sunrise industries" of high tech'. The quotations marks in the *Washington Post* report indicate that it must still have been a newish phrase. The *Economist* had, however, been using it in February 1980.

Superbrat. Nickname of John McEnroe (*b* 1959), the American tennis player and Men's Champion at Wimbledon. Notorious for his spoilt-child behaviour on court, arguing with umpires, linesmen, crowds, anybody.

sure as eggs is eggs. Meaning 'absolutely certain, safe', the derivation for this expression is obscure, unless it is a corruption of the mathematician or logician's 'x is x'. Known by 1699. It occurs also in Charles Dickens, *The Pickwick Papers*, Chap. 43 (1836–7).

Svengali. A mentor, agent, inspirer (often with sinister implications) – from the character in the novel *Trilby* by George du Maurier (1894). He enables a young female singer to become a famous performer – but her powers evaporate when he dies. Used allusively by 1914.

swansong. A farewell appearance. The legend has it that swans 'sing' once only in their lives – just before they die. In fact, they never sing at all. The phrase is now broadly applied to anyone's last appearance or act before retiring from almost any activity. Originally a German phrase, known in English by 1831.

sweet Fanny Adams/sweet FA/sweet f***-all. There actually was a person called Fanny Adams from Alton in Hampshire, who was murdered, aged eight, in 1867. At about the same time, tinned meat was introduced to the Royal Navy, and sailors – unimpressed – said it was probably made up from the remains of the murdered girl. 'Fanny Adams' became the naval nickname for mutton or stew, and then the meaning was extended to cover anything that was worthless. The abbreviation 'sweet FA' being re-translated as 'sweet f***-all' is a more recent coinage.

swing a cat. *See* NO ROOM TO . . .

swinging. 'Swinging' had been a musician's commendation for many years (certainly by 1958) before it was adopted to describe the free-wheeling, uninhibited atmosphere associated with the 1960s. By extension, 'swinging' came to denote sexual promiscuity. 'A swinger' was one who indulged in such activity. One suggestion is that 'swinging' in the sense of changing partners derives from the caller's use of words in square dancing.

How the phrase caught on is not totally clear. Frank Sinatra had had an album entitled *Songs for Swinging Lovers* (1958), Peter Sellers, *Songs for Swinging Sellers* (1959), and Diana Dors *Swinging Dors*. Could the square-dancing use of 'swing your partners' have contributed to this?

The coming together of 'swinging' and 'London' may first have occurred in an edition of the *Weekend Telegraph* Magazine on 30 April 1965 in which the words of the American fashion journalist Diana Vreeland (*c.*1903–89) were quoted: 'I love London. It is the most swinging city in the world at the moment.' In addition, a picture caption declared, 'London is a swinging city.' One year later, *Time*

Magazine picked up the angle and devoted a cover-story to the concept of 'London: The Swinging City' (15 April 1966).

swings and roundabouts. *See* ROUNDABOUTS AND SWINGS.

swoop. *See* AT ONE FELL . . .

— syndrome. A somewhat unnecessary elaborative suffix, applied to any set of actions, behaviour or opinions. Originally a medical term for a concurrence of several symptoms (as in Down's Syndrome), though the Greek-based word has been known in English since the 1540s), the clichéd use has been around since the 1950s. Recent use was perhaps encouraged by the film title *The China Syndrome* in 1979.

> Robert Harris, he of massive global sales for his 'what if?' novel, *Fatherland*, gets to further hype his latest *Enigma*, using the excuse of a film on the problems of 'second-novel syndrome'.
> *Independent* (25 September 1995)

T

T. *See* FIT TO A . . .

table. *See* HAVE ONE'S FEET UNDER THE . . .

tables. *See* TURN THE . . .

tabloid. This word now used for a newspaper with smaller pages than a 'broadsheet' and written in a downmarket, popular style, was coined by the chemist Sir Henry Wellcome in the 1880s to describe a small new tablet he had invented. 'Tabloid' was registered as a trademark, but in a short space of time came to be applied to anything that was miniature. Newspaper magnates Alfred Harmsworth and Lord Northcliffe both used the word to describe the new small popular papers at the start of the twentieth century, and the name stuck. Known by 1918. Hence, **tabloid television**, a coinage of the late 1980s to reflect TV programming akin to the popular newspaper approach.

> *Night Network* is in the front of ITV's battle to capture the attention of Britain's viewers, especially young ones, using the latest technique in the broadcasting world: tabloid television.
> *Sunday Times* (28 February 1988)

take a rain-check, to.   Originally, in the US, a rain-check (or -cheque) was a ticket for re-admission to a sporting event when the event had had to be postponed because of rain. The person to whom it was given would be able to produce it at a later date and claim free admission. Now broadened, the expression is used to mean 'let's put this "on hold", let's not make any arrangements about this until the time is more opportune'. Obviously, the phrase can be used as a polite way of postponing something indefinitely, but basically there is some kind of commitment to 'renegotiate' at a later date. Known by 1959.

An Australian source states that 'rain-check' was used of someone's action in putting a licked finger on a cake to reserve it for later – 'Unhygienic, but I am talking about perhaps the late 1930s, when I was but a teenager.'

take a shufty, to.   To take a look. Probably after the Arab word *shufti* which occurs in phrases like *shufti bint*, an available woman. Known since 1943. Hence, in military slang, a shuftiscope was the name given to a telescope or similar instrument for looking through.

take down a peg, to.   To humble, to reduce a person's self-esteem. The phrase probably comes from its nautical use in connection with flags, which were raised and lowered with pegs. A flag flying high would carry more honour than one lower down. Known by 1664.

take French leave, to.   To do something without permission. Originally, to leave a reception without announcing one's departure. In Smollett's *Humphrey Clinker* by 1771. One of many anti-French coinages which exist to snub the French (compare **French gout** = veneral disease).

take someone for a ride, to.   (1) To deceive or trick a gullible person. (2) To entice a person to their death – US underworld expression. Those who fell foul of gangsters were invited to 'take a ride' with the boss in his car. Flattered they might have been, but it was possible they might not return (another form of the phrase is 'taken for a *one-way* ride'). Both meanings known by 1925.

take someone's idea(s) on board, to.   To receive and accept new ideas. Obviously from the original sense of taking material on board a ship. Known by 1984. Probably in business language at first.

take something with a grain of salt, to.   Meaning, 'to treat something sceptically', just as food is sometimes made more palatable by the addition of a pinch of salt. This comes from the Latin *cum grano selis*. Known in English by 1647.

take the mickey, to.   Meaning 'to send up, tease'. Known by 1952. Possibly from rhyming slang, 'Mickey Bliss' = piss. But who was Mickey Bliss to be so honoured? The Rev. Geoffrey Knee wrote to *Radio Times* (in April 1994) thus: 'I have long understood that the phrase is a less vulgar form of "Taking the p***" [his asterisks] and that it's derived from the term "p*** proud", meaning an erection caused by pressure in the bladder and not, therefore a sign of sexual prowess; hence, someone who is "p*** proud" has an exaggerated sense of his own importance. Such a one might be to told to "p*** off", meaning, not "go away", but "get rid of the p***" and stop boasting. Thus, to "take the p*** out of someone" means to deride him into lowering his self-esteem.'

However, with all due respect to the reverend etymologist, an earlier form – **to take the Mike** – is remembered by some from the 1920s and would seem to demolish his origin. More recently, the verbose and grandiose 'are you by any chance **extracting the Michael**?', and '**extracting the urine**' have become reasonably common. Another explanation is that the 'mickey' = 'piss' derives from the word 'micturition' (the overwhelming desire to urinate frequently).

talent to amuse.   A quotation from Noël Coward's song 'If Love Were All' in *Bitter Sweet* (1932): 'I believe that since my life began/ The most I've had is just/A talent to amuse.' *A Talent To Amuse* became the title of Sheridan Morley's biography of Coward in 1969. But compare this in Byron's *Don Juan*, Canto 13, xxxvi (1819–24):

'There was the *preux Chevalier de la Ruse*,/Whom France and Fortune lately deign'd to waft here,/Whose chiefly harmless talent was to amuse.'

talk nineteen to the dozen, to.   To talk very quickly. A very literal derivation comes from the Cornish tin mines of the eighteenth century. When pumps were introduced to get rid of flooding, they were said to pump out 19,000 gallons of water for every 12 bushels of coal needed to operate the engines.

But, surely, one can be even more basic than that: to speak 19 words where only 12 are needed gets across the idea very nicely. Nineteen may be a surprising number to choose. Oddly, however, it sounds right and better than any other number. 'Twenty to the dozen', for example, sounds rather flat. The phrase was in use by 1785.

'Thirteen to the dozen' was in use in the sixteenth century to indicate a long measure. Sir Walter Scott seems to have had his own version:

There is a maxim for thee! … hang it up amidst thy axioms of wisdom, and see if it will not pass among them like fifteen to the dozen.
Castle Dangerous, Chap. 45 (1831)

talk turkey, to.   To get down to business, to talk seriously. Although a widely used expression, this originated in the US and was known by 1824. Robert L. Shook in *The Book of Why* (1983) says it first appeared in American colonial days when the Pilgrim Fathers always seemed to want turkeys when they traded with the Indians. So familiar did their requests become that the Indians would greet them with the words, 'You come to talk turkey?'

This seems rather more to the point than the tale usually given as the origin of the phrase: in colonial days, a white hunter and an Indian made a pact that they would share equally between them anything they caught. However, at the end of the day, when they came to share out what they had bagged – three crows and two turkeys – the white man first handed a crow to the Indian and a second turkey to himself. At which point the Indian is said to have remarked, 'You talk all turkey for you. Only talk crow for Indian.'

talking heads.   British broadcasting term for the type of TV programme which is composed mainly of people talking, shown in 'head and shoulder' shots and sometimes addressing the camera directly. Often used critically by those who would prefer a programme to show more physical action or to get out of the confines of the studio. Granada TV's booklet *Some Technical Terms and Slang* (1976) defined the term solely as 'a documentary programme which uses the technique of people talking directly to the camera'. Earlier (*c.*1968), the term 'talking head' seems to have been applied to anyone addressing a camera in a presenter's role.

The US/UK pop group with the name Talking Heads flourished from 1981. Alan Bennett wrote a series of monologues for TV with the title *Talking Heads* (1987).

tarantula. *See under* COCKROACH.

task force. 'An armed force organized for a special operation under a unified command, hence ... any group of persons organized for a special task' – *OED2*. Known by 1941, possibly of American origin. A 1949 film called *Task Force* was a 'flag-waver' (according to *Halliwell's Film Guide*) portraying an admiral about to retire recalling his struggle to promote the cause of aircraft carriers. In the early 1970s (according to *Halliwell's Television Companion*), there was a BBC TV series 'rather clumsily' entitled *Softly, Softly: Task Force*. Then, finally, in 1982, the Falkland Islands were liberated from the Argentinians by what was widely referred to as the British Task Force.

taters. Very cold. Another of the more obscure rhyming slang derivations: 'taters' or 'taties' are potatoes. The rhyming phrase is 'potatoes in the mould' = cold. But what is that supposed to mean? One of the meanings of 'mould' is easily broken-up surface soil. Perhaps this conveys the idea of earth which is liable to be colder than that deep down. Known by the mid-twentieth century.

tawdry. The word meaning 'cheap; trashy' comes from 'St Audrey' (otherwise Etheldreda, Abbess of Ely in the seventh century AD). She developed a breast tumour which she blamed on wearing rich jewel necklaces as a child, and she died of it in 679. Much later, in the sixteenth and early seventeenth century, women wore necklaces of *silk* which they called 'St Audrey's lace'. Alas, poor imitations of the lace drove out the good and, by an unfortunate process, her name came to be given to something of a gaudy nature. 'Tawdry' in this derogatory sense was in use by 1676.

taxi. A vehicle for hire. The *taximètre* (i.e. *taxe*, meaning tariff plus *mètre*, meaning meter) was a French word for the device invented (*c*.1898) for clocking up the cost of hiring a cab. The abbreviation 'taxi' for the vehicle itself was soon applied (by 1907) and English speakers adopted it, from the French.

This explanation may come as a surprise to those who, like C.H. Manning (writing to the *Observer*, 23 December 1990), believe: 'Sometime early in the century a Thurn und Taxis was Interior Minister of the Austro-Hungarian Empire and decreed that all licensed vehicles plying for passenger hire in Vienna should be fitted with meters. This splendid idea spread and soon motorcabs worldwide were equipped with taxi-meters.'

teach. *See* DON'T ... YOUR GRANDMOTHER TO SUCK EGGS.

teddy bear. A child's cuddly toy. The nickname 'Teddy', the inevitable shortening of any man called Edward or Theodore, was well established by the year 1903. One of the most notable bearers of the nickname was Theodore Roosevelt, the US President (in office 1901–9). The 'teddy bear' was named directly after him because of an incident the year after they were imported from Germany into the US (1902), when he was on a bear shoot in Mississippi. His hosts stunned a small brown bear and tied it to a tree so that he would be sure to make a kill. After this, he gave the Ideal Toy Company permission to use his name and manufacturers of stuffed toy bears generally renamed their product.

teetotal. Someone who is teetotal (i.e. abstains from alcohol) may indeed drink a lot of 'tea', but the word probably comes from a simple emphasis on the initial 't' of 'total'. The totality of abstaining became important when the American Temperance Union extended its ban beyond hard liquor to include beer, wine and cider in 1836. However, three years before, the word 'teetotal' had been used in this context by Richard Turner of Preston, England and, indeed, credit for the coinage is on his gravestone:

Beneath this stone are deposited the remains of RICHARD TURNER, author of the word *Teetotal* as applied to abstinence from all intoxicating liquors, who departed this life on the 27th day of October, 1846, aged 56 years.

His coinage of the word is said to have taken place at a meeting in the Preston Cock-pit in September 1833. 'Dicky' Turner evidently had a way of emphasizing words and, when it came to the need for 'entire' abstinence, he declared that 'nothing but the te-te-total will do'. 'That shall be the name!' declared a colleague, and so it was.

Probably the UK and US uses arose independently. Stuart Berg Flexner in *I Hear America Talking* (1976) says the word 'teetotally' had been used in the US as early as 1807 by Parson Mason Locke Weems in the 'T – totally' rather than abstinence sense.

Compare from Richard Erdoes, *1000 Remarkable Facts About Booze* (1981): 'Members of abstinence societies sang "Dash the Bowl to the ground" and signed pledges to "refrain forever from ingesting spirituous and malt liquors, wine, or cider." On some pledges a letter was put after each signature indicating how far a pledger wanted to go. *M* stood for moderation; *A* stood for abstinence from ardent spirits only; *T* stood for total abstinence, hence the expression "*tee*total".'

tell it/that to the Marines.   Meaning 'don't expect us to believe that'. This apparently dates from the days, in Britain, when Marines were looked down upon by ordinary sailors and soldiers. Working on land and sea, the Marines were clearly neither one thing nor the other, and thus stupid. So perhaps they would believe a piece of unbelievable information. The phrase was current by 1806. In 1867, *Notes and Queries* discussed it in the form, 'Tell that to the Marines for the sailors won't believe it.'

Brewer derives it from an occasion when Samuel Pepys was regaling Charles I with stories from the Navy. An officer of the Maritime Regiment of Foot (the precursors of the Marines) gave his support to Pepys when doubt was cast on the existence of flying fish. Said the King, 'Henceforward ere ever we cast doubts upon a tale that lacks likelihood we first "Tell it to the Marines".' In fact, this story was originated by Major W.P. Drury in *The Tadpole of an Archangel* (1904). He subsequently admitted that it was an invention and a 'leg pull of my youth'.

The phrase is also well known in the US. Sometimes it takes the form, 'Tell that to the *horse*-marines.'

ten-gallon hat. *See under* STETSON.

terminate with extreme prejudice, to. To kill, execute, assassinate in American CIA parlance. It became known to a wider audience in 1972 and was used in the film *Apocalypse Now* (US, 1979). Also, in a weaker sense, simply to dispose of, get rid of.

> Taylor is the design supremo who stood at the right hand of Harold Evans for 15 years, accompanying him from the Sunday Times to refashion the Times. His relations with Times Newspapers terminated with extreme prejudice after he had collected a staff petition in support of the sacked Evans.
> *Guardian* (31 August 1985)

that and a — will get you —. An American expression of the obvious where the object mentioned is clearly of no value: 'That, and a dollar, will get you a cup of coffee', 'That, and a token, will get you on the subway'... An early example of the format appears in Shakespeare's *A Midsummer Night's Dream*, V.i.277 (1594): Theseus says – 'This passion, and the death of a dear friend, would go near to make a man look sad.'

theatre piece. A theatrical work which is not substantial enough to be called a 'play' or which its devisers feel requires something other than the conventional name. Rather an irritating innovation. Or, in ballet and musical concerts, a dramatic rather than abstract work. Current by the early 1980s.

> Isadora arrived and sent a quiver through many very delicate sensibilities. It might seem that Kenneth MacMillan was mounting a Red Brigade assault on the fairy-fanciers, but Isadora was an attempt at a theatre piece to break the mould of balletic traditionalism (and, like dance works here and in New York, it suggested a renewed interest in the forms and possibilities of narrative).
> *Financial Times* (7 January 1982)

> Thea Musgrave's The Last Twilight, a theatre piece for large chorus, semichorus, 12 brasses and percussion, a setting of D.H. Lawrence's 'Men in New Mexico,' was not well performed (in the Brooklyn Academy of Music), but not so badly as to conceal a large, romantic vision.
> *Financial Times* (1 July 1982)

them. *See* ONE OF ...

think tank. (1) the brain (US origin). *Punch* (10 June 1903) has the word. In 1964, former President Harry S Truman said on his eightieth birthday that he wanted to live to his ninetieth, 'if the old think tank is working'. (2) an organization often devoted to deep strategic thinking on behalf of a government. Known by the 1960s.

> The work of think tanks is often similar to work done by universities, industrial research-and-development departments and management consultants.
> *New York Times* (1967)

thirtysomething.   There was nothing new about giving someone's age as '—something' when you didn't know the exact figure, but the title of a US TV drama series, *thirtysomething* (from 1987) – about couples around this age – helped popularize the usage.

> Eighties pop for the thirtysomethings.
> Advertisement in *Barclaycard Magazine* (1989)

> Judy is a successful and attractive businesswoman toward the far end of her thirtysomething decade. Yet she feels frustrated, alone and angry about her failed relationships with men.
> *Washington Post* (13 March 1990)

Adaptable, of course.

> My generation, the twentysomethings, were fortunate enough to catch the golden age of American TV detectives.
> *Guardian* (3 May 1991)

three sheets in the wind.   Drunk. The 'sheets' in question are not, as you might expect, sails but the ropes or chains attached to sails to trim them with. If the sheet is free, the sail is unrestrained. As Robert L. Shook in *The Book of Why* (1983) puts it, 'if these sheets are loose, the ship will be as unstable on the water as a thoroughly drunk man is on his feet'. Sometimes 'three sheets *to* the wind'. Known by 1821.

through the keyhole.   A phrase for how one obtains information about a person or household secretly or illicitly. *Through the Keyhole* has been used as the title of a feature on British TV since 1983 in which the homes of celebrities are revealed to the camera's gaze. Known by 1592 (Marlowe, *The Jew of Malta*).

throw in the towel, to.   To give up some enterprise, usually in disgust or frustration. To admit defeat. From the traditional gesture by the losing participant in a boxing match. Whether the towel was originally thrown into the ring or into the wash-bucket is not clear. Known by 1915.

throw one's hat in the ring, to. To join an enterprise or at least show that you intend to. To pick up a challenge. From the days when a challenge to a prize fighter at a showground or fair was delivered in this manner. Known since 1847.

> Mr Secretary Hoover has been forced to throw his hat into the ring for the Presidency, but he does not mean to follow it there.
> *Observer* (4 March 1928)

thumbs down. *See* GIVE THE . . .

thunder. *See* STEAL ANOTHER'S . . .

tich. 'Little Tich' was the stage name of Harry Relph (1868–1928), a popular British music-hall comedian. Probably invented by his family when he was a baby, the nickname derived from the sensational Tichborne case – about the claim made in 1866 by a man from Australia that he was the missing heir to a Hampshire baronetcy and fortune. The Tichborne Claimant (Arthur Orton), who was imprisoned for perjury, was plump – as no doubt was Harry Relph as a little boy. Relph remained small in stature and, at first, called himself 'Little Tichborne'. 'Tich' then became the nickname for anyone small (also **titchy**).

tiddly (or **tiddley**). Lightly drunk, tipsy. This may be rhyming slang: tiddlywink = drink. Rather a pleasant euphemism. Known by 1905, though 'titley' for a drink was current by 1859.

Tin Lizzie. Nickname of Henry Ford's Model T motor car, the first mass-produced vehicle, inelegant but efficient and comparatively cheap. Fifteen million were produced between 1908 and discontinuation of the model in 1927. Ford is said to have encouraged jokes about them for the sake of publicity as they rattled around the world. 'Lizzie' may be a contraction of 'limousine' or be from the name applied to a domestic servant. The term 'Lady Lizzie' was used about the car in a 1913 advertisement. 'Tin Lizzie' was known by 1915, the 'tin' probably referring to the fact it was produced for the masses.

The Irish pop group Thin Lizzy (which, being Irish, pronounced itself 'Tin Lizzy') flourished 1973–83.

Tin Pan Alley. The name given, by 1908, to the area in Manhattan where most music publishers worked – because the noise of countless pianos being tinkled must have sounded like tin pans being bashed. A 'tin pan' was also (*c.*1900) the name given to a cheap tinny piano. In London, the equivalent area around Denmark Street, off Charing Cross Road, was so known by 1934.

tin-pot dictator. 'Tin-pot' as a dismissive adjectival phrase referring to the cheap quality or noise of something has been around since the 1830s. The *Daily News* (23 March 1897) used the phrase 'tin-pot politicians'. The inevitable linkage to dictators probably has more to do with the repetition of the 't' sound.

> Severn Trent was also attacked by the Labour Party for behaving like a 'Third World tin pot dictatorship' over the issue.
> *Independent* (1 September 1995)

tired and emotional. Meaning 'drunk'. A pleasant euphemism, ideally suited to British newspapers which have to operate under libel laws effectively preventing any direct statement of a person's fondness for the bottle. The expression 't. and e.' (to which it is sometimes abbreviated) is said to have arisen when *Private Eye* printed a spoof Foreign Office memo suggesting it was a useful way of describing the antics of George Brown when he was Foreign Secretary (1966–8). On 29 September 1967, the *Eye* described him as 'tired and overwrought on many occasions' and a cover showed him gesticulating while Harold Wilson explained to General de Gaulle: '*George est un peu fatigué, votre Majesté.*' There was never any question that Brown *did* get drunk. Peter Paterson entitled his biography of Brown, *Tired and Emotional* (1993).

Private Eye may not actually have coined the phrase, though it undoubtedly popularized it. It has been suggested that a BBC spokesman said of Brown 'He was very tired and emotional' after the much-criticized appearance he made on TV on the night of President Kennedy's death in November 1963. In fact, it was ITV Brown appeared on and the remark, even if it was made, has not been traced.

tiswas. *See* ALL OF A . . .

Titanic. The name of the large British ship which famously sank when it hit an iceberg on its maiden voyage in 1912. The name comes from the Titans, twelve giants of classical mythology, but the word has long been used to describe anything massive. In a speech on 22 May 1909, Winston Churchill said: 'We have arrived at a new time . . . and with this new time strange methods, huge forces and combinations – a Titanic world – have spread all around us'.

titchy. *See under* TICH.

to boot. In addition, besides, moreover. Not a verb but a little phrase that gives added emphasis. 'He is a very good friend of mine, to boot'. This has nothing to do with footwear but more to do with 'boot' meaning 'advantage, good'. Known in Old English *c.*1000.

to the nth degree. To any extent. This derives from the mathematical use of 'n' to denote an indefinite *number.* Twentieth century.

> In America the film-cutter is a man with a sub-editorial mind developed to the *n*th degree.
> *Sunday Express* (18 March 1928)

toady. A sycophant, flatterer, servile dependant. This is short for 'toad-eater'. A charlatan or quack-doctor would employ a toad-eater to appear to eat a 'poisonous' toad so that he could be 'cured' with the medicines the quack had for sale. Known since 1826.

toast. *See* PROPOSE/DRINK A . . .

tod. *See* ON ONE'S . . .

Tom cat. A male cat. In 1760 there was published an anonymous story called *The Life and Adventures of a Cat* which was very popular. The male cat was called Tom and soon every male cat was so called.

Tony. This is the name given to the annual series of awards presented by the American Theatre Wing (New York) for excellence in the theatrical arts. From their inception, the awards have been called Tonys, after the nickname of Antoinette Perry (1888–1946), the actress and manager. She died the year before the first awards were made in 1947.

The word may gain something from the fact that 'tony' is also an informal American adjective, derived from 'tone', for 'stylish, distinctive, classy'.

toodleoo!   Parting cry. Possibly connected with 'toot', as though one were to go 'toot, toot', like a horn, on leaving. Or perhaps it has something to do with 'toddling off' or 'tootling off'. Could 'I must tootle-o' have led to it?

Another suggestion is that the word derives from the French *à tout à l'heure* [see you soon]. In *Punch* on 26 June 1907.

tooth.   *See* LONG IN THE ...

top.   *See* OVER THE ...

top hole!   Excellent. Probably referring to holes or notches cut in a board to record the points scored in some games. The top hole represents the highest, best score. Known by 1899.

touch someone/thing with a bargepole, not to.   To keep one's distance, avoid at all costs. From the *length* of the bargepole used to propel a barge. Known by 1893. Eric Partridge, *A Dictionary of Clichés* (5th edition, 1978) dates it late nineteenth-/early twentieth-century.

Hideous little beast! I wouldn't touch him with the end of a barge pole.
A.H. Gibbs, *Persistent Lovers* (1915)

She has begun to campaign on behalf of other badly hit Names concentrated on the so-called 'spiral' syndicates – those which provided reinsurance against large-scale losses for other Lloyd's syndicates. 'If I knew then what I know now I wouldn't touch [Lloyd's] with a bargepole,' she says.
Financial Times (1 May 1993)

'Frankly, I wouldn't touch any of the men I have met in nightclubs with a bargepole,' says Jane, 23, who lives in Surrey.
Today (24 August 1993)

towel.   *See* THROW IN THE ...

tower of strength.   Someone who is a great help or encouragement. A possible origin lies in Shakespeare, *King Richard III*, V.iii.12 (1592–3):

'Besides, the King's name is a tower of strength.' Compare: Tennyson, *Ode on the Death of the Duke of Wellington* (1852): 'O fall'n at length that tower of strength.' In the Bible, God is often called a 'strong tower'.

> Special mention must be made of Miss Dorothy Swerdlove who ... has proved a tower of strength on the details of the American theatre.
> Phyllis Hartnoll, Preface, *Oxford Companion to the Theatre* (1983 ed.)

> Though doubtless willing to swap his personal triumphs for the right result, Simon Langford, the veteran full-back, was a tower of strength, scoring all Orrell's points and defusing just about everything that Catt kicked at him.
> *Daily Telegraph* (30 January 1995).

toy! toy!   Theatrical good-luck wish. Before the opening of his production of *Don Giovanni* at the English National Opera in 1985, Jonathan Miller explained that 'the cry is age-old, either from kissing or spitting, no one seems really sure'. But it is probably an onomatopoeic reference to knocking on wood to ward off evil (as in 'touch wood'). Some suggest a Jewish or Yiddish origin, but *toi* in German is apotropaic = 'Good luck!' Lutz Röhrich in his *Lexikon des sprichwörtlichen Redensarten* (1973) gives *Unberufen, toi-toi-toi!* as meaning 'touch wood ...' and says it was popularized by a song in 1930 (though current since 1900). The word *toi!* may represent the sound of spitting – which has the same superstitious function. In G.L. Apperson's *English Proverbs and Proverbial Phrases* (1929) there are two mentions of the phrase 'John Toy'. *Notes & Queries* in 1856 had 'Like lucky John Toy' among 'Cornish Proverbs'. And C.H. Spurgeon in *John Ploughman's Pictures* (1880) had: 'The luck that comes to them is like Johnny Toy's, who lost a shilling and found a two-penny loaf.' Surely too much of a coincidence for there not to be some connection.

tree.   *See* BARK UP THE WRONG ...

trees are tall (but they do not reach to the sky).   In other words, 'trees may be tall, but they're not that tall' or, metaphorically, 'no person is that important, however grand he or she may appear'. Winston Churchill's favourite proverb. In Wolfgang Mieder & George B. Bryan's *The Proverbial Winston S. Churchill. An Index to Proverbs in the Works of Sir Winston Churchill* (1995), there are listed no less than thirteen occasions on which Churchill used the 'trees' proverb in his writing or speeches. Mieder and Bryan note how close the meaning of the words is to 'Pride goeth before a fall' (based on Proverbs 16:18), how it derives from a German original '*Est ist dafür gesorgt, daß die Bäume nicht in den Himmel wachsen*' (though this is most usually in the form '*God* takes care that the trees don't grow up to the sky'), and how, although Goethe did not originate it, he used the proverb in his autobiography *Dichtung und Wahrheit* (1811). Earlier, it occurs in Martin Luther's *Tischreden* [Table Talk] and in one of the collections of proverbs of Johannes Agricola (1528–48).

trick-cyclist. A psychiatrist, jokingly mispronounced. Known since the 1930s.

> It was at Didcot this afternoon that I first heard the name given by the Army to the psychiatrists now being taken on by the R.A.M.C. The boys call them "trick-cyclists". Which, of course, is what they are.
> James Agate, *Ego 5* (1942)

trillion. *See under* BILLION.

trowel. *See* LAY IT ON WITH A . . .

T-shirt (or **tee-shirt**). So named, because this simplest of garments is, if you think about it, shaped like a letter T. Originally from the US, the word describes a form of cotton shirt, simple to cut out and make. Known by 1920.

Tunbridge Wells. *See* DISGUSTED, . . .

turkey. *See* TALK . . .

turn the tables on someone, to. To obtain advantage over someone, bring a complete reversal in a state of affairs. This derives from playing games (like chess or draughts) which require the use of marked boards or the moving of pieces about on table-tops. If one player is not doing well, then were he to 'turn the table' on his opponent, he would be in the winning position. Known by 1634.

turn up for the book(s). *See* WHAT A . . .

tutu. A ballerina's small dress, sticking out stiffly from the waist. 'Tutu' is a corruption of *cucu* which is French baby talk for *cul-cul*, the equivalent of English 'botty-wotty' or 'bum-bum'. *Cul* is French slang for 'arse' or 'bum' and derives from the Latin *culus*, buttocks. Known by 1910.

tuxedo. A type of jacket, part of male evening dress. Made of light-weight wool, the tuxedo was introduced to the US from Europe by one Griswold Lorillard. He did so at an Autumn Ball held on 10 October 1886 at the Tuxedo Club, Tuxedo Park, a fashionable country club in Orange County, New York State. So much more convenient to wear than tails, the garment obviously took its name from the scene of its first appearance.

There are other claimants as to who introduced it, but there is no mistaking why Tuxedo (the place) gave its name.

twerp/twirp. A foolish fellow. T.W. Earp (1892–1958), the English art critic, matriculated at Exeter College, Oxford, in 1911. The *OED2* produces a couple of citations (one, be it noted, from J.R.R. Tolkien) to demonstrate that this man gave rise to the common use of the word 'twerp'. It is not totally clear what Mr Earp did to make his unfortunate gift to nomenclature (if indeed he did – it is not proven).

The Speaker of the House of Commons added the word 'twerp' to the list of unparliamentary expressions in May 1987.

> I frequently heard this word used, by working-class people, in south-east Lancashire more than thirty years ago. It generally denoted one who was considered to be an extremely silly or foolish young man.
> *Notes & Queries*, clxxxii (1942)

If the correspondent's memory was accurate this would make it most unlikely that T.W. Earp was the origin. Most likely it was just an unfortunate coincidence for him. Perhaps his parents were unworldly people when it came to giving him initials.

twitcher. A birdwatcher. This term became popular during the late 1970s and onwards and is said to derive from the nervous tics or twitches such enthusiasts have when they get to hear of rare birds arriving *or* when they do not manage to sight them. One would have thought some combination of 'watcher' and 'twitch' more likely.

Some birdwatchers dislike being given the name as they feel it denotes a mindless enthusiasm for spotting birds (just as a trainspotter pursues trains, merely to add to his tally). They prefer to be thought of as serious ornithologists.

two shakes.   *See* IN . . .

U

up a gum tree.   Stuck, isolated, in a difficult position. Presumably because not only could a person (or animal) be trapped by pursuers if he went up a tree, but his position would be made doubly difficult if the tree was of the type he would stick to. Known in the US by 1829. The phrase is also used in Australia, which must have more gum trees to the square mile than anywhere else. A correspondent writes: 'The characteristic of many gum trees, as opposed to other Australian trees, is that it is a long way to the first branch, and therefore difficult to climb, either up or down.'

up and running.   *See under* HIT THE GROUND RUNNING.

up the garden path.   *See* LEAD SOMEONE . . .

up the river.   *See* SEND SOMEONE . . .

up to snuff, to be.   To be of a proper standard or quality. Perhaps literally, if a person is up to snuff it means he is able to follow a scent. Known by 1811. As for the similar **up to scratch**, this has a probable sporting origin – from the line scratched on the ground, especially in boxing, to which contestants are brought ready to start. Known by 1821.

usual suspects.   The people you would expect, the customary lot. At the end of the 1942 US film *Casablanca*, 'Round up the usual suspects' is a line spoken by Claude Rains as Captain Louis Renaud, the Vichy French police chief in the Moroccan city, who is, in his cynical way, appearing to act responsibly in the light of the fact that a German officer, Major Strasser, has been shot. In fact, Renaud knows full well that the killing has been committed by Rick (the Humphrey Bogart character) because it was carried out but a few moments before in front of him.

It is remarkable that, of all the many memorable lines from *Casablanca*, it has taken until quite recently for this one to catch on, but it is currently verging on the cliché – as was perhaps confirmed by the release of a film called *The Usual Suspects* (1995) which involved a police identity parade.

All the usual suspects will be out at Fontwell tomorrow, when the figure-of-eight chase course will throw up its usual quota of specialist [racing] winners.
Independent on Sunday (17 January 1993)

U-turn. *See* MAKE A . . .

V

Valley Girl. An American pubescent teenage girl (aged thirteen to seventeen) of a type first observed and indentified in California's San Fernando valley in about 1982. She is from a fairly well-to-do family, her passions are shopping, junk food, cosmetics, and speaking in a curious language, Valspeak – 'for sure' (pronounced 'fer shurr'), 'totally' (pronounced 'todally' or 'toe-dully'), 'gag me with a spoon' (expression of disgust – 'you make me feel sick'), 'grody to the max' ('unspeakably awful to the maximum').

Valspeak is the latest teentalk craze to surface in the real world, brought to adults' attention in the usual way: a hit record, Valley Girl, by Frank Zappa and his 15-year-old daughter Moon Unit.
Guardian (26 October 1982)

vamp. The name for a flirtatious, predatory woman, much in vogue in early silent films, the 'vamp' character reached her final form in the performances of Theda Bara. In *A Fool There Was* (US,

259

1914), Bara played a *femme fatale* who lures a European financier. He forsakes all for her and dies in her arms.

However, the idea of a woman who behaves towards men as a vampire behaves towards its victims predates the coining of 'vamp'. Known by 1911.

velvet revolution. Name for the process which led to the end of Communist rule in Czechoslovakia at the end of 1989. It signifies a non-violent transition and was apparently originally coined in French. The Czechs themselves had talked of a 'gentle revolution'.

> Even in Czechoslovakia's 'velvet revolution', the most peaceful and perhaps the most complete of all the transformations, the middle ranks of the new order are staffed by those who kept their heads down during the long nights of normalisation.
> *Observer* (21 January 1990)

vote. *See* ONE MAN, ONE . . .

W

wage a battle royal, to. Meaning, 'to take part in a keenly fought contest; a general free-for-all', this term originated in cockfighting, or at least has been specifically used in that sport. In the first round, sixteen birds would be put into a pit to fight each other, until only half the number was left. The knock-out competition would then continue until there was only one survivor. Known by 1672 in general use; 1860 in cockfighting.

wagger pagger bagger. A wastepaper basket (sometimes just **wagger** or **wagger pagger**). Known by 1903. From Act II of John Dighton's *The Happiest Days Of Your Life* (1948): 'If you don't mind, therefore, I shall deposit them in the wagger-pagger-bagger [*He drops the flowers into the wastepaper basket*].' This is an example of the (now rather dated) slang popular at the University of Oxford in the early years of the twentieth century. A whole range of words was transformed into different ones ending in 'agger'. The then Prince of Wales (who studied at the university for a while) was the 'Pragger Wagger'. Jesus College was known as 'Jaggers'. And a curious working-class character who used to hang around Oxford and was known as 'the British Workman' came to be called the 'Bragger Wagger'.

The whole scheme is a variant upon the old English Public School custom of adding '-er' to everything: rugby becoming 'rugger', football becoming 'footer', and so on. Silly, but rather fun.

walk in the woods.   Name given to a negotiating tactic employed by high officials in Strategic Arms Limitation Talks (SALT) between the United States and the USSR. A play inspired by the compromise achieved on a specific occasion by negotiators in 1982 and showing how they might have talked through their personal and political differences was accordingly entitled *A Walk in the Woods*. Written by Lee Blessing, it was first performed on Broadway in 1988.

> The package that Mr Nitze and Mr Kvitsinsky worked out in their now famous 'walk in the woods' near Geneva last July involved equal ceilings for both sides' medium-range nuclear weapons in Europe.
> *Financial Times* (9 March 1983)

> In the summer of 1982 Perle sabotaged the formula agreed between Nitze and the Soviet negotiator, Kvitsinsky, during their famous 'walk in the woods'.
> Denis Healey, *The Time of My Life* (1989)

wally.   Meaning 'a foolish, inept or ineffectual person', this was a vogue word in Britain *c.*1983, and many origins have been put forward for it. In Cockney a 'wally' is a pickle. Or it may be Scottish and possibly derives from the name 'Walter' (though, in Scots, it can have the more positive meaning of 'handsome, fine, admirable' – as in 'that's a wally dog you've got there'). In 1969, 'wally' was defined as 'out of fashion' and in 1974 there were some 'vulnerable individuals' who liked to be known as the 'Wallies of Wessex'.

One of the newer theories is this: in the early nineteenth century, *valet* seems to have been pronounced 'wally' in the colloquial speech of both England and Scotland. In June 1818, Byron wrote a letter in the character of his servant William Fletcher, a Nottinghamshire man, and used the phrase 'if you know any Gentleman in want of a Wally'.

An opera by Catalani called *La Wally* was first performed in 1892. Here it is just the name of the heroine without any relevant implication. Arturo Toscanini, the conductor, so esteemed it that he named his daughter Wally.

Walter Plinge. In British theatre, when an actor plays two parts, he traditionally uses this name rather than his own in one of them. It is said that the original Mr Plinge was a stage-struck pub landlord from near the Theatre Royal, Drury Lane, in the nineteenth century. Having his name so used was the nearest he ever came to being on the stage.

> I took over the role of A.B. Raham in *Home and Beauty* [in 1969], in which for policy reasons ... I put myself down in the programme as 'Walter Plinge'. (This is a professionally though not generally well-known *nom de theatre* used for various reasons, from uncertainty of final casting to merely wishing to even up the columns on a bill.)
> Laurence Olivier, *Confessions of an Actor* (1982)

The US equivalent is **George Spelvin**.

wannabe. Someone who aspires to be something else, from the American pronunciation of 'want to be'. First encountered when teenage girls emulated the pop singer Madonna in the mid-1980s.

> The bright side of this phenomenon is that these Wanna Be's (as in "We wanna be like Madonna!") could be out somewhere stealing hubcaps.
> *Time* Magazine (27 May 1985)

—watch. The '—watch' suffix is now a cliché – designed, apparently, to add dignity and status to almost any vigil, regular study or observation. Perhaps one should distinguish between two families of '—watch' words. In one family, the second element of the word means 'an organization set up to police something' and the first element tells you what it is that is being policed (town-watch, night-watch, fire-watch, and so on).

In the other family, the second element means an 'organized and continued act of watching, a keeping vigilant to observe something' (though sometimes with an admixture of the policing sense), and the first element tells us what is being looked out for. The fashion may have been set by the BBC TV programme *Doomwatch* which ran from 1970. The *OED2* shows the word quickly escaping from the TV listings and being used in such phrases as 'his latest piece of political doomwatch' (*The Times*, 3 July 1973).

Used in earnest in the UK from about 1985, the suffix was popularized by Neighbourhood Watch (sometimes Home Watch) schemes, which had been started by police in the UK a year or two before this – schemes in which residents were encouraged to 'police' their own and each other's properties. The coinage originated, however, in the US in the early 1970s.

> Camden Council employs a lone inspector to walk the pavement on the lookout for citizens allowing their dogs to foul it. In a sane society he would command a department called Shitwatch.
> *Observer* (6 July 1975)

> I'm fed up with Agewatch and Childwatch. I'm thinking of founding a society against potential suicide called Wristwatch.
> Russell Harty, quoted by Alan Bennett in a memorial address (14 October 1988)

Waverley. The title of the first novel (1814) by Sir Walter Scott, which was then given to the whole series of his novels set in Scotland. The name of the hero of the novel was taken from Waverley Abbey, near Farnham, in Surrey. From the Scott association, the main railway station in Edinburgh was named Waverley Station. There is an overture, 'Waverley' (1828) to an uncompleted opera by Hector Berlioz.

way the wind blows. *See* KNOW WHICH ...

Weathermen. The original name of a violent radical group in the US (*fl.* 1969), which then became the Weather Underground. It derived from the lyrics of 'Subterranean Homesick Blues' (1965) by Bob Dylan:

> Keep a clean nose
> Watch the plain clothes
> You don't need a weather man
> To know which way the wind blows.

well. *See* I'M NOT ...

wellerism. A form of comparison in which a saying or proverbial expression is attributed to an amusingly inapposite source. E.g.

'"That's an antelope," observed the small boy when he heard that his mother's sister had run away with the coachman.' Mieder and Kingsbury in their *Dictionary of Wellerisms* (1994) note that a wellerism usually consists of three parts: a statement, a speaker who makes this remark, and a phrase or clause that places the utterance in a new light or an incompatible setting: '"Every little helps," quoth the wren when she pissed in the sea.' This last was recorded in 1605 and demonstrates that the type was known long before Charles Dickens gave a fondness for uttering these jocular remarks to the character Sam Weller in *The Pickwick Papers* (1836). This popularized the form which came to be known as 'wellerism' (the word known by 1839).

Wellington.   The 1st Duke of Wellington (1769–1852) most famously gave his name (by 1817) to Wellington boots, now waterproof rubber boots but originally military boots that came over the knee or short boots worn under the trousers. His name has also been bestowed upon: a coat, a hat, trousers, a cooking apple, a bomber, a chest of drawers, a term in card-playing, a public school and, as Wellingtonia, to a type of coniferous tree.

welsh rarebit.   Name of a type of food made of melted cheese and butter mixed with seasoning and poured over buttered toast. The *OED2* finds it being called 'Welsh rabbit' by 1725, but 'rarebit' by 1785. It describes this process as 'etymologizing', i.e. someone too learned for his own good, finding that the dish had nothing literally to do with rabbit, had turned its name into something more sensible.

But why 'Welsh rabbit' in the first place? Had it something to do with the shape or the look of it? Well, Bombay duck is a fish, and mock-turtle soup has nothing to do with turtles (it is made from calf's head), so why not?

Wendy.   Girl's name invented by J.M. Barrie and given to a character in his play *Peter Pan* (1904). A friend of Barrie's was the poet W.E. Henley who, indeed, used to call him 'Friend'. Henley's daughter, four-year-old Margaret, echoed this but, unable to pronounce her r's, distorted it to 'Fwendy' or 'Fwendy-Wendy'. Margaret died at the age of six, but her expression lives on through the play, and the subsequent novel, and all the 'Wendy' houses that followed.

west. *See* GO ...

wet one's whistle, to. To have a drink. One of the oldest idioms of all. It appears in the 'Reeve's Tale' in Chaucer's *Canterbury Tales* (1386): 'So was hir ioly whistle wel y-wet.'

wets. (1) States opposed to Prohibition in the US. Those who were in favour were 'drys'. (2) The name for British Conservative politicians who took a cautious middle-of-the-road line (by 1980, although privately spoken as early as 1976).

> 'Wet' is a public schoolboy term meaning 'feeble' or 'timid', as in 'he is so wet you could shoot snipe off him.' The opponents of government economic policy in the early 1980s were termed 'wets' by their opponents because they were judged to be shrinking from stern and difficult action. As often happens with pejorative political labels (cf. Tory, which originally referred to Irish political bandits), 'wet' was embraced by the opponents of our economic strategy, who in turn named its supporters 'the dries'.
> Margaret Thatcher, *The Downing Street Years* (1993)

WFMs (White F***-Mes). A name for a type of open-toed shoe worn by women and understood, by some, to signify sexual availability. Known by 1990.

> A feminist of the younger school ... hair bird's-nested all over the place, f***-me shoes and three fat inches of cleavage ... So much lipstick must rot the brain.
> Germaine Greer, quoted in the *Independent* (20 May 1995)

what a turn up for the book(s)! What an unexpected outcome, what a surprise! The 'books' here are those kept by bookies to maintain a record of bets placed on a race. Does the bookie have to turn up the corner of a page if a race has an unexpected outcome? No, the phrase merely means that something unexpected has 'turned up'. Known by 1873.

what in the Sam Hill ...? What in Hell's name ...? This euphemistic expression enrols the name of Sam Hill, a nineteenth-century American politician, to avoid having to say the worst. Known since the early twentieth century.

Characters [in 1936 production] are given to Will Rogerisms like 'What in Sam Hills is the matter with her?' and 'Creeping Jesus!' (which got them into hot water with the censors).
Simon Callow, *Orson Welles: The Road to Xanadu* (1995)

What the Sam Hill you yelling for, George?
Film soundtrack, *It's A Wonderful Life* (US, 1946)

wheel. *See* PUT A SPOKE IN SOMEONE'S ...; PUT ONE'S SHOULDER TO THE ...

whelk-stall. *See* COULDN'T RUN A ...

when I was in Poona. Phrase typical of an old British India hand. Included in Partridge/*Catch Phrases* as 'Gad, sir, when I was in Poona'. It can be found in the story 'Reginald' (1901) by 'Saki' as, 'When I was at Poona in '76 –.'

when push comes to shove. At the critical moment, when action must back up words, when matters become serious or crucial. Known in the US by 1958. Especially in American business language of the 1970s.

We used to say rude things about them and they used to say rude things about us but, when push came to shove, they waded in when we were in the shit and I've got to thank them for it.
Independent Magazine (9 September 1995)

when the chips are down. Meaning 'at a crucial stage in a situation', the phrase alludes to the chips used in betting games. Known by the 1940s. The bets are placed when they are down but the outcome is still unknown.

when the wind blows. *See under* KNOW WHICH WAY ...

whipping boy. A person punished because of another person's mistakes. From the custom of having a boy educated at the same time as a royal prince, who received the prince's punishments because it was not allowed for a tutor to strike a royal prince. Known by 1647.

The superintendents claim that their present reports are not designed for

reading by other than experienced senior police officers. They also fear that they will become the whipping boys in any change of procedure.
Guardian (10 September 1974)

Whisky à gogo. Name of clubs all over France since the 1960s. Curiously, they take the name from the French title of the film *Whisky Galore* (UK, 1948) – source Philip Kemp, *Lethal Innocence: The Cinema of Alexander Mackendrick* (1991). Hence **à go-go** as a term for 'in abundance', 'no end of' (by 1965).

This is really nothing but Leninism à go-go!
New York Times (24 September 1966)

whistle. *See* WET ONE'S . . .

white elephant. Something which turns out to be of no value or an expensive mistake. From Siam/Thailand where elephants were sacred. The king would bestow one on awkward courtiers who then had the bother of its upkeep. Known by 1851.

white hope. A great hope. Jack Johnson was the first black boxer to be the World Heavyweight Champion (1908–15). A 'white hope' was, originally, a white boxer who might have been hoped to be able to beat Johnson. From there, the phrase came to refer to anyone who might be able to bring about a much-desired end, and upon whom hopes were centred. Known by 1911.

white knight. A corporation that comes to the aid of another in a takeover fight. Known as Stock Exchange jargon by 1981.

The knight rescues the embattled firm by agreeing to acquire it on better terms than the pursuer would provide. The improved provisions can include a higher purchase price for the company's stock, and assurances that executives of the acquired corporation will not be forced to use their golden parachutes.
Time Magazine (4 March 1985)

whiter than white. Of extreme purity, innocence or virtue. Known by 1592 – Shakespeare *Venus and Adonis* (l. 398): 'Teaching the sheets a whiter hew than white.' In modern times said to have been popularized by an advertising slogan for (Persil?) washing powder in the UK (1950s?)

whodunit. A detective story where the perpetrator of a crime, especially murder, has to be identified. The phrase is probably of US origin. Known there (also as 'whodunnit') by 1930.

whole nine yards. The entire problem – so defined in an article about Pentagonese in *The Times* (2 April 1984). Everything, the whole lot. Of American origin and known by 1970. A consensus has developed that the phrase comes from concrete mixing – presumably the distance it would be possible to cover using one truck load.

wick. *See* GET ON ONE'S . . .

wild oats. *See* SOW ONE'S . . .

wild-goose chase. A pursuit of something which it is impossible to capture or find; a hopeless enterprise. From a sixteenth century horse race in which each horse had to follow the leader on an erratic course. But also a wild goose is very difficult to follow. Shakespeare uses the term in its figurative sense in *Romeo and Juliet* (1594).

will. *See* I DO.

willies. Meaning 'the effect of being frightened; nerves' – as in 'that gave me the willies'. *OED2* suggests a US nineteenth-century origin. Another possible source is 'wiffle woffle' meaning stomach-ache. Note also that in the ballet *Giselle* (Paris, 1841) there are things called *Wilis* – spirits of maidens who die before marriage. The fairy chorus in the Gilbert and Sullivan opera *Iolanthe* (1882) sings: 'Willahalah,! Willaloo', and this has been compared to the wailing of the Rhinedaughters in Wagner's *Das Rheingold* (1869): 'Wag-a-la-weia, Wa-la-la, Wei-la-la, Weia'. Could there be some common thread running through all these wails?

wimp. Meaning 'a weak, ineffectual man', this word is probably a shortened form of 'whimperer'. The Wymps were characters in children's books written by Evelyn Sharp in the 1890s. They were fond of playing jokes but apt to cry when jokes were played on them. The US author George Ade wrote in his *Handmade Fables* (1920): 'Next day he sought out the dejected Wimp'. In *Arrowsmith* (1925) by Sinclair Lewis, we find: 'Wimpish young men with spectacles, men whose collars do not meet'. Then came J. Wellington

Wimpy, a character in the Popeye comic strip. He was very corpulent, but sloppily dressed and always forgot to pay for his hamburgers. (He gave his name *to* **Wimpy** hamburgers in Chicago in 1935.) The word 'wimp' resurfaced in the 1980s, for some reason, and George Bush, before he became US president, was said to worry about suffering from the Wimp Factor.

wind. *See* KNOW WHICH WAY THE ...

window of opportunity. A period of time during which something can be achieved. Something of a cliché latterly, this phrase grew out of the use of 'window' to describe the limited opportunity to launch a space rocket when weather and other conditions were right, in the late 1960s. The figurative sense had evolved by 1979.

> Unexpected changes in price or volatility might provide sudden and short-lived windows of opportunity to reduce costs or generate profits.
> *Energy in the News* (1988)

with flying colours. With triumphant ease, great outward success. From the naval use of colours to mean flags. A victorious ship might sail into harbour with all its flags still flying. Known by 1706 (in Farquhar's *The Beaux' Stratagem*).

> 'We've come off with flying colors,' as the ensign said when he ran from the enemy.
> *Yankee Notions* (1854)

> Not only did he pass that test with flying colours, but he also found a trump lead, an essential prerequisite for his side extracting the maximum penalty.
> *Daily Telegraph* (24 February 1996)

with knobs on. As in the similar phrases **with bells on** and **with brass knobs on**, this is a way of saying (somewhat ironically) that something comes with embellishments. British use only. *OED2* has a 1931 citation from J.J. Farjeon. There is a 1932 one in a theatre review by Herbert Farjeon (perhaps if they were related, it was a family expression?). It goes: 'A massive company has been assembled at His Majesty's Theatre to restore what is called "the Tree tradition" with an overwhelming production of *Julius Caesar*, which I need hardly tell anyone who knows anything about the Tree tradition means plenty of lictors and vestal virgins or, to sum the matter up in the base vernacular, *Julius Caesar* with knobs on.'

'Same 'ere, wi' knobs on!' occurs in a *Punch* cartoon (17 July 1918).

women and children first!   Catchphrase used jokingly in a situation where people might appear to be behaving as though caught in a shipwreck (in a crowded bus or train perhaps). It originated in the incident involving HMS *Birkenhead*, one of the first ships to have a hull of iron, in 1852. She was taking 476 British soldiers to the eighth 'Kaffir War' in the Eastern Cape of South Africa when she ran aground 50 miles off the Cape of Good Hope. It was clear that the ship would go under but only three of the eight lifeboats could be used and these were rapidly filled with the 20 women and children on board. According to tradition, soldiers remained calm and did not even break ranks when the funnel and mast crashed down on to the deck, with the loss of 445 lives. Thus was born the tradition of 'women and children' first. In naval circles, this is still known as the Birkenhead Drill.

Somerset Maugham said he always chose to sail on French ships: 'Because there's none of that nonsense about women and children first!'

wool.   *See* DYED IN THE ...; PULL THE ...

word of mouth.   One person telling another by speech, not by writing. Usually applied to a recommendation to see some entertainment or other. Known by 1553; the secondary use by 1951.

Of the three chances in her favour, on which she had reckoned at the outset of the struggle – the chance of entrapping Magdalen by word of mouth ...
Wilkie Collins, *No Name* (1862–3)

An award-winning Glasgow hotelier and restaurateur who is expanding east ... Eventually the problem was solved by word of mouth recommendations by well-known people.
Scotsman (1 February 1994)

The life of the impresario is not all bouquets and sell-out shows ... For real exposure, though, you need to rely on more than friends and word of mouth.
Independent (2 February 1994)

worse things happen at sea.   Mildly ironic expression of comfort – 'things could be worse'. First recorded in 1829 (Pierce Egan, *Boxiana*) in the form 'Worse accidents occur at sea!' *Worse Things Happen at Sea* was the title of a play by Keith Winter, presented in London in April 1935.

worth one's salt, to be.   To be of worth, of strong character and worth employing on any task or in any job. Neil Ewart in *Everyday Phrases* (1983) states that 'before money was introduced, soldiers and workers in ancient Roman times had their wages paid in salt'. One wonders whether they really liked this procedure. After all, what did they put the salt on if they did not have the money to buy food?

A *salarium* was what was paid to soldiers *for the purchase of* salt. From *salarium* we get our word, 'salary'. If a man was not worth his salt, therefore, he was not worth his salary.

Brewer takes a middle course and says that a *salarium* was a salt ration which was later replaced by money but retained the same name. Known by 1830.

wrap.   *See* IT'S A . . .

wrong side of the bed.   *See* GET OUT OF THE . . .

WYSIWYG.   'What you see is what you get' – an acronym from computing, meant to suggest that what the operator sees on the computer screen is exactly how the material will appear when printed out (i.e. with correct typefaces, artwork, etc.) In use by 1982. Now an expression used to suggest that a person is not deceiving by appearances. President Bush said the full version on the first day of the Gulf War (16 January 1991) when asked how he was feeling.

Y

yob/yobbo.   Thug, brute, lout. Maybe from 'lob', a bumpkin. Also backslang (i.e. word reversal) of 'boy' has been suggested. Known since 1959.

yomp, to.   To march over difficult terrain carrying heavy equipment. This word became general knowledge from its use by Royal Marines during the 1982 Falklands campaign. Clearly, it is akin to the word 'stomp' which means much the same thing. But one explanation is that it like 'yump', a Scandinavian pronunciation of 'jump', familiar in motor rallying where Scandinavian drivers predominate. It is used to describe the action of a car that takes a corner at high speed and leaves the ground.

> Our troops have foot-slogged it to lay siege to Port Stanley. 'Yomping', the men call it. You won't find the term in military manuals.
> *Daily Mail* (4 June 1982)

yoof.   Youth, when associated with its particular culture in Britain in the late 1980s. Derived from the Cockney pronunciation given to the word by social arbiters like Janet Street-Porter (a TV executive and journalist).

Yorkies.   The name applied to long-distance lorry drivers, after the chocolate bars introduced in the early 1980s. Originally these were promoted with commercials showing lorry drivers eating them.

> Every lorry driver in Britain was supposed to sound his horn at noon ... The *Sun* even devoted its Friday front page to a large picture of a clock so that Yorkies would recognise noon.
> *Independent on Sunday* (13 May 1990)

Earlier, a 'Yorkie' was a nickname for a Yorkshireman or the Yorkshire terrier.

Yorkshire Ripper. *See under* JACK THE RIPPER.

you heard it here. *See* (AND REMEMBER) . . .

you know? *See under* KNOW WHAT I MEAN?

you're a star. Meaning, 'You have done something out of the way for which I am exceedingly grateful!' Noted 1995; probably of American origin. Possibly an extension of the literal (show business) sense as in the title of a song (1979).

young fogey. A man below the age of 40 who dresses and behaves as if he were prematurely middle aged. The species was fashionable in Britain from 1984 onwards although observed and commented on as early as 1909 (by the philosopher C.S. Peirce). Obviously, a play upon the phrase 'old fogey' (a Scots word from the 1780s) applied to a person displaying all the attitudes of old age.

yuppie. Meaning 'Young Urban Professional People/Person', this was one of a stream of acronyms created in the late 1970s and 1980s designed to identify select groups. This one lasted longest in the UK because it answered a need for an (eventually pejorative) term describing young, brash money-makers of the period. The term originated in the US, as in Piesman and Hartley's *The Yuppie Handbook* (1983), and may have been coined by syndicated columnist Bob Greene that same year. It featured prominently in reports of Senator Gary Hart's bid for the Democratic nomination in the 1984 presidential race. He and his supporters appeared to belong to the Yuppie tendency. The launch of the word was slightly confused by the similar-sounding **yumpie** ('Young Upwardly Mobile People').

Z

Zitat. *See* GOETZ.